Sino-Japanese Relations

In recent years, there has been increasing interest in the relationship between China and Japan, particularly as a way of understanding contemporary political, economic and security developments within the whole East Asia region. Caroline Rose presents a thorough, balanced and objective examination of one of the most vexing issues that continues to plague the Sino-Japanese relationship – that of the legacy of history. Using models of reconciliation as a framework, the book considers the different ways in which historical events have been represented and remembered, and how the governments and peoples of both countries have attempted to come to terms with the past. This will be of great interest to academics and policy-makers in the United Kingdom and the United States, as well as to professionals working in Chinese and Japanese communities.

Caroline Rose is Senior Lecturer in Japanese Studies and Head of the Japanese Section at the Department of East Asian Studies, University of Leeds. Her current research interests are contemporary Sino-Japanese relations, Japan's foreign policy, nationalism in China and Japan, Japan and China in the Asia Pacific and reconciliation between China and Japan.

RoutledgeCurzon Advances in Asia-Pacific Studies

Sino-Japanese Relations

Facing the past, looking to the future?

Caroline Rose

Routledge
Taylor & Francis Group

LONDON AND NEW YORK

First published 2005
by Routledge
2 Park Square, Milton Park, Abingdon, Oxon OX14 4RN

Simultaneously published in the USA and Canada
by Routledge
270 Madison Ave, New York, NY 10016

Transferred to Digital Printing 2005

Routledge is an imprint of the Taylor & Francis Group

© 2005 Caroline Rose

Typeset in Times by RefineCatch Ltd, Bungay, Suffolk
Printed and bound in Great Britain by
TJI Digital, Padstow, Cornwall

British Library Cataloguing in Publication Data
A catalogue record for this book is available from the British Library

Library of Congress Cataloging in Publication Data
A catalog record for this book has been requested

ISBN 0-415-29722-2

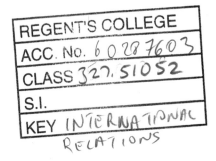

For Marcia Rose

Contents

Acknowledgements

This book could not have been completed without the cooperation and patience of many people. A research grant from the British Academy and Chinese Academy of Social Sciences provided me with the funding and opportunity to make what was to be an invaluable research visit to China. Staff at the Institute of Japanese Studies (Beijing Academy of Social Sciences), Heilongjiang Academy of Social Sciences, the Institute of Asian Pacific Studies (Shanghai Academy of Social Sciences) and at Fudan University and Shanghai Teachers' University provided invaluable insights. Particular mention must be made of Bu Ping, Wang Xiliang, Xin Peilin, Yang Yulin, Rong Weimu, Wang Xiusheng, Su Zhiliang, Li Xiushi, Gao Lan and Jin Xide who were most generous with their time and work. Hu Peng took particularly good care of me in Beijing, for which I remain most grateful.

In Japan, staff at the National Diet Library and the Ministry of Foreign Affairs Public Records Office helped me to navigate my way around catalogues and databases. Takeda Tadashi at the Japan–China Friendship Association provided me with invaluable information unavailable elsewhere, and Margaret Kosuge inspired me to think more deeply about the topic of reconciliation and helped me see things more clearly.

Penny Francks and Hugo Dobson were kind enough to read through a previous draft of the book, and gave me the encouragement to complete it! Thanks also go to my colleagues in the Department of East Asian Studies, University of Leeds, and of course to my very kind editor at RoutledgeCurzon, Peter Sowden, whose patience never ran out. I am also grateful to the editorial team at Routledge for their efforts. Needless to say, all remaining errors in the book are my own.

Finally, I must thank my family who have had to put up, once again, with my moods, and absences over the last two years and who never seem to make demands of their own. Mum and Gabby – what would I do without you?

Abbreviations

ACLA	All China Lawyers' Association
ACWF	All-China Women's Federation
APEC	Asia-Pacific Economic Cooperation
ARF	ASEAN Regional Forum
ASEAN + 3	Association of South-east Asian Nations plus China, Japan and South Korea
AWF	Asian Women's Fund (Asia Peace and Friendship Fund for Women)
CASS	Chinese Academy of Social Sciences
CCP	Communist Party of China
CCTV	China Central Television
CPPCC	Chinese People's Political Consultative Conference
CWC	Chemical Weapons Convention
DPJ	Democratic Party of Japan (Minshutō)
DSP	Democratic Socialist Party
EEZ	Exclusive economic zone
FDI	Foreign Direct Investment
GEAW	Greater East Asia War
GHQ	General Headquarters (of SCAP)
GMD	Guomindang
IMTFE	International Military Tribunal of the Far East
JCP	Japan Communist Party
JNP	Japan New Party (Nihon Shintō)
JSP	Japan Socialist Party (renamed SDP)
JTU	Japan Teachers' Union
LDP	Liberal Democratic Party
MoE	(Japanese) Ministry of Education
MoFA	(Japanese) Ministry of Foreign Affairs
NCRR	Nikkei for Civil Rights Redress
NGO	Non-governmental organisation
NPC	National People's Congress
NPO	non-profit organisation
ODA	Overseas Development Assistance

PFT	Treaty of Peace and Friendship
PoW	prisoner-of-war
PRC	People's Republic of China
RoC	Republic of China
SCAP	Supreme Commander of the Allied Powers
SDP	Social Democratic Party (formerly the Japan Socialist Party)
SFPT	San Francisco Peace Treaty
TARC	Textbook Authorisation Research Council
VAWW-NET, Japan	Violence against Women in War Network, Japan
UN	United Nations
UNSC	United Nations Security Council
WTO	World Trade Organisation
WWII	World War Two

Glossary

1972 Joint Statement   Marked the normalisation of diplomatic relations between the PRC and Japan.

Hanaoka incident   Refers to an uprising by Chinese forced labourers at the Hanaoka mine run by Kajima-gumi (now Kajima Corporation) in Akita prefecture in June 1945 which was brutally put down by Japanese military police.

Heiwa Izokukai   National Council of Bereaved Families for Peace.

Hoshū Shintō   New Conservative Party. Formed in 2002 as a splinter group of the DPJ. Merged with LDP in 2003.

ianfu   'comfort women' (in Japanese; *weianfu* in Chinese).

Izokukai   Japan Association of War Bereaved Families.

Jinja Honchō   National Association of Shinto Shrines.

Kōmeitō   Clean Government Party. Formed in 1964, disbanded in 1994 to join the Shinshintō (New Frontier Party), but then re-formed in 1998 as New Kōmeitō.

kyōkasho kentei   textbook authorisation.

kyōsei rōdo   forced labour.

Marco Polo Bridge   The site of the outbreak of fighting between Chinese and Japanese troops in July 1937 on the outskirts of Beijing at Wanping which marks the beginning of the Sino-Japanese war.

New Kōmeitō   English title for re-formed Kōmeitō in 1998.

owabi   apology.

September 18th incident   (Manchurian or Mukden Incident) Marks the beginning of Japan's occupation of China's northeast in 1931 when the Japanese Kwantung army blew up a section of the railway line as a pretext for launching an attack on Chinese troops.

shinryaku   aggression/invasion.

Shinseitō   Japan Renewal Party, formed in 1993 by a group of LDP defectors.

Shinshintō   New Frontier Party, a merger of Shinseitō, DSP, Kōmeitō and JNP in 1994.

(Shintō) Sakigake   (New Party) Harbinger, formed in 1993.

Tsukuru kai   Atarashii kyōkasho o tsukuru kai [The Japanese Society for History Textbook Reform].

Unit 731   One of Japan's wartime chemical and biological experimentation
centres, located on the outskirts of Harbin at Pingfang, and headed by
Ishii Shirō.

Note on style

Japanese and Chinese names are given with surname first. Japanese (J:) and Chinese (C:) terms are given in *romaji* and *pinyin* respectively. Macrons indicate long vowels in Japanese words and are used throughout, except for words which have become standard in the English language, e.g., Tokyo, Shinto.

Introduction

The year 2002 marked the thirtieth anniversary of the normalisation of Sino-Japanese relations. Allowing for the exuberant tone that is characteristic of statements by politicians and the press on such key anniversaries, the reviews of the relationship issued in the run-up to the anniversary were markedly upbeat and highly complimentary about the progress made in all aspects of the relationship. Furthermore, they made frequent reference to the potentially bright future of the relationship based on an understanding of the past. In a message to Chinese Premier Zhu Rongji, Prime Minister Koizumi expressed the desire to strengthen co-operative relations with China and talked of the promotion of mutual understanding and trust among the younger generations in China and Japan. Premier Zhu Rongji, in his message, expressed the hope 'that we will both seize the opportunity of the thirtieth anniversary of the normalization of relations, in accordance with the spirit of "taking history as a mirror and looking toward the future"'.[1]

The positive tone of speeches, policy reviews, and the numerous celebratory activities of 2002 were, however, overshadowed by a series of issues that suggested a slightly different picture of the state of affairs. The main indication that something was awry in 2002 was the absence of Prime Minister Koizumi from the celebrations in China in September to celebrate the anniversary of the signing of the 1972 Joint Statement. Although there had been plans for him to attend the celebrations, a number of diplomatic incidents put a strain on the relationship and rendered the visit inappropriate as far as the Chinese and Japanese foreign ministries were concerned. Although no specific reasons were offered for his absence, China's dissatisfaction with Koizumi's visit to the Yasukuni Shrine[2] in April could have been a contributory factor, in addition to the row over the Shenyang consulate issue, which also threatened to stall the celebration plans.[3] Other diplomatic problems such as the 'mystery ship' incident,[4] and visits by Japanese Cabinet ministers to the Yasukuni Shrine on 15 August also marred the celebratory mood during the year.

The presence of such problems between the two countries comes as no surprise to the student or observer of Sino-Japanese relations. Previous years had also been marked by a string of incidents which tested the diplomatic patience of both sides. Since the 1980s, many of the issues have been related to what the Chinese call 'problems remaining from the war' (*zhanzheng yiliu wenti*). In this regard, the Chinese Ministry of Foreign Affairs website refers specifically to three categories of outstanding problems: (1) the history problem; (2) war reparations, and (3) disposal of abandoned chemical weapons. The frequent recurrence of these war-related problems on the Sino-Japanese political agenda, and the way in which the Chinese and Japanese governments and peoples have been trying to come to terms with their past, are the focus of this book.[5]

References to 'the history problem' (C: *lishi wenti;* J: *rekishi mondai*) or 'history consciousness' (*lishi ishi; rekishi ishiki*) began to appear more frequently in Chinese and Japanese official statements and documents, in the media, and in academic accounts of the state of the relationship in the 1980s and 1990s. The history problem comprises a set of issues relating to the legacy of history and the very different interpretations in China and Japan of the events of 1931–45. Emerging in the 1980s, problems reappeared on an almost annual basis in the form of protests over textbook content, the nature (or lack of) Japanese apologies to the Chinese, gaffes by Liberal Democratic Party (LDP) Diet members relating to the events of the war, Japanese prime ministerial visits to the Yasukuni Shrine, and so on. As the chronology (Table 1) shows, similar problems continued into the 1990s and early twenty-first century, sometimes threatening to disrupt other aspects of the relationship. To cite a few examples, Li Peng cancelled a visit to Japan in 2001 because of the textbook problem. After Koizumi's April 2002 visit to the Yasukuni Shrine, the Chinese cancelled a trip to China by the Director General of the Japanese Defence Agency. Similarly, the fledgling security dialogue between Japan and China was interrupted between 2001 and 2002 because of the textbook and Yasukuni Shrine issues (Ching 2002; Przystup 2002a). In addition to problems over the interpretation of history, the issue of war reparations (re-)emerged in the 1990s in the form of growing demand upon the Japanese government and companies for compensation to be paid to individuals or groups of Chinese, and the disposal of chemical weapons abandoned by the Japanese army at the end of the war also became an issue on the political agenda.

The longevity of some of the issues, and the way in which the Chinese and Japanese governments have dealt with them, are notable, since they have tended to appear intermittently, emerging as crises in some years, only to be resolved temporarily through some *ad hoc* arrangement or agreement between the two governments. As this book will show, none of the issues has yet been fully resolved, and this is partly to do with the failure of both governments to reach agreements satisfactory to both sides, often because of domestic political pressures and constraints. The problems were further complicated by the involvement of other, non-state, actors that put pressure on both governments to act. The involvement of domestic, regional, and international non-governmental groups and activists reflects the fact that the

Table 1 Issues in Sino-Japanese relations: 1982–2002

1982	Jul.–Sep.	Textbook issue (also 1984 and 1986)
1985	Aug.	PM Nakasone visits Yasukuni Shrine
1989	Jun.	Tiananmen Square incident: Japan reluctant to isolate China
1992	Oct.	Visit of Emperor Akihito to PRC
1994	May	Nagano Shigeto (Minister of Justice): 'Nanking Massacre is fabrication'
	Aug.	Sakurai Shin (Environment Minister): 'not a war of aggression'
1995	May	Chinese nuclear tests – Japan freezes aid
	Jun.	Diet 'no war' resolution
1996	July	PM Hashimoto visits Yasukuni Shrine
	Sep.	Senkaku/Diaoyu Islands dispute
1997	Sep.	China protests about revised USA–Japan Defence Guidelines
	Nov.	Jiang Zemin–Obuchi Keizō summit in Tokyo – problems over wording of apology
1999	May	Japan protests over Chinese naval/research activity near Senkaku Islands
	July	China concerned about Senkaku Islands discussion in Diet
	July	Obuchi–Jiang Zemin/Zhu Rongji summit in Beijing
2000	Jan.	China raises concern about conference on Nanjing Massacre held in Osaka by right-wing groups
	Oct.	Zhu Rongji visits Japan, adopts forward-looking stance on history
2001	Apr.	China criticises approval of *The New History Textbook*; Japan sends delegations to explain
	Aug.	PM Koizumi visits the Yasukuni Shrine (also Apr. 2002, Jan. 2003, Jan. 2004)
	Oct.	PM Koizumi visits China, visits Marco Polo Bridge and Anti-Japanese War Museum, offers 'heartfelt apology'
	Dec.	'Mystery ship' incident
2002	May	Shenyang incident (at Japanese consulate)
	Sep.	ceremonies to mark the 30th anniversary of normalisation

Sources: various issues *Comparative Connections*, *Japan Echo*, *Japan Times*.

problems between the two sides can no longer seen within the narrow confines of Sino-Japanese state-to-state relations, but have broader implications for conflict resolution, human rights and gender issues. By the late 1990s there appeared to be a growing rift between the way in which the two governments were attempting to deal with the issues (which increasingly involved an agreement to disagree in the interests of developing other aspects of the relationship), and the attempts of the domestic and regional non-governmental groups to keep history-related problems firmly on the agenda. These diverging approaches meant that by the beginning of the twenty-first century, resolution of the history problem and related issues seemed more elusive than ever.

Problems remaining from the war and their impact on Sino-Japanese relations

The two sets of issues with which this book is concerned are the history problem, and the pursuit of civilian compensation for Chinese former forced labourers, comfort women,[6] and those harmed by Japan's wartime biological warfare programme or abandoned chemical weapons. This section will explain in more detail what is meant by each of these problems, before examining the ways in which they are seen to affect the relationship between China and Japan as described in the literature on Sino-Japanese relations. It then introduces the theoretical framework and objectives of the book.

The first set of issues relates to the history problem, defined here as encompassing problems relating to the content of Japanese school history textbooks since the 1980s, revisionist interpretations of the war in Japan in the 1990s, and the very different understandings of the events of the war as depicted in war museums and memorials in both countries. It also refers to the problems relating to the attempts by various Japanese governments to settle the past with China (which includes apologies, educational initiatives, and official visits to Chinese memorials and museums), while simultaneously attempting to satisfy the needs of Japanese citizens to commemorate the war and memorialise their own war dead.

The official Chinese view of the history problem is as follows:

> The correct understanding of history is a sensitive political issue in the [sic] bilateral relations. How to acknowledge and recognize the history of Japanese militaristic invasion against China was a focal point at the negotiation table in the process of the normalization of bilateral diplomatic relations early in 1972. The explicit explanation has been made in the Joint Statement and the Treaty of Peace and Friendship, which served as the political basis for bilateral relations. The Chinese side has all along stated that 'The past, if not forgotten, can serve as a guide for the future'. On the basis of respecting the history, the Chinese side wishes to look to the future and develop friendly relations between the two peoples from generation to generation. Nevertheless, the prerequisite for long-term bilateral cooperation is to face and recognize the history.[7]

In sharp contrast, the official Japanese view tends to play down history-related issues. The Japanese Ministry of Foreign Affairs website has a page devoted to 'Topics Related to Post-war Issues' which lists statements and agreements made between Japan and the Chinese and Korean governments on such issues as textbooks, comfort women and the Yasukuni Shrine issue, but does not provide any details about the origins of these issues or the measures taken to try and resolve them.[8] The *Diplomatic Bluebook 2002* refers very briefly, and in a matter-of-fact way, to the 'Main Causes for Concern' in Japan–China relations in 2001, which included the textbook problem and Prime Minister Koizumi's visit to the Yasukuni Shrine (Ministry of Foreign Affairs 2002: 58).

The second set of issues with which this book is concerned relates to civil compensation cases. Although the question of war reparations was settled when Sino-Japanese normalisation took place in 1972 (with China waiving reparations), nonetheless the pursuit of restitution in the form of civil compensation, acknowledgement, and official apologies by some hundreds of individual Chinese has become a marked trend in recent years. New research into Japan's biological and chemical warfare programme in China, the Nanjing Massacre, and so on, have provided a great deal of evidence to support the plaintiffs' cases. It is now thought that the number of Chinese women who were forced into sexual slavery by the Japanese military could have been in the region of 200,000. There are very few survivors left, but some have begun to talk about their experiences and joined with comfort women of other nationalities to seek compensation and an apology. Approximately 40,000 Chinese labourers were shipped to Japan to work in mines and factories affiliated with Japanese companies such as Mitsui and Mitsubishi. Many of these former forced labourers have sought compensation from such companies in recent years, in addition to demanding an apology from the Japanese state. Other compensation cases relate to the injuries and illnesses caused by the accidental discovery of chemical weapons and bombs since the end of the war. Chemical weapons were introduced into China by the Japanese military during the war, but were abandoned or crudely disposed of as the Japanese withdrew. The Japanese government acknowledged its responsibility for disposing of the vast amounts of chemical weapons in the 1990s, and, albeit slowly and intermittently, joint efforts between Japanese and Chinese teams to locate, identify and eventually destroy the weapons have made some progress since 1997. In the meantime, however, accidents continue to happen and much research is still being undertaken in China about the extent of injuries caused by the abandoned weapons.

The compensation cases have been brought to the attention of the international community with the help of Chinese, Japanese, regional, and international non-governmental organisations (NGOs), which provide financial and moral support for what are very often gruelling and lengthy experiences. Compensation cases against the Japanese state and companies have been brought in Japanese, American, and Chinese courts, but as yet few have met with success for the plaintiffs.[9] Both the Chinese and Japanese governments have adopted a 'hands-off' approach to the compensation cases, maintaining that the state-to-state agreements resolved such issues, but the movement for civil compensation continues to gather speed and groups within each country have begun to put pressure on their own governments to act.

While it is perhaps the first set of issues – Japanese school textbooks, visits of Japanese ministers to the Yasukuni Shrine, and so on – which appear often on the diplomatic agenda of the Sino-Japanese relationship, all the war-related problems are detrimental to the bilateral relationship, and all are closely connected. The history problem centres on an inability to agree on a shared version of history (both within Japan and between Japan and China), and causes problems for Chinese victims of the war who are now seeking acknowledgement and justice in Japanese courts, and for those who are calling upon the Japanese government to issue a 'genuine apology'. In turn, the problems relating to compensation cases have highlighted the failure of Japanese courts to order the Japanese government to accept legal and financial responsibility for the suffering inflicted upon former forced labourers and comfort women. For some, this simply reinforces the view that the Japanese government is evading its war responsibility.

The negative impact of problems remaining from the war can be seen in a number of aspects of the Sino-Japanese relationship, and is frequently referred to in the existing literature on Sino-Japanese relations. That the two countries have not yet fully reconciled the past has broader repercussions in the region, and the tension caused by diplomatic disagreements on such issues has the potential to impact upon the stability and development of the East Asian region.

China and Japan are undoubtedly the chief contenders for economic, political, and/or military power in East Asia. This is, of course, not just a phenomenon of the twenty-first century – their rivalry throughout the centuries as their relative economic, political and military strengths have waxed and waned has been well documented. But in the view of one Chinese academic, the problems emerging between the two countries at the end of the twentieth century and the beginning of the twenty-first are worthy of particular note, given that China and Japan are now approaching a more equitable balance of power than ever before: 'In the past when China was strong, Japan was weak; and when Japan was strong, China was weak. Now China and Japan are both strong' (Jin 2002: 51).

The strength of the two countries can, of course, be viewed positively. The economic aspect of the relationship, for example, is particularly strong and there is little doubt that the two countries benefit from increasing economic interdependence, that their policies converge in terms of their general interests (for example, in matters to do with the environment, energy and resources, peace, stability, prosperity, etc.), and both countries appear to be accepting of regional and international norms (for example, ASEAN + 3, ARF, WTO) (Austin and Harris 2001). The Chinese and Japanese economies together represent a formidable force in the region. China's impressive record of modernisation and economic growth in the past ten to fifteen years looks set to continue, but it still has a long way to go to 'catch up' with Japan, which, despite its record of negative economic growth in same period, remains a powerful economy, accounting for 66 per cent of the region's GDP in 2001 – over four times China's 15 per cent (Jin 2002b: 222). The volume of trade between the two countries has been increasing annually to reach its highest level in 2003 of over $130 billion. In 2002 Japan's imports from China exceeded those from the USA, while its exports to China increased by 32 per cent (Przystup 2003b). Japan's aid and direct investment continue to be an essential, and increasingly valued, source of funding for China's modernisation programme, in particular the 'Western development' plan (aimed at developing the Chinese hinterland). At the regional level, there are signs of a willingness to discuss greater economic integration – the idea of an East Asia Free Trade Association, for example, was suggested by Zhu Rongji during the ASEAN+3 meeting in Phnom Penh in October 2002 (Przystup 2003a).[10]

But while many opportunities for cooperation exist between the two countries, the legacy of the Sino-Japanese war is often seen as a hindrance to the smooth development of the relationship. The duality of the relationship – where periods of tension alternate with periods of relative calm – receives much attention. A survey of recent literature on Sino-Japanese relations finds that the phrases like 'complementarity and conflict', 'cooperation or rivalry', and 'cooperation, competition and conflict' appear frequently in titles and subtitles.[11] The 'conflict' to which the titles refer stems from the lack of trust and understanding between the two countries, itself a product of the war and a reflection of the failure to resolve issues of war and war responsibility. This, according to some, impacts more widely on other aspects of the relationship. Thus, despite the strength of the economic relationship noted above, Yahuda argues that there are limits to how far economic interdependence between China and Japan can compensate for the 'thinness' of other aspects of the relationship, and that it is impossible to separate political considerations from economic activity (Yahuda 2001). Yahuda views the constant misunderstandings over history, for example, as the 'failure of empathy on both sides'. Failing even to try to understand each other's stances on the history issue bodes ill for the future which, in Yahuda's formulation, will be dictated by traditional balance-of-power considerations as Chinese and Japanese elites each consider the other's growing military clout. In addition, a widespread lack of interest in their neighbouring country among the younger generation, he argues, further removes the proximity and closeness that used to exist in the form of a set of personal links between leading politicians, scholars and key businessmen.

Studies of East Asian security tend to place much emphasis on the role of Chinese and Japanese mutual images and perceptions, and also raise concerns about the legacy of the war on the security aspect of the Sino-Japanese relationship. Zhao Quansheng's view of the relationship as having deteriorated throughout the 1980s and 1990s, casting 'a shadow over regional and global affairs in the post-Cold War era', is not untypical (2002: 43). In particular, Zhao identifies problems such as Taiwan, territory (Diaoyu/Senkaku islands), and 'the potential resurgence of Japanese militarism, *memories of which stem from past Japanese aggression*' (ibid.: 41, italics added). Indeed, he argues that 'sometimes it appears that wartime history has become a leading factor in China's Japan policy' (ibid.: 44). Christensen considers Chinese and Japanese mutual perceptions – that is 'historically-based mistrust and animosity' – to be important to an understanding of the security dilemma facing

North-east Asia in the 1990s.[12] China's 'historically rooted and visceral distrust of Japan', or 'Tokyo's refusal to respond satisfactorily to Chinese requests that Tokyo recognize and apologize for its imperial past', are, according to Christensen, at the heart of the problem, and will prevent China and Japan from forming close ties in the near future (1999: 52). A similar view is expressed by Kim Taeho who argues that rivalry and distrust are linked to 'deeply ingrained cultural, historical and perceptual factors' rather than shared economic or strategic interests, and are therefore more difficult to control (Kim 1998: 361). Wu Xinbo also accounts for the strong mutual suspicions between China and Japan in terms of history, memory and lingering negative perceptions – China's memory of Japan's aggression and perception of Japan's national character as 'exclusivist and resistant to external pressure' are set against Japanese suspicions that China still 'embraces the traditional "Middle Kingdom mentality"' (Wu 2000: 308). Midford argues that China's reaction to the USA-Japan decision to revise the defence guidelines in the mid-1990s revealed the perception, based on 'robust cognitive roots', that Japan possessed malevolent intentions regarding regional security (2000: 21). Based on these assumptions, the PRC responded with alarm to the threat of a Japan potentially free from, or at least enjoying greater autonomy within, the US alliance. In this context, the balance-of-threat theory relies on the idea that Chinese perceptions and beliefs about the Japan threat, themselves based on the events of history (i.e., a Japanese capacity for militarism), impact upon Chinese behaviour towards Japan.[13] Finally, Drifte argues that 'many Chinese fear that an unrepentant Japan is bound to repeat its past aggression, echoing the widespread historical deterministic idea of many Chinese that a country that does not acknowledge past misdeeds "correctly" is bound to repeat them' (2003: 15).

One need not read only the academic literature on Sino-Japanese relations to find examples of mutual mistrust, misunderstanding and dislike. Opinion polls taken to mark the 30th anniversary of normalisation highlighted the attitudes of Chinese and Japanese towards each other. On the Japanese side, a *Yomiuri shinbun* poll of August 2002 revealed that 55 per cent of the respondents said they could not trust China.[14] The first-ever joint poll, carried out by the Chinese Academy of Social Sciences and *Asahi shinbun* in September 2002, showed that 45 per cent of Japanese respondents, and 50 per cent of Chinese respondents thought that the China–Japan relationship was only going 'okay', and when asked to qualify this answer, the stated reasons on the Japanese side were a lack of mutual understanding, and, on the Chinese side, the Japanese failure to understand history (Chinese Academy of Social Sciences 2002). The results of the Chinese side of the poll provide some interesting details. A total of 43.3 per cent felt unfriendly or very unfriendly towards Japan (47.6 per cent had ordinary feelings; 5.9 per cent felt friendly, 3.2 per cent did not know). The main reason for unfriendly feelings was Japan's lack of remorse for its aggression in China (63.8 per cent). The predominant image of the Japanese was the war of aggression (53.5 per cent), and among the most important issues for the smooth development of Sino-Japanese relations in the twenty-first century were trade (46.8 per cent), the history problem (46 per cent), the territory problem (12.8 per cent), and Taiwan (25.8 per cent) (multiple answers were allowed). On the issue of what policy the Japanese government and companies should adopt in dealing with unresolved issues such as forced labourers and comfort women, the responses were largely split between 'apology and compensation from the Japanese government' (43.3 per cent), and 'apology and compensation from the Japanese government and companies concerned' (45.3 per cent). 50.9 per cent of the respondents felt that official visits to the Yasukuni Shrine by the Japanese prime minister 'should not take place under any circumstances', and 60.4 per cent felt concerned about the possibility that Japan could once again 'go down the militarist road' (Chinese Academy of Social Sciences 2002; Jiang 2002). These results are perhaps hardly surprising given the heavy diet of anti-Japanese sentiment expressed in the Chinese press over the last half century, but there is also evidence of a more spontaneous, grass-roots-led sense of injustice. There is, on the other hand, a growing frustration among some Japanese people and politicians with the ongoing demands from the Chinese for compensation and apologies. The results of such polls seem to indicate a growing awareness among the public in both countries that war-related problems are far from resolved.

Aims and framework of the book

It is clear that the problems discussed above cast a shadow over the Sino-Japanese relationship, and it is therefore important to understand why they continue to emerge over fifty years after the end of the war. The impact of the history problem on Sino-Japanese relations has been the focus of a great deal of academic and popular attention in recent years. A number of studies have been undertaken which help to shed light on the politics of particular aspects of, for example, textbook disputes, prime ministerial visits to the Yasukuni Shrine and so on. For example, Johnson (1986), Rose (1998), Dirlik (1996), Kim (1983), Beal *et al.* (2001), among others, have written on the various instalments of the textbook issue; the significance of the Yasukuni Shrine has been analysed by Whiting (1989), Nelson (2003), Bix (2000), Harootunian (1999) and others. There are a number of very useful studies of Japanese and Chinese approaches to history, memory and war responsibility in general (for example, Awaya 1994; Barmé 1993; Orr 2001; Yoneyama 1999 *et al.*), and issue-specific studies, such as discussions of the debate on the Nanjing Massacre (Fogel 2000; Yamamoto 2000; Yang 1999) and the apology issue (Field 1995; Mukae 1996) are also enlightening. Japanese and Chinese language sources on war-related subjects have proliferated in recent years, and I have drawn heavily on studies carried out by Tanaka Hiroshi, Tawara Yoshifumi, Su Zhiliang, Bu Ping, and Jin Xide. Issues such as compensation cases have not yet received much attention in the English-language literature, and this book aims to fill that gap by discussing the origins, aims and progress of some of the cases brought by Chinese groups and individuals in the 1990s, making use of some of the transcripts of the court cases, Chinese and Japanese media reports, and publications produced by lawyers' groups and support groups.

The main purpose of the book is to build upon the existing body of literature on the various war-related problems in Sino-Japanese relations, by considering them all within an overarching framework of reconciliation. The framework will be explained in more detail in Chapter 1, but briefly, it makes use of models of reconciliation which demonstrate the way two former enemies attempt to reconcile the past. There is no one ideal model, but there are certain patterns common to the process of coming to terms with the past. These generally include: an acknowledgement of wrongdoing; acceptance of legal and moral responsibility; retribution; apologies; forgiveness and redress. Reconciliation between two parties is not guaranteed and is prone to setbacks and numerous obstacles as the case of China and Japan highlights. As the book demonstrates, reconciliation between China and Japan began soon after the end of the war, and continues today. The book splits the reconciliation process into two broad phases or cycles: the Cold War period up to the late 1970s, by which point China and Japan had achieved diplomatic normalisation; and the 1980s onwards which saw much greater political, economic and social interaction between the two countries. During the first cycle, reconciliation was carried out at governmental or judicial level, through war crimes trials and treaties. It was, therefore, a predominantly top-down process, although numerous individuals and groups were also actively involved in re-building the relationship below the level of the state. During the second phase, however, reconciliation became pluralised and began to incorporate other, non-governmental, actors – an essential element if the process is to have broad success. While the two governments continued to implement measures favourable to a settlement of the past (or at least pay lip service to the process), it is perhaps the bottom-up element of this phase of the reconciliation process that is significant since it involves much greater interaction between groups and individuals on both sides than in previous years. The role of these groups in the reconciliation process between China and Japan will be a recurrent theme in the book.

The book has two main aims: first, it seeks to explain why the war-related issues emerged in the 1980s and, more importantly, why they have continued into the 1990s and beyond; second, it examines the ways in which the governments and peoples have attempted to resolve the issues, considering the successes and failures.

In terms of the first objective, there are a number of reasons for the occurrence, and recurrence, of war-related problems between China and Japan in the 1980s and beyond, but fundamentally, the argument throughout the book is that attempts by the two sides to reconcile the past have been flawed and are, as yet, incomplete. The first reason can be traced back to the early post-war period, the onset of the Cold War, and the evolution of the relationship between the two countries under a particular set of domestic and international constraints. As Chapter 2 will explain in more detail, the Chinese and Japanese governments progressed through various, standard, stages of reconciliation in almost textbook fashion: war crimes trials were carried out; post-war reparations were discussed (and waived), and a peace treaty was signed. On the whole, these measures were deemed appropriate and satisfactory at the time, but by the early 1980s when a different set of domestic political and international circumstances prevailed, problems harking back to the war began to emerge. The textbook issue of 1982 was the first major diplomatic incident between China and Japan (and Korea and Japan) and was to set the tone of the diplomatic agenda for the next few years, during which a string of minor (and major) history-related problems developed. As Chapter 3 will demonstrate, some of these problems emerged largely because there was now the political space for them to do so – in other words, more open discussion in both China and Japan (and between Chinese and Japanese academics and politicians) about hitherto taboo topics relating to the war meant that debates which had been stifled for so long were finally out in the open, and able to be contested. Thus, for example, greater academic and political freedom in China allowed researchers to access archives and reinterpret the events of the war free (or at least freer) of the constraints imposed by the CCP's official line; and the death of Emperor Hirohito in 1989 revitalised the debate on war responsibility in Japan. What problems like the textbook issues highlighted was the contrasting interpretations of the war that had emerged in the early post-war period as a result of the very different domestic political circumstances in each country, and the attendant need for governments to create a grand narrative for legitimation purposes. These different views of history were also a result of Japan and China's relative isolation from one another during the early part of the Cold War. The kind of joint history projects undertaken by Germany and Poland which aimed to produce a shared view of the past, and which helped to heal the past between the two countries, have only recently begun in China and Japan.

   A second reason for the emergence, and persistence, of the history problem relates to its political utility, as several academics have observed. The elevation of the textbook and other issues into diplomatic spats have much to do with domestic politics, and politicking, in both China and Japan. In the 1980s and early 1990s, the various instalments of these recurring problems tended to follow a particular formula whereby the Chinese government protested at some Japanese insult or gaffe, the Japanese government denied there was a problem until the Chinese protests became sufficiently persuasive, at which point both governments reached an agreement which resolved the matter temporarily. This is not to say that the reasons for the protests of the Chinese government were not legitimate or genuine – a diplomatic response is, no doubt, appropriate when a Japanese cabinet minister denies the Nanjing Massacre (as Minister for Justice Nagano Shigeto did in 1994). But often one, or indeed both, governments, have sought a short-term objective (to do with political legitimacy, perhaps, or a domestic power struggle), by playing what has come to be called the 'history card'.[15] Some of the case studies in this book highlight the use of the history card, but they also show that since the late 1990s, the response of each government to the various history problems has started to change.

The third reason for the persistence of war-related issues in the 1990s and up to the present day is due to the nature of the issues themselves, in addition to changing domestic and international environments. As Chapter 4 will explain in more detail, in the 1990s, a different set of problems emerged between the two countries, specifically the movement for civil compensation from Chinese individuals and groups. The struggle for compensation for former comfort women, forced labourers and others who suffered during the war, developed from grass-roots initiatives and is being played out in courtrooms rather than embassies. International and regional developments in the form of trans-national activism on human rights and gender issues certainly helped the compensation movement to develop, but it was also driven by the rise of civil society in both China and Japan, and by the need of now elderly individuals (or their families) to seek recognition and restitution. The compensation movement had the effect of temporarily shifting the emphasis away from the role of the state in the reconciliation process, but both the Chinese and Japanese governments started to come under pressure from domestic and international groups to take up the cause of victims of the Sino-Japanese war whose suffering was not acknowledged or avenged in the war crimes trials or taken into account in state-level discussions about reparations in the 1970s. The issue of the disposal of chemical weapons abandoned in China by the Japanese military, was informed by international developments (the signing of the Chemical Weapons Convention in 1993), and is being dealt with, albeit slowly, at the political level. Similarly, other international trends, such as the vogue for offering apologies, the 'memory boom' which saw a surge in commemorative acts, a fashion for reflection on, and re-writing of the past as the end of century approached could also be seen in China and Japan. As Chapter 5 shows, in many cases this served only to reinforce the gulf between Japanese and Chinese views of history, but it was attended by a perceived need to at least attempt to breach that gulf to enable the two governments and people to move forward, positively, into the twenty-first century.

The second aim of the book is to consider the way in which the governments and people of China and Japan have attempted to resolve the war-related problems in the 1980s and 1990s, and why these efforts appear not to have been entirely successful (hence their persistence). The book divides the war-related problems noted above into three categories: (1) the battle for history writing (Japanese school textbooks, historical revisionism in Japan and the search for a shared history); (2) the quest for justice via individual claims for compensation and apologies; and (3) problems surrounding Japanese apologies, (re-)presentations of the past (for example, in museum exhibitions), and commemoration of the dead (remembrance ceremonies, visits to the Yasukuni Shrine, and so on). These categories correspond roughly to different stages of the reconciliation process described in the literature, that is, seeking the truth, seeking justice and reparations, and settling the past through apologies and commemoration. Thus, all three categories relate to the way in which Chinese and Japanese governments and people are trying to come to terms with, or reconcile, the past, and the failure to resolve one particular issue often explains the failure to resolve the others.

A noticeable trend in recent years is the divergence between the governmental approach to the history problem and that of domestic and transnational civil society. Specifically, it seems that both governments would very much like to avoid discussion of the past, and concentrate more on talking about the future. Although there are exceptions, the Chinese government and individual leaders, for example, have tended to be *comparatively* restrained in their criticisms of Japan's various transgressions over textbooks and Yasukuni shrine visits. For their part, Japanese prime ministers seem increasingly willing to offer (verbal) apologies to the Chinese for the events of the war. The problem, however, is that while the governments may be more willing to put history to rest by adopting a more conciliatory stance than in previous years, or else by skirting around it entirely, the Chinese and Japanese people are becoming more interested in seeking solutions to those problems which they feel have not yet been fully resolved, and on which they feel their respective government should be taking a stronger position. Ironically, the patterned, almost ritualised behaviour of the two governments on history-related issues in the past has, in the long term, exacerbated the problem because it has created certain expectations amongst the domestic audiences and interest groups of how their government should respond. In addition, it has hindered serious discussion of the important issues of historical consciousness and war responsibility. By the late 1990s, when it became apparent that both governments were increasingly willing to put the history problem to one side in the interest of developing a more forward-looking relationship (or, more cynically, when they began to find that the history card lacked the potency of previous years), they had to deal with the heightened expectations of people who, in China's case, for example, had become accustomed to the government taking a hard stance on Japan. If the Chinese government adopts too pragmatic a stance, it runs the risk of being criticised for being weak. If the Japanese government adopts an apologetic stance, it is condemned in conservative circles for being weak-kneed, but if it takes a hard-line stance, it is criticised by pro-reconciliation groups for not facing up to its post-war responsibility. Needless to say, this complex interplay of the pressures of domestic politics on the one hand, and the need to find an accommodation with an important neighbour, on the other, influences the outcome of history-related problems.

Structure of the book

Chapter 1 considers the literature on the process of reconciliation and how it can be applied to the case of China and Japan. It suggests that China and Japan, like other countries formerly at war, have undergone various stages of the process since the end of the Second World War, and that renewed efforts in the 1990s by both Chinese and Japanese governments and societies to resolve war-related issues conform to models of reconciliation where the role of grass-roots organisations is seen to be of growing importance. Chapter 2 outlines what I refer to as the first phase of reconciliation in Sino-Japanese relations from 1945 up to the 1970s. This historical background, which covers the impact of the Cold War on Sino-Japanese reconciliation, the agreements reached between China and Japan on the wording of an apology and on reparations in the 1970s, and the evolution of different views of the Sino-Japanese war in each country, is important since it helps to explain why some of the war-related issues remain unresolved today. The remainder of the book then deals with the second phase of reconciliation from the 1980s to the present. Chapter 3 considers the ongoing process of uncovering the 'truth' about what happened during the war. It focuses on the very different interpretations of the war in China and Japan, problems of Japanese historical revisionism and history textbooks, and recent attempts to find a version of history acceptable in both Japan and China. Chapter 4 considers the quest for justice by individual victims of Japanese atrocities, by looking at the Chinese 'compensation movement' (*suopei yundong*) of the 1990s and the support activities of Japanese and other NGOs. Chapter 5 considers the difficulties of settling the past, looking at the apology issue and other contentious issues such as Yasukuni Shrine visits, commemorative activities and the way in which the past is presented in museums and exhibitions. The Conclusion in Chapter 6 considers how far the two sides have come in the lengthy process of reconciliation, and how much further there is to go.

1 Reconciliation and Sino-Japanese relations

It may seem odd to discuss reconciliation in the context of a relationship between two countries which ceased hostilities nearly sixty years ago, which normalised relations thirty years ago, and which are actively pursuing a friendly, cooperative partnership at the beginning of the twenty-first century. Indeed, as will be discussed below, China and Japan have been undergoing reconciliation for the past fifty years. But as the introduction illustrated, despite the efforts of leaders and citizens alike, fundamental problems relating to the war between China and Japan still exist, and appear to pose a formidable obstacle to settlement of the past and, therefore, to the smooth running of the relationship in the future. The aim of this chapter is to provide a framework for the book as a whole, and some context for the case studies that follow. It considers the process of reconciliation as a means of explaining and understanding the efforts made by the Chinese and Japanese governments and society to settle the past. The literature on reconciliation describes a series of stages through which two parties must pass in their attempts to overcome past problems. The issues covered in this book – textbook problems, compensation cases, and a range of activities associated with commemoration and memorial – can be seen as different stages along the path of reconciliation.

There are a number of historical reasons for the difficulties faced by both sides in coming to terms with the past. These reasons will be discussed more fully in Chapter 2, but, briefly, the domestic political climates in each country following the war, the outcome of war crimes trials, and the onset of the Cold War had the effect of halting nascent debates about the war within each country, as well as dialogues between the two countries. Domestic constraints or political struggles over history (for example, the education battle between the Left and Right in Japan or the relative lack of academic freedom in China until the late 1970s) further hampered efforts to settle sensitive issues to do with the past. As Carol Gluck points out in reference to Japan, the 'early mastery of the past ... froze condemnation of the war into orthodoxy at a stage when the division of villains and victims seemed starkly clear' (1992: 13). This could apply equally to China where the communist lore on the War of Resistance against Japan was established very early in the PRC's history.

There was no dialogue about the war between the Chinese and Japanese until normalisation took place in the 1970s, and even then, the issues of an apology and reparations seemed to be resolved fairly quickly and amicably. But the ease with which normalisation between China and Japan was achieved in 1972 masked a deeper problem which would emerge in the 1980s and 1990s and which stemmed from the very different ways in which the war had come to be remembered in both countries. The result is an ongoing process of reconciliation between the two countries which encompasses a renewed search for the 'facts' of history, the discovery of hitherto hidden evidence of wartime activities, the need for individuals to seek recognition of their wartime experiences and justice for their suffering, and the desire of individuals and groups to make amends for and commemorate the past through apologies, memorials, and so on. These activities closely resemble those described by academics and practitioners working on conflict resolution and transitional justice in their analyses of the ways in which former conflicting parties attempt to come to terms with the past and create the conditions for a stable social and political environment for the future. The next section outlines the relevant literature with a view to constructing a framework applicable to Sino-Japanese reconciliation.

Approaches to reconciliation

While the topic of the way in which countries like Germany and Japan have attempted to settle their past has been the focus of much academic attention for many years, less has been written about Sino-Japanese reconciliation. The political and social changes brought about by the collapse of Communism and the end of the Cold War revitalised general debates about war, justice, memory and commemoration. There is now a sizeable literature which considers the way in which countries previously split by civil war or whose peoples have been the victims of brutal regimes or discrimination have attempted to settle the past (for example, South Africa, Eastern Europe, Rwanda, Latin America). In addition, the efforts of minority groups to seek amends for past injustices have become an important area for study (for example, Native Americans and Australian aborigines). Germany's ongoing Holocaust restitution and Japan's handling of the comfort women issue in the 1990s are also recurring themes in the recent literature (for case studies of these and more, see Barkan 2000; Brooks 1999; Neier 1998; Rigby 2001). The literature produced in the 1990s reflected seemingly universal trends which can be split into three types of activity. Using terms coined by academics working in the field, these can be summarised as the 'memory boom' (Huyssen 1995), the 'rush for restitution' (Barkan 2001), and the 'age of apology' (Brooks 1999), and are discussed below.

The memory boom

The end of the Cold War and the effects of globalisation brought about a world-wide revival of debates about history, national identity, memory, and so on. States and sub-state groups (for example, ethnic or religious groups) began to review their histories as part of a re-affirmation of their local or national identities. Huyssen talks about a 'memory boom of unprecedented proportions' in the last fifteen years of the twentieth century, marked by debates about memory and identity in political, social and cultural spheres, the proliferation of memorials, museums, celebrations of national heritage, and anniversary events (1995: 5).

Nowhere was this more apparent than in Germany. Niven (2002), for example, refers to a 'veritable explosion of discussion' in the 1990s amongst the German media, intellectuals, politicians of all parties and the general public about the National Socialist past prompted by key anniversaries (e.g., the 50th anniversary in 1995 of the end of the war), new interpretations and images of the past (for example, Goldhagen's *Hitler's Willing Executioners*, exhibitions and concentration camp memorial sites), Hollywood films (*Schindler's List*), unification, and the 'right timing' for Germans to (re-) consider the past (Niven 2002: 1–2). Of course, German debates about the country's past had been ongoing for a number of years – the 'historians' dispute' (*Historikerstreit*) of the mid-1980s is perhaps the best-known episode. But for Niven, the remarkable thing about the latest phase of Germany's ongoing process of facing the past was its *inclusiveness* both in terms of the 'broader awareness of the true extent of National Socialist criminality and of the range of victims' (ibid.: 5), and in the audience it reached:

> The task of coming to terms with the past, long the preserve of histor-ians and politicians, was taken up by the population at large. Freed from Cold War politicisation, the period 1933–1945 was 'released' into the public realm for re-evaluation. Only once in the pre-1990 period, in West Germany with the showing of the American TV series *Holocaust* in 1979, had the wider German public been so shaken by the theme of German atrocities. In the course of the 1990s, a sense of shock was the hallmark of an intense public interest and discussion.
>
> (ibid.: 4)

This inclusiveness is seen in a positive sense, with a more critical understand-ing of Germany's past and an acceptance of the mistakes providing a basis for a democratic national identity. To an extent, a similar phenomenon could be discerned in China and Japan where, by the 1990s, history and identity were becoming far more popular and populist topics, and were no longer the preserve of academics. In Japan, this produced some controversies and bitter conflicts between the 'traditional' progressive academics and popular new groups such as the Japanese Society for History Textbook Reform (Atarashii kyōkasho o tsukuru kai, hereafter Tsukuru kai) which introduced revisionist, and, many argued, dangerous, narratives to a young mass audience. In China, the War of Resistance against Japan and the continuing problem of Japan's 'incorrect interpretations' of the war grabbed the interest of a wide section of the population, often reinforcing negative images of the Japanese. Films, television documentaries, museums and memorials also formed part of this history and memory boom in both countries. Chapters 3 to 5 show how, in some respects, these developments in China and Japan appeared only to push the Chinese and Japanese even further apart on the history problem, since the interpretations of wartime events remained poles apart. But they also had the effect of encouraging academics, students, journalists, film-makers, and so on to work even harder to reach a common understanding, and for the first time since the end of the war there emerged a dialogue between civil groups on both sides rather than two (or more) separate debates raging in isolation.

The rush for restitution

The 1990s also saw a marked increase in calls for compensation or justice for human rights violations of the Second World War which had not been addressed previously. This was in part a corollary of the renewed focus on history. The discovery of archival evidence, revised interpretations of the past, and the establishment of new international institutions, laws and norms provided greater opportunities for victims of war crimes or crimes against humanity to seek justice. It was also part of a broader trend, described by Barkan as 'a sudden rush of restitution cases all over the world', which testified to a 'new globalism that pays greater attention to human rights' (2001: 46).

Barkan defines restitution as a process where 'victims and perpetrators [come] face to face to barter the suffering and responsibility for the past and create a future, which both sides can subscribe to' and it can encompass compensation to victims, an admission of guilt, recognition of suffering, and forgiveness by the victims (ibid.: 49). An important element is the 'willingness of governments to admit to unjust and discriminatory past policies and to negotiate terms for restitution or reparation with their victims based more on moral considerations than on power politics' (Barkan 2000: 317). Restitution has potential benefits for both sides – the perpetrators 'hope to purge their own history of guilt and legitimise their current position, the victims hope to benefit from a new recognition of their suffering and to enjoy certain material gains' (ibid.: 321). Material gains derive from compensation claims for damages or loss of life, repayment of wages, veterans' pensions, medical support, and so on. In the 1990s such claims were brought by non-governmental groups, human rights lawyers, and trans-national civil society. WWII-related cases include German compensation for forced labourers and plundered art, Swiss compensation for the handling of Nazi gold, and American compensation of Japanese internees. In Japan's case, Asian and non-Asian victims (former prisoners of war, Korean and Taiwanese veterans, 'comfort women', forced labourers and victims of biological and chemical weapons, and so on) began to demand acknowledgement and individual compensation, but faced fundamental problems in the form of a Japanese government and judiciary unwilling to admit to past injustices, or, initially, to negotiate based on moral considerations.

The age of apology

Another global pastime of the 1990s, in addition to remembering one's past, was to apologise for it. Roy Brooks (1999: 3) refers to the 'age of apology' characterised by 'a matrix of guilt and mourning, atonement and national revival' and symbolised by statements of remorse and apology from heads of state or political leaders such as Queen Elizabeth II, Bill Clinton, F. W. de Klerk and so on. Dudden refers to the 'demands for official state apologies [which] brought about a transnational explosion of national contrition, and heads of state were transformed into articulators of new national histories' (2001: 598). The apology is considered deeply significant since it provides international recognition of the victims' own memory and suffering, and an admission of guilt by the perpetrator and thus helps the healing process. As part of the reconciliation process, apologies are sometimes more important to the injured parties than material compensation. Indeed, offers of compensation are often rejected by victims if an apology is not considered sufficiently sincere, or if no apology is forthcoming. Tavuchis categorises apologies into four types: one to one, one to many, many to one, many to many. The type of apology we will be most concerned with is from one state (acting as a collectivity) to another, or 'many to many' (Tavuchis 1991: 48). Such an apology must satisfy certain conditions: it must be offered with the backing and authority of the collectivity so that the apology is official and binding; it must be made publicly and on the record: and it should acknowledge the violation, accept responsibility, and indicate that there will be no repetition of such acts in future. The wording of an official apology is often very different to that of a personal apology, tending to be 'couched in abstract, remote, measured and emotionally neutral terms' (ibid.: 102). The expression of sorrow, a central component of a personal apology, appears to be lacking in the collective variety, but according to Tavuchis is not as essential to the apology as 'putting things on the record' (ibid.: 109). For an apology to be effective it must also be accepted and acknowledged by the injured party. As Jeong warns ' no reconciliation is achieved without forgiveness not only because the hurts of the past cannot be undone but also because any harm cannot be truly compensated' (1999a: 25–6).

The visit of Emperor Akihito to China in 1992, and a change of government in 1993, which ushered in the first non-LDP prime minister (Hosokawa) for thirty-eight years, are often seen as the starting point of a more apologetic attitude by the Japanese government towards its neighbours, but there had been earlier examples of an acknowledgement of Japan's aggression during the war from some individuals (most notably Prime Minister Nakasone in 1983). In China too there were signs that the government was willing to accept Japan's apologies and adopt a more forgiving stance than had been evident in the 1980s. But many Chinese doubted the sincerity of official apologies by Japanese prime ministers, and, as Chapter 5 will illustrate, Japanese governments were often reluctant to put an apology on the (written) record, even if they did offer verbal apologies. On the other hand, the Chinese too showed an inconsistency in their approach to the apologies that were offered by Japanese prime ministers, thus further exacerbating the problem.

When viewed within the context of the literature on reconciliation, what have been described above as distinct trends are, in fact, all part of the reconciliation process as a whole. General models of reconciliation are of relevance to this study of Sino-Japanese relations since they help to demonstrate that the various, and continuing, attempts by the Chinese and Japanese governments and people to reconcile the past fit with patterns observed elsewhere, and that the war-related problems that (re-)emerged between the two countries from the 1980s onwards reflected, or were informed by, the international trends noted above. These models are described in the next section.

Patterns of reconciliation

A word on definitions is perhaps necessary here, since there is some variation in the use of terms such as reconciliation, restitution and reparation. Lee defines reconciliation as:

> an effort to establish a new and constructive relationship between the perpetrators and the victims based on shared principles of justice, equity, and mutual respect. Without reconciliation, conflicting parties may come to some sort of accommodation, perhaps an uneasy truce, but seldom an enduring peace. In reconciliation, the parties involved take steps to ensure that justice be served. They then work to remove the residues of mistrust, which, if unaddressed, would linger as latent sources for future conflicts.
>
> (Lee 2003: 21)

Cairns' description of the process of 'coming to terms with the past' encompasses a similar set of activities:

> It means seeing the behaviour of our predecessors, and sometimes of our earlier selves, in terms of its consequences for contemporary generations. This may include trying those responsible for shameful acts and punishing them if found guilty. It includes apologizing to the victims or their successors; paying reparations; and providing symbolic recognition by plaques and memorials.
>
> (2003: 66)

Rigby (2001) discusses a number of possible approaches to reconciliation including amnesia, trials, purges and the pursuit of justice, truth commissions, and compensation and reparations. Barkan uses the word restitution to describe 'the entire spectrum of attempts to rectify historical injustices' which includes restitution (in the narrow sense of the word), reparations and apology (2000: xix). By contrast, however, Torpey (2003) understands restitution in the traditional, narrower sense to mean the return of specific items of real or personal property. Torpey instead uses the concept of 'reparations politics'[1] to refer to similar sorts of activities to those described by Rigby and Barkan, including justice, reparations, apologies, and commemorative history. In this book, the word reconciliation is used to indicate the process whereby states and societies interact over time and aim to resolve the past through such activities as trials, reparations (from one state to another), compensation (to individuals or groups), apologies (and acceptance of them), commemorative activities, and agreements on the interpretation of historical events.

The research carried out by scholars working in the areas of peace studies, conflict resolution and transitional justice agrees that reconciliation is a future-oriented, joint endeavour between the victims and perpetrators, but one that is lengthy, complex and prone to failure. There is no single, ideal model for reconciliation, and in some cases reconciliation is impossible to achieve. Different groups, and different individuals, approach the process in different ways with different results. Activities contributing to reconciliation can be official or unofficial, private or public, top down or bottom up. Kriesberg's elements of reconciliation illustrate this. He identifies, for example, several types of 'units' or agencies (individuals, officials, groups and peoples), 'dimensions' or models (acknowledgement, acceptance, apology, redress and forgiveness), and degrees of reconciliation (full, partial, accommodation, coexistence) (1999: 105–8). He suggests that while some individuals may be able to be reconciled with each other, 'most members of the enemy groups remain hostile' and that the degree of reconciliation varies according to 'proportion of people on each side who behave and have attitudes that are reconciliatory' (ibid.: 106–8). He further offers a series of alternative paths of reconciliation which depict different patterns in the way reconciliation takes place over time. For example 'linear progress' indicates steady progress, 'incremental steps' indicates progress 'made in little steps that are consolidated before the next steps are taken', and the 'wave progression' shows 'a few steps of improved relations . . . followed by one or two steps backward and then followed by a few steps forward again' (ibid.: 110–11). This latter pattern of progression seems most applicable to the case of Sino-Japanese relations.

The process of reconciliation cannot be unilateral, and to prevent future recurrence of crimes against humanity 'both perpetrators and victims [should] develop a commitment to share a common future in which mutual trust and harmony reign' (Lee 2003: 23). In the case of reconciliation between two countries, it is usually governments that create the conditions necessary to stimulate reconciliation on a mass scale (for example, by agreeing with the other state on reparations or by an acknowledgement of wrongdoing), but the activities of private groups or individuals are equally important to re-build trust and understanding. In Rigby's words, reconciliation 'requires *active participation* of those who were divided by enmity' (2000: 12). Rather than it being left to states to deal with issues such as compensation or trials, it is increasingly recognised that other actors, in particular, those who suffered directly (or their representatives), should play an active role if the process is to be successful. Thus, Rigby argues that:

> *the process should not be confined to a narrow strata of society*. The differ-ent dimensions and values that together contribute to any healing process must be deepened and broadened to encompass *all levels of society*, creat-ing in the process a new culture of respect for human difference and human rights.
>
> (2001: 183, italics added)

Barkan argues that although it is more likely that liberal societies will 'recog-nize past public injustices ... *other governments, NGOs, commercial com-panies, and even individuals* may take the burden of the past upon themselves (2000: 315, italics added). Winter and Sivan also stress the importance of individuals and groups who act as 'agents of remembrance' – whether the state is liberal or totalitarian (1999: 29).

But even if citizens, NGOs, companies and the like do become involved in the process, it does not guarantee full reconciliation. As Kriesberg points out, 'it is not to be expected that reconciliation will be universal among all mem-bers of the opposing sides' (1999: 106), and the degree of reconciliation can vary according to the particular experiences of the injured parties. In China, for example, it is perhaps more difficult for people (either those with direct experience, or their descendants) in the North-eastern provinces (formerly Manchuria) or in Nanjing to achieve reconciliation than it is for those who were not so directly affected by Japanese actions.

A further element of the process is time. Rigby states:

> The necessary conditions for reconciliation between formerly antagon-istic parties can only be realised over time. Moving beyond the divisions of the past is a *multidimensional process that can take generations*, and the *different constitutive elements involved in the journey toward reconciliation can rarely be pursued all at the same time*
>
> (2001: 183, italics added)

The sequence in which activities contributing to reconciliation take place is not always agreed upon in the literature, but the elements are usually the same, and echo the trends of remembrance, restitution, and apology men-tioned above. Fisher argues for acknowledgement, apology, forgiveness and assurance (1999: 97), Montville suggests acknowledgement of grievances, acceptance of responsibility, expression of contrition, and seeking and receiving forgiveness (1993, cited in Fisher 1999: 98), whereas Tavuchis suggests that an official apology is the 'prelude' to reconciliation (1991: 109). Rigby's ideal-type reconciliation process, describes four stages. Once peace has been secured between the two parties, one pressing task is to uncover the truth. There are various means by which this can be achieved, for example, through trials or truth commissions. It is then necessary to seek justice on behalf of the victims, again perhaps through trials of those responsible for their suffering or through reparations, which can either be symbolic or material in form. Eventually it should be possible to settle the past, or 'put the past in its proper place' through an apology to the victims, or through some form of memorial to honour the memory of war dead (Rigby 2001). In addition, assurances that past actions will not be repeated are important in order to reduce the fears of the injured party. Forgiveness would be another element at this stage, and one which many believe to be the key to resolving conflict (Fisher 1999: 100).

Torpey's concept of 'reparations politics' describes a set of activities depicted as a series of concentric circles. Central to the process are activities relating to 'transitional justice', where identification and/or punishment of the perpetrators is carried out through criminal trials, truth commissions, political purges, and so on. Here the reference is to national reconciliation undertaken by those regimes in Latin America, Eastern Europe, the Soviet Union and South Africa whose collapse in the 1980s and 1990s led to truth commissions and trials of those held culpable for crimes against their own peoples, and which were replaced by new, usually democratic, governments. Clearly this does not apply in the case of China and Japan where the problem is between two sovereign states with very different political systems, but the elements of uncovering the truth, identifying those responsible for victimisation of others, and putting them on trial are certainly applicable. Justice is followed by reparations, usually of the material kind, and then apologies from the perpetrators (or their descendants) to the victims (or their descendants). The final set of activities involves 'a concern with "collective memory"' and

> the pursuit of a 'communicative history' – that is, a history oriented toward a mutual agreement by the various parties that participate in re-writing historical narratives on the basis of a claim that they are (most) directly affected by the history in question.
>
> (Torpey 2003: 6)

These activities do not necessarily occur in strict chronological order, but the conceptualisation nonetheless provides 'an analytical grid distinguishing "ideal types" of activities germane to coming to terms with the past that may, in practice, be found lumped together' (ibid.: 7). Both Rigby's and Torpey's descriptions of reconciliation or reparations politics are useful in understanding the stages through which China and Japan have progressed since the end of the Second World War in attempting to come to terms with the past. This book therefore uses a combination of the models suggested by Rigby and Torpey and identifies three stages relevant to Sino-Japanese reconciliation: seeking the truth; seeking justice; and settling the past.

The two cycles of Sino-Japanese reconciliation

The book argues that reconciliation between China and Japan resembles patterns observed elsewhere, but that the process has gone through two cycles, each of which encompasses similar activities: seeking truth and justice through trials and/or historical enquiry, reparations (or compensation), and settling the past through apologies, commemoration and communicative history. What I refer to as the first cycle of reconciliation took place during the early post-war period and the Cold War. As we know, governments are charged with the task of settling wars, seeking justice through trials, agreeing on war reparations, making official apologies, and so on. The Chinese and Japanese governments (the latter under the tutelage of the USA and the Allies between 1945 and 1952) addressed these steps at various points between the 1940s and 1970s. This involved attempts to reveal the truth and provide justice through the International Military Tribunal in the Far East (IMTFE) and other war crimes trials held in China, to agree upon war reparations (which were waived by the PRC in 1972), and to settle the past (that is, provide apologies and a reflection on Japan's wartime activities) through the agreements signed in the 1970s (the Joint Statement of 1972, and the Treaty of Peace and Friendship of 1978). In so doing, the two countries appeared to satisfy the sort of ideal-type models of reconciliation described above.

By the 1980s, however, the inadequacies, partiality, omissions and even injustices of earlier settlements were becoming apparent. 'Residues of mistrust', to use Lee's phrase, became increasingly obvious, and indicated that reconciliation between the two sides was incomplete or partial. While some of the reasons for the emergence of war-related problems can be attributed to power politics and the attempts of one government to gain leverage over another, this does not fully explain the problem. One explanation is that the first cycle of reconciliation was largely a top-down process, whereas the second cycle has been driven increasingly by non-governmental groups seeking to resolve issues that the governments have failed to, or refuse to, deal with.

From the 1980s, then, the reconciliation process entered a second cycle, with an expansion of activity that still included diplomatic measures, but also involved non-state actors. This included renewed efforts to uncover the truth (through historical investigation based on newly discovered documentation and oral evidence); to seek justice through Japanese (or US) courts (compensation cases for individual victims) and through mock tribunals (the Women's International War Crimes Tribunal on Japan's Military Sexual Slavery[2]); and to settle the past (apologies and assurances, ceremonies and memorials in honour of the war dead). Clearly these developments were not the result of some cohesive plan by the governments and people to bring about reconciliation. Rather, a number of factors brought war-related issues into the open, but the efforts made by diplomats, politicians, citizens' groups and individuals to resolve the problems in the 1990s and early twenty-first century were, in effect, attempts to face the past and move on. Domestically, changes in the political and social environments in both countries had a big impact. The easing of constraints during the 1980s and 1990s facilitated much greater discussion of the past both within and between China and Japan. Research on the war proliferated, academic exchange increased, the war responsibility debate in Japan was revived, Chinese academics were allowed greater freedom to conduct war-related research, and civil society in both countries grew and became more involved in addressing human rights issues and reconciling the past. International trends also impacted upon developments in China–Japan relations, such as the growth of transnational society, changes to international laws, greater access to information via the world-wide web, and so on, and illustrate that what was happening within and between the two countries was also part of a global trend.

The bulk of this book focuses on the second cycle of reconciliation, in particular the renewed attempts to seek justice (through compensation cases or settlements with companies), to seek agreement on the writing and telling of history, to elicit apologies and statements of regret, to commemorate past suffering in a manner acceptable to both sides, and to move beyond the history problem. The case studies consider the role of both the Chinese and Japanese governments in this second cycle, but they also pay attention to the role of domestic, regional and international non-governmental groups. To that end some background on each government's foreign policy *vis-à-vis* the other is useful to understand their basic strategies on how to deal with the past. Similarly, an overview of the rise of civil society in both countries, and the development of transnational civil society will also help to provide some background for Chapters 3, 4 and 5.

Chinese and Japanese future-oriented foreign policies

There can be no doubt that both the Chinese and Japanese governments have at least paid lip service to the idea of settling the past, and at most have tried to implement specific measures intended to bring about greater exchange and interaction between the Chinese and Japanese peoples. While this has been an ongoing process since the late 1970s, it was particularly marked in the late 1990s when leaders in both countries went about re-formulating their foreign policies with a view to ensuring a peaceful and stable region in the next century. For China this meant in large part a reiteration of the independent foreign policy of peace which had provided the framework for China's foreign policy since the early 1980s and which stressed security, development and reunification (that is, of Hong Kong, Macau, and eventually Taiwan). To this end China's military modernisation, stability in the Asia Pacific, and an expansion of China's economic links regionally and globally became key policies in the 1980s and 1990s. Added to this basic framework was Jiang Zemin's 'own vision for a post-Deng foreign policy in a changing post-Cold War, "cross-century" world order' which included new themes. It stressed the need for 'strategic partnerships' between great powers such as the USA, Russia, China, Japan, and the EU to commit to a stable international system; it promoted a broader definition of security to include political, economic and technological dimensions; and it stressed the importance of economic globalisation and economic security (Miller and Liu 2001: 143–4). The 1990s thus saw China become more involved in multilateral institutions, while developing bilateral relationships with, for example, Russia and France.

Japan's foreign policy has evolved too. For many years, Japan's foreign policy was considered reactive and passive, but since the 1980s globalisation has been one of the dominating factors in the direction of Japan's foreign policy, and the nature of Japan's role in regional and global affairs has broadened and deepened.[3] Foreign policy strategies produced by Japanese think-tanks stressed the importance of Japan developing a robust foreign policy for the twenty-first century. For example, the report entitled *Challenge 2001: Japan's Foreign Policy toward the 21st Century*, produced in 1999 by a team of leading foreign policy scholars, suggested that 'The way for Japan to secure its national interests amid this trend is to develop and present ideas and act as a global player in pursuit of stability and prosperity of the international community' (Inoguchi *et al.* 1999). The means by which Japan could act as a global player, according to the recommendations of *Challenge 2001*, included enhancing the total strength of its foreign policy by involving the public through open discussion, encouraging more research, and facilitating closer links between the government and NGOs; enhancing national power through inventiveness, technology and a review of the nation's responsibilities; and reinforcing diplomatic networks with a view to building a secure and prosperous world. The report referred to the need to move forward with Japan's foreign policy, stressing the need for 'an overall review of the basic stance of Japan and Japanese foreign policy without being bound by the past', and to have:

> an open discussion on the role of a nation in ensuring the security of its citizens, to avoid falling into such extreme arguments as interpreting a dispatch of the Self-Defence Force units to rescue Japanese citizens from areas of conflict as a resurgence of Japanese militarism.
>
> (ibid.)

The forward-looking stance of the Chinese and Japanese governments of the 1990s was clearly reflected in their policies towards one another. In the late 1990s, Chinese leaders, especially Jiang Zemin and Zhu Rongji, frequently stressed the need to settle unresolved issues so that the relationship could move forward. During his visit to Japan in 1998 Jiang expressed the hope that:

> China and Japan can use history as a mirror to build the future (*yishiwei-jian, kaichuang weilai*) . . . We must work hard together to take a healthy, stable and developing relationship into the twenty-first century, and enable the peoples of both countries to live in friendship for generations to come.
>
> (*Renmin Ribao*, 28 November 1998)

Ironically, Jiang's visit was marred by a dispute over the wording of the statement due to be signed by the President and Prime Minister Obuchi. This episode is discussed in more detail in Chapter 5, but it was the failure of the Japanese side to agree to the insertion of a written apology into the document that caused great indignation on the Chinese side. Such incidents may occur less frequently as the new leadership in China is keen to continue the future-oriented approach to China's Japan policy instigated by Zhu Rongji and Jiang Zemin. In 2002, Beijing began to map out a long-term diplomatic strategy toward Japan in preparation for the change in leadership. As the official hand-over of top positions took place in China in March 2003, the Japanese press commented on the pro-Japan tendencies of this new group. Individuals such as Hu Jintao, Zeng Qinghong, Wen Jiabao, Huang Ju, and Tang Jiaxuan would prefer to stop dwelling on the past and construct a Japan-policy more geared to future development (*Asahi Online*, 19 March 2003).

On the Japanese side, while there has been a tendency to view China's economic and political development in the 1990s as a threat, policy has focused on developing closer, mutually beneficial links through trade, aid, direct investment, and student and cultural exchange. Prime Ministers Hashimoto, Obuchi and Koizumi all implemented important China packages (as had a number of their predecessors such as Prime Ministers Ōhira, Nakasone and Takeshita), encouraged by think-tanks, big business and the Ministry of Foreign Affairs. A report produced in late 2002 by Prime Minister Koizumi's 'Task Force on Foreign Relations' identified China as Japan's top foreign policy concern in the immediate future (Przystup 2003a; Taigai kankei tasuku fōsu 2002). With specific reference to the history problem, it stated that 'it is important that both countries, while learning from history, must break the "spell of history" (*rekishi no jubaku*) and build a future-oriented (*mirai shikō*) relationship' (Taigai kankei tasuku fōsu 2002). Prime Minister Koizumi spoke in the Upper House of the Diet in February 2002 of the importance of strengthening relations with China for future generations, given that the China–Japan relationship was one of Japan's most important bilateral relations (*Kokkai kaigiroku*, Sangi'in honkaigi 154 (5), 4 February 2002), and he has reiterated on a number of occasions that he sees China not as a threat, but an opportunity.

At state level, then, there has been much talk of putting the past in the past, and both the Chinese and Japanese governments have shown some restraint in recent years in the way they have approached the history problem. But these efforts have been marred on the Japanese side by 'slips of the tongue' by LDP ministers, textbook policy, and attitudes to the Yasukuni Shrine issue, and on the Chinese side by inconsistencies in the handling of the history problem and a tendency to 'use the history card' when it is politically expedient. The contradiction between what some politicians say and what they do as far as the history problem is concerned poses a serious problem, and produces the 'wave progression' described by Kriesberg, where some progress is made only to be checked by other events. Another factor impeding reconciliation has been, until recently, the lack of interaction between victims and perpetrators (or their families or other representatives) at grass-roots level. As the reconciliation literature highlighted, this is increasingly acknowledged as an important factor in the reconciliation process. For China and Japan, the broadening and deepening of the reconciliation process to include individuals and groups below the level of the state represent one of the dominant features of the 1990s. Thus, since the early 1990s, both the Chinese and Japanese governments have come under increasing pressure from grass-roots organisations to deal with war-related problems. This pressure has increased in recent years as the groups have gained influence by joining with regional and international organisations. In this respect, then, attempts to settle the past are beginning to take place from the bottom up in a manner consistent with some of the patterns described in the reconciliation literature. The next section provides some background to the growth of civil society in Japan and China in the 1990s, and describes the ways in which their activities have contributed to the reconciliation process.

Civil society and Sino-Japanese reconciliation

It was only in the 1990s that Japan started to experience the rapid growth of civil society, defined as 'a spontaneous, concerned group of citizens who interact independently of government, while collaborating with it at certain times and opposing it at others' (Yamamoto 1999: 14). The relatively late emergence of civil society is ascribed to the public–private split in Japanese governance and society. Traditionally the 'public' referred to officialdom which took on the task of providing the people with what they needed and acted in the public interest. The 'private', on the other hand, referred to the people (or rather 'the masses') who were 'permitted the pursuit of private gain, personal welfare, and individual happiness insofar as these things lie within the legal and political frameworks dictated by government' (Iokibe 1999: 51). While citizens' groups existed, they were seen to be, at best, 'trespass[ing] the boundaries of their status in society and interven[ing] in the realm of activity deemed to belong to the government' (ibid.: 52), and at worst, opposing the state (except for a brief blossoming of liberalism during the Taisho democracy period when there was a proliferation of private-sector groups). These attitudes and structures persisted to a certain extent after 1945, but by the end of the 1960s citizens' movements had formed to pursue welfare and environmental campaigns. As a result of the economic setback of the 1970s these tendencies were 'dampened', but revived again in the 1980s with the development of international cooperation and volunteer pro-grammes, and groups concerned with global environmental issues (ibid.: 87). These trends developed even further with the Rio de Janeiro UN Conference on Environment and Development of 1992, but particularly with the Kobe earthquake of 1995 which created a spontaneous movement of volunteers. Japanese groups involved in pursuing reconciliation with China originate mainly, but not exclusively, from the left, and include anti-war groups, educa-tion-related groups, lawyers' associations, war veterans' associations, organ-isations run by teachers, academics, journalists, union representatives, and so on.

The recent history of civil society in China shares some similarities with Japan, despite the very different political environments, insofar as there was a rapid growth in the number and type of 'non-governmental' organisations in the 1990s. The opportunity for the growth of civil society in China came about through the reforms of Deng Xiaoping and his successors and 'found expression in an official strategy of political liberalization which decreased the degree of direct politicization of society and provided greater space for intellectual debate, cultural creativity, professional expertise, and economic entrepreneurship' (White *et al.* 1996: 26). The activities of civil groups are still highly restricted, but the extent to which the state continued to exercise con-trol over them began to weaken in the 1990s when 'social organisations' started to proliferate and the Internet facilitated greater exchange of ideas and opinions.

The terms 'civil society' and 'NGOs' are perhaps slightly misleading in China's case. As White *et al.* point out, 'it is difficult to find ideal-type "civil society" organizations that fully embody the principles of voluntary partici-pation and self-regulation, autonomy and separation from the state' (ibid.: 29). Traditional mass organisations (for example, the All-China Women's Federation) are the best-known type of organisation. A new sector of 'incorporated social organisations' (*shehui tuanti*) (i.e., registered and allowed a legal status) emerged in the 1990s. These groups moved beyond the activ-ities of the mass organisations to include national and local level groups ranging from 'associations' (*xiehui*) to friendship societies (*lianyihui*), profes-sional associations, trade groups, and issue-oriented groups,[4] but they were still restricted and subject to government control (ibid.: 31, 133). A third type of association is the informal, non-incorporated 'interstitial associations' which proliferated in the 1980s and 1990s, for example, women's groups, artists, journalists, musicians, professionals, religious groups, and so on. The groups involved in Sino-Japanese reconciliation belong to this latter group in that they are issue-oriented. They have no official status, receive no funding, and cannot, therefore, be referred to as *social* organisations, merely 'organisa-tions' or 'groups' (*tuanti*). They tend to be quite small and fluid in their membership. They have the freedom to hold conferences, workshops and meetings. They are often referred to by Chinese academics and those involved in them as spontaneous (*zifa de*) or grass-roots organisations, and there seems to be no aim to seek incorporated status or official funding. Indeed, it was the consensus among those I spoke to in China that these groups would have problems finding official sponsorship, because of the nature of their activities.

There are a number of ways in which civil society in China and Japan has contributed to the reconciliation process. One is to do with 'civil society memory' and the way in which the war is remembered and re-presented; another is to do with the development of transnational civil society.

The frequent reference of Chinese and Japanese government leaders in recent years to the need for a co-operative, future-oriented partnership based on mutual understanding and trust was noted above. But as problems over textbooks or the apology issue illustrate, the two states seem unable (or unwilling) to reach a compromise on such issues. After all, to do so would be to relinquish the tight grip on the officially sanctioned version of the events of the war, the one thing that, for the CCP at least, continues to secure its legitimacy and national unity. The LDP too benefits politically by adhering to the conservative view of history. Beyond party politics, collective memory, a set of shared notions about the past, ideas, values, goals of a group, society or country in which one lives, plays a central role in a group's identity and unity. It does not necessarily equal 'truth' since shared memories (as indi-vidual memories) can be highly selective or open to manipulation. It is per-haps more accurate to refer to collective memor*ies*, since there is often more than one collective memory, depending on whose 'collective' is referred to. Official (national, or state-sanctioned) memory is a fundamental underpin-ning of the state, and is essential to the construction of a national identity and government legitimacy. Thus, Japanese national memory for many years rested on the perception of Japan as victim of the nuclear attacks rather than as aggressor in East and South-east Asia. Chinese official memory rested on the perception of China as victim of Japanese aggression and the colonial powers, with the CCP liberating the Chinese people from national humili-ation. Official memory is embodied in academic and popular historical accounts, textbooks, museums, memorials, exhibitions, ceremonies, literature, and the media, but it can, and does, change over time in response to shifts in political regimes, or international developments.

'Civil society memory', on the other hand, refers to the way groups try to 'work out their own strategies of remembrance alongside the state, sometimes against it' (Winter and Sivan 1999: 30). Remembrance or memory work car-ried out by civil society can have various aims, from the personal (to cope with trauma or grief) to the public-minded (to achieve recognition of, or material gain for, a minority or persecuted group as a whole). Groups involved in such memory work tend to start on a small-scale (individuals meeting to share memories, negative or positive, of a particular event), but often expand their activities to take on bigger issues, sometimes to compensate for the lack of action on the part of the state. While in China and Japan the state remains dominant as the 'major producer and choreographer of commemoration' (ibid.: 38), the role of civil groups in either contesting or supporting the form and content of that commemoration became more noticeable in the 1980s and 1990s. Thus sections of society in Japan and China became increasingly engaged in 'remembrance work', sometimes for the purpose of trying to resolve those issues that the states consider settled, sometimes as part of a struggle between domestically contested versions of history.

In terms of reconciliation between China and Japan, one reason for the growing dissonance between what the two states consider to be important (i.e. moving on, and looking to the future) and what groups within each country consider important (i.e., justice and recognition for those who have been overlooked by the Chinese and Japanese governments) is that until recently the 'interactive process between victims and perpetrators' described by Rigby has been lacking at the *grass-roots level*. The broadening and deepening of the reconciliation process to include individuals and groups below the level of the state fit with Winter and Sivan's description of 'memory work'. Chinese and Japanese groups involved in such work have often linked up with groups based in other countries to form sometimes very influential networks of organisations campaigning on similar issues.

The growth of civil society and the interaction of organisations across borders have been a key feature of the post-Cold War, globalised, era. Florini suggests some additional factors that have facilitated this trend, including technological advances, issues of global concern, funding, and 'the ability of transnational civil society coalitions to learn from and build upon previous efforts' (2000a). But as Iriye Akira points out, 'cross-national exchanges among nonstate actors have been going on for quite some time' (1999: 147), a statement particularly true of Chinese and Japanese groups which have worked hard to maintain links throughout the post-war period in spite of the ideological and political constraints imposed by the international system and their respective governments. The importance and longevity of informal groups in China and Japan, and their influence on policy-makers in both countries, have long been recognised. These groups can be seen as the precursors or ancestors of the 'new' networks of the 1990s and beyond and are worth outlining in brief.

In the absence of normal political relations between 1952 and 1972, interaction between the Chinese and Japanese governments took place 'by proxy' via friendship groups, cultural missions, private trade organisations, trade unions, and so on. The utilisation of such groups by the Chinese government enabled the Chinese to conduct 'people's diplomacy' (*minjian waijiao*) and kept the channels of communication open. It enabled Japan's China-watchers and China's Japan-watchers to interact frequently. Individuals such as Sun Pinghua, Liao Chengzhi, Matsumura Kenzō and the groups they represented played a crucial role in maintaining a level of mutual understanding between both sides. These groups and their activities were important from the 1950s to the 1980s. In the 1990s, some observers lamented the weakening of key groups such as the Parliamentary League for China-Japan Friendship or the Japan-China Friendship Committee, arguing that their decline adversely affected the nature of interaction between the Chinese and the Japanese government and people (Osaki 1998: 93, Yahuda 2001). Generational change is seen to be a factor. Jin Xide, for example, argues that in the early 1990s the younger generation in both countries became more assertive and nationalistic and exchange channels between the older generation of leaders were fading (2000: 4). But the old groups did not disappear entirely, and there are still at least one dozen friendship-related organisations. In addition, leaders in both countries have been keen to try to broaden cultural and people-to-people exchange. For example, the agreement reached by President Jiang and Prime Minister Obuchi in 1998 injected new life into Sino-Japanese exchange, the year 2002 was designated 'Japan–China Year', and numerous activities were arranged for the 30th anniversary celebrations. New channels of communication developed in the 1990s in line with international trends. Track Two diplomacy brought Chinese and Japanese together in such bodies as the Pacific Economic Cooperation Council, the Conference for Security and Cooperation in the Asia Pacific (CSCAP), the CSCAP North Pacific Working Group, and the Northeast Asia Cooperation Dialogue (NEACD).[5] In addition, there emerged a number of Japanese or Chinese-run organisations or think-tanks which regularly brought Chinese and Japanese together.[6] These groups enabled officials (acting in a private capacity), academics and journalists to debate sensitive or important issues, including security, energy, the environment, trade and so on.[7] Jin comments on the proliferation from 1996 onwards of scholarly exchange between Chinese and Japanese academics who were 'actively working on drafting the possible blueprints for [the] China-Japan relationship in the years to come (2000: 4). Cooperation between Chinese and Japanese NGOs is encouraged at an official level. At a meeting of 53 NGOs held in Beijing in January 2002, Jiang Zemin expressed his hope that the NGOs 'would make new contributions to bilateral friendship in the new century' (*China Daily Online*, 29 January 2002).

Zhang Jinshan remarks upon the continued importance to Sino-Japanese friendship of people-to-people exchange since the end of the Cold War, and considers it to be an essential factor in the smooth running of the relationship in future, as long as it is allowed to deepen and broaden its activities. In particular, he describes the 'grass-roots-ification' (*cao gen hua*) and the spontaneous nature (*zi faxing*) of countless exchanges between individuals or groups (Zhang 2002: 46–8). The case studies in this book will demonstrate how this is now taking place. Of particular importance is the way in which Chinese and Japanese groups interested in dealing with the history problem or compensation cases have created links with each other, and have in turn developed links with other like-minded groups to raise international awareness of their issues. The sort of groups and organisations that have taken an interest in Chinese, and indeed Asian, compensation cases, for example, include bodies such as the International Labour Organisation and the UN Commission on Human Rights, and North American activist groups such as the Global Alliance for Preserving the History of World War II in Asia, and Canada Alpha. The networks developing between these groups have contributed to an increasing awareness of the issues both within and across borders. As the book will show, transnational networks between Chinese, Japanese and US-based groups are, as Florini suggests with regard to transnational networks in general, 'particularly good at getting otherwise-neglected issues onto the agendas of national governments, inter-governmental organizations and, increasingly, corporations' (2000a). Examples of such success can be seen in the activities of the networks that have coalesced around comfort women, forced labourers and Unit 731 victims in their quest for compensation. As the activities of each of the groups have gathered momentum, they have grabbed the attention of Chinese, American and Japanese politicians and institutions and put these issues firmly on domestic and international political agendas.

This chapter has suggested that the literature on reconciliation provides a means of explaining the ways in which China and Japan have tried, and in many instances failed, to come to terms with the past since the end of the war. By looking at the various stages of reconciliation, at the actors involved, and at the domestic and external pressures impacting upon policy-makers and non-state actors alike, the remainder of the book explores the potential for a more complete reconciliation at the beginning of the twenty-first century. The next chapter considers the first phase of reconciliation between China and Japan from the end of the war to the 1970s.

2 Sino-Japanese reconciliation during the Cold War

As the previous chapter suggested, the fact that certain issues were not fully resolved during the first phase of Sino-Japanese reconciliation has led to ongoing problems in the relationship ever since the textbook issue of the 1980s. This chapter explains in more detail the different stages that encompassed the first phase of reconciliation as a means of explaining why problems arose in the 1980s and 1990s, relating to a perceived lack of justice, compensation and apology by the Japanese for what happened during the war. The different stages of the reconciliation process as described by Torpey (2003) and Rigby (2001) are present in this first phase: war crimes trials (in Tokyo and China) sought to uncover the facts of Japan's transgressions during the war and produce definitive versions of how things happened; the trials also brought to justice some of those who were considered responsible for Japanese wartime policies and conduct; negotiations on reparations aimed to bring about an agreement between both governments on material redress (which was waived) for Japanese actions, and, during the normalisation process, the way in which Japan should express its regret was discussed and agreed. The problem, however, is that each element of this early phase of reconciliation, though deemed satisfactory at the time, has since been questioned. This chapter describes the various stages of the first phase of reconciliation, and highlights in particular the shortcomings of war crimes trials (held in Japan and China), differences in the way the war came to be written and remembered in China and Japan, problems with the treaties and joint statement signed between Japan and the Republic of China, and Japan and the People's Republic of China, and the inadequacies of the wording of apologies and other statements of regret.

War crimes trials and the telling of history: justice and truth?

In theory, war crimes trials aim to 'police the past' by bringing to trial those guilty of committing crimes against humanity. They bring the perpetrators to account, and also help to 'individualise the guilt' by identifying the crimes of individual leaders or soldiers (Rigby 2000: 4).[1] Trials are also about uncovering the facts about wartime conduct and policies, and have the potential to promote mutual understanding and reflection. Minear reminds us, for example, that one of the aims of the trials in Nuremberg and Tokyo was 'the writing of official history' (2001: 126). In practice, however, there can be problems with war crimes trials, as the IMTFE highlighted. The war crimes trials carried out to deal with Japan's conduct during the war went some way towards identifying and punishing individuals responsible for particular policies and decisions, but this in itself is controversial and remains a topic for debate. In addition, the desire of Joseph B. Keenan (Chief Prosecutor) to establish an authentic record of pre-war and wartime events in the Asia Pacific was, according to many, ill-fated and the project 'failed miserably' (Minear 2001: 158).[2] The Tokyo War Crimes Trial (hereafter Tokyo trial) held between 1946 and 1948 was charged with the task of identifying and bringing to account Class A war criminals (i.e., those responsible for crimes against peace). In addition, military tribunals carried out throughout Asia prosecuted thousands of Class B and C war criminals (i.e., those responsible for conventional war crimes, crimes against humanity or 'planning, ordering, authorization, or failure to prevent' crimes against humanity) (Dower 1999: 443–7). There is a large amount of literature on the Tokyo trial, less so on the B/C trials, but there is little agreement on the nature and outcome of the trials.

The Tokyo trial in particular has been criticised as an example of victor's justice or for promoting a view of Japan's actions as particularly evil. The trial is seen by some as deeply flawed in legal, political and historical terms, as unfair, hypocritical, rushed, and biased, while others consider it highly successful in its pursuit of justice and commitment to the punishment of inhumane crimes.[3] Although some of Japan's war criminals and the crimes they perpetrated were prosecuted, many individuals, notably the Emperor, evaded responsibility. More important for our purpose is that certain crimes against humanity, mainly those committed against Asians, were not fully dealt with during the Tokyo trial. At the Tokyo trial, 23 of the defendants were found guilty on the charge of waging war against China, seven of them being sentenced to death. Of these seven, two individuals, Hirota Kōki (former foreign minister) and Matsui Iwane (commanding officer of the Japanese forces in Central China), were found guilty in connection with atrocities in Nanjing.[4] But no charges were brought against those thought to be responsible for the capture and enslavement of Chinese forced labourers (for example, Kishi Nobusuke). Information about crimes committed at Unit 731 and other chemical and biological warfare (CBW) facilities was never introduced to the court because of the desire of the USA to acquire information about the programme and keep it secret.[5] This was despite a mounting set of evidence about Japan's CBW programme gathered throughout the period of the trial based on information from other governments (notably China), Japanese informants, and non-Japanese witnesses. While the reasons for the US cover-up of the chemical and biological experimentation are well documented, the reasons behind the lack of pressure from the Nationalist

(Guomindang, hereafter GMD) government to ensure that those responsible be brought to trial are less clear, but may be related to Jiang Jieshi's growing need to accommodate American policy, which was changing in favour of speeding up the trials as a whole as the communist threat loomed. Harris states that the 'Kuomintang government showed little interest in Ishii [Shirō, Unit 731] or his confederates' but also that 'Neither Mao nor any of his spokespersons raised the issue of prosecuting BW experts' (1994: 225–6).[6]

The marginalisation of Chinese, and indeed other Asian, victims during the Tokyo trial meant that the suffering of 'comfort women', forced labourers, and victims of biological experimentation was completely overlooked.[7] The (current) Chinese view of the Tokyo trial is that the process was severely weakened by the absence of Emperor Hirohito from the witness box, the cover-up of the CBW activities, and failure to prosecute Ishii Shirō (Tian 2002: 63). The B/C trials held in China went some way to redressing the balance, but they were just as constrained by domestic and international politics as was the Tokyo trial. In China, trials by the Nationalists led to the execution of approximately 200 Japanese and imprisonment of many more (Dower 1999: 447–9). Military tribunals were held in various cities in China and Taiwan, including Beijing, Nanjing, and Shenyang (formerly Mukden), and Taibei, between 1946 and 1949. According to Chinese statistics, 517 Japanese were tried as war criminals, 148 were given the death sentence, 81 life sentences, 229 fixed sentences and 59 were acquitted (Tian 2002: 64–5).[8] These figures are low when compared with convictions made in trials held by the British or the Dutch, and the Nationalist government seemed more interested in trying Chinese collaborators than Japanese war criminals (Dower 1999: 447; Eykholt 2000: 22). Furthermore, the ongoing conflict between the Nationalists and Communists in China meant that the focus of the Guomindang's attention was devoted more to 'preventing the Communists from reclaiming previously occupied territory' than to the trials. By 1947, as the Communists gained the upper hand, and Cold War divisions began to emerge, Jiang Jieshi 'hurried the trials' (Eykholt 2000: 21, see also Piccigallo 1979).

There were further trials run by the Communist government in 1956 which took place in Shenyang and Taiyuan. On trial were some of the 969 Japanese soldiers held as PoWs by the Soviets since 1945, and released to the Chinese in 1950. Most of the prisoners were incarcerated in Fushun Prison (near Shenyang), where they underwent 'ideological education'. Forty-five men were put on trial for actively implementing aggressive policies in China, supporting a war of aggression, and violating international law and humanitarian principles. By the time it came to the trials, most had confessed their crimes and were repentant. In line with Zhou Enlai's instructions – and China's 'magnanimous policy' of the 1950s – none were given capital sentences. Instead they received prison sentences from between 8 and 20 years (to include the time they had already spent in prison) (Sō 2000: 66–7). These, and the remaining prisoners who were released without trial, were repatriated to

Japan between 1956 and 1964. On their return, some established the Chinese Returnees Association (*Chūkiren*), a vocal advocate for Sino-Japanese friendship.[9]

There is some agreement that the trials in Tokyo and in China were *partially* successful in bringing to account those responsible for Japan's actions in China during the war and those who personally committed crimes against humanity. The trials also provided a rich source of information (albeit some of a dubious quality) about hitherto little-known events, contributing to a greater understanding of the nature of the war and Japan's role in it. But the omissions of the trials (both A and B/C trials), whatever their causes, have become the focus of attention in the intervening years, and continue to impact upon relations between Japan and its neighbours, as victims now seek the justice they did not receive in the 1940s and 1950s.

Japan's 'collective amnesia'

The trials had a further outcome, leading to what many have described as Japan's collective amnesia about the war. The Tokyo trial, in particular, had a profound influence on the interpretation of the war and the way Japanese were able to 'forget' their wartime practices. In the words of Ienaga Saburō:

> there has been a tendency to reject the Tokyo trial *in toto* as unfair, and this tendency is linked inseparably with a second tendency: to assert the legitimacy of the war waged by Japan and to suppress or obliterate the aggressive nature of that war and the inhuman criminal activity that took place.
>
> (1986: 167)

Yoneyama talks about the 'remarkable indifference about Japan's pre-war and wartime legacy' (1999: 5), and Japan is often accused of a 40-year silence on the subject of the war and the issue of war responsibility. Collective amnesia is not a uniquely Japanese approach to dealing with the past. Examples of collective amnesia can be found in the 'Cambodian approach to dealing with the pain of the past' or in Spain's collective forgetting of Franco's regime after his death in 1975. Indeed, covering up the past, argues Rigby, can be the wish of leaders and the people alike 'particularly if so many of them share a past that they would rather forget because of their active involvement in, or complicity with, the evil that was perpetrated' (2000: 2), but it rarely lasts longer than one generation. Much has been written on Japan's national forgetting, and Japan is often compared, unfavourably, with Germany in this regard. Germany's success in dealing with its past is held up by Japanese and Chinese alike as the model which Japan failed to emulate. But the case has perhaps been over-stated, and it is worth remembering that the events of the war, and the issue of war responsibility, were debated in Japan very early in the post-war period, and sporadically ever since. In Orr's words, 'the amnesia was intermittent and often only partial' (2001:173). Dower recounts the 'general mood' of the Japanese people in the immediate aftermath of the war, as described by the US State Department in 1945, as being in favour of 'fixing war responsibility'. Furthermore, there was a growing conviction that 'Japan should not have undertaken aggressive warfare' (1999: 476). As the Tokyo trial revealed more and more about the shocking conduct of Japanese troops overseas (particularly in China), so too did the discussion develop among the Japanese public and left-leaning press and intellectuals about who should be held responsible. This debate, admittedly, did not last long. Once again *realpolitik*, and SCAP, intervened: 'as the Cold War intensified and the occupiers came to identify newly communist China as the archenemy, it became an integral part of American policy itself to discourage recollection of Japan's atrocities' (ibid.: 508). This in turn enabled the Japanese to 'forget' the war, or specifically the role of Japan as victimiser during the war, a process no doubt welcomed by those who failed to see Japan's war as anything but one of liberation from the West. Nonetheless, the battle lines for the debate on the interpretation of the war and war responsibility in Japan had already been drawn by 1948, with those on the left supporting the war of aggression point of view, and those on the right and in ruling circles preferring to defend the Emperor and lay the blame on military-clique politics (ibid.: 476–8).

The debate re-surfaced after the Occupation. In the mid-to-late 1950s, for example, the publication of books questioning the role of intellectuals' war responsibility or whether the 'post-war era [was] over' re-ignited discussion of war guilt (Wilson 2001). The history of the war in China, or the 15-year war (*jūgonen sensō*) as coined by Tsurumi Shunsuke, had received some attention during this period too, but it was not until the 1970s that it became a greater focus of popular attention. Since then, those committed to what Yoneyama calls 'counteramnes(t)ic practices' in Japan, for example, academics, journalists, teachers, grass-roots peace and anti-war groups, have constantly sought to raise a critical awareness about the past and made 'various efforts to counter the hegemony of historical amnesia' (1999: 8).

Of particular note in relation to remembering the war in China is journalist Honda Katsuichi's account, published in 1972, of the China war and the events surrounding the fall of Nanjing, based on his interviews with Chinese survivors (*Chūgoku no tabi*). Honda's account provoked a backlash and was countered by denials of the Nanjing Massacre.[10] The debate about the Nanjing Massacre has continued ever since, with an increasing amount of academic and popular attention being paid to it in China, Japan and the West. The 1990s saw the publication of many new books on the subject, prompted in part by various denials of Japanese ministers that the Nanjing Massacre took place, and the publication of Iris Chang's controversial *Rape of Nanking* (1997).[11] Other aspects of Japanese war conduct were debated during the 1970s, and have undergone a revival in the 1990s. The issue of (Korean) comfort women was the subject of a book by Japanese journalist Senda

Kakō, written in 1973 (*Military Comfort Women* (*Jūgun Ianfu*)), and Kim Il Myon's *The Emperor's Forces and Korean Comfort Women* was translated into Japanese in 1976 (*Tennō no guntai to Chōsenjin ianfu*). In the 1990s the work of academic Yoshimi Yoshiaki was instrumental in raising awareness of the comfort women issue in Japan, and a number of autobiographical accounts of former comfort women were translated into Japanese. In the 1980s the internationalisation of the problem of Japanese history textbooks brought the long-running Japanese domestic conflict out into the open (described in the following chapter), and the publication of personal accounts of the war (by victims, army staff, Thai-Burma railway survivors and soldiers, and so on) further raised public consciousness of the Japanese as victimisers, not victims. Developments in the late 1980s and early 1990s, not least the death of Emperor Hirohito in 1989 and the subsequent revisiting of the issue of his role in the Second World War, also informed the debate on Japan's war responsibility. Nonetheless, these various efforts to pursue the issue of war guilt are generally seen as quite weak, never having 'coalesced into a single movement strong enough to effect changes in postwar Japan' (Kinoshita 1986: 146). By the 1990s, however, there were signs that such a movement was gaining strength and pace, largely in response to the growing neo-nationalist, revisionist trend in Japan. We will return to this topic in Chapter 3.

China's collective amnesia?

In the early post-war period, the official Chinese view of the War of Resistance against Japan (*Kangri zhanzheng*) was dictated by the sheer practicalities of domestic politics (the civil war in China) and other, more pressing foreign policy concerns (the Korean war). When Chinese historians came to study the details of the war, they did so under the strict guidelines set by the state, which emphasised the role of the Communists but downplayed the contribution of Nationalists or ignored such events as the Nanjing Massacre (see Waldron 1996; Eykholt 2000).

Historiography during the Mao period, Jenner explains, though drawing upon Marx, Engels and Stalin, was nonetheless 'profoundly traditional' in that Mao took a state-centred, unitary view of history. 'Maoism developed and propagated a modified traditional historiography, changing it only enough to enable it to continue and flourish' (1992: 15). Communist Party leaders, as centuries of Chinese leaders before them, 'were determined to control the messages imparted in works of history- to bend those messages in ways favourable to official policy lines' (Unger 1993: 2). Eykholt provides an excellent example of the manipulation of one event, the Nanjing Massacre, as a political tool to whip up patriotism during the Korean war *against the United States* during the early 1950s (2000: 24).[12] Research on the Nanjing Massacre by Nanjing University academics was held 'hostage to political ideology' in the 1960s, and was kept classified so as not to focus 'attention back on a time of weakness and invasion, thereby drawing away from China's revolutionary progress' (2000: 25–6).

In the late 1970s, Deng Xiaoping's re-evaluation of China's recent history (including Mao's role, and the role of the bourgeoisie in China's development) allowed historians some freedom to *be* historians. The unitary view of history favoured by Mao gave way to a certain amount of pluralism, but limits were still imposed on how far historians could go, and Deng Xiaoping still emphasised the need for 'unity and stability'. Disagreements between the top leaders over interpretations of the past were echoed in different appraisals produced by historians who nonetheless still 'served one political mentor or another' (Barmé 1993: 261). From the mid-1980s, 'mass media historians' (such as Liu Binyan) 'created a semi-official and at times even unofficial forum for the airing of controversial questions' (ibid.: 270), such as the history of the Communist Party. The 'creation myths' of the War of Resistance against Japan and the strengthening of Communism during the Yanan period had been inviolable until this period, but new developments in Chinese cinema caused controversy because they reinterpreted those periods of Party history. Yet the Party was itself also engaging in a reinterpretation of the same period. During the mid-1980s, for example, the GMD's role in the war was represented in a far more favourable light in officially sanctioned films and publications (e.g. *The Battle of Taierzhuang*, a film produced in 1986). This interpretation was in sharp contrast to that of the 1960s, for example, when memoirs of former GMD generals who had remained in China after 1949 were published with the purpose of criticising the GMD's weak defence of Nanjing (and, by extension, China) against the Japanese (Eykholt 2000: 26). As Barmé points out, this development was to have a major impact on the public's consciousness of Party history: 'Prior to this, although specialist historical materials had gradually acknowledged that the Communists did not prosecute and win the war against Japan single-handedly, this was a watershed in terms of the mass media' (1993: 278), and it would have a knock-on effect in a new genre of neo-nationalist literature (discussed in Chapter 3).

Uncovering the truth is a crucial stage in the reconciliation process, but one of the most difficult. As Chapter 3 will show, one of the long-running disputes between China and Japan, and within Japan itself, is the search for the 'truth' about what happened to whom during the war. The question is, of course, whose truth? As Rigby notes, 'The different parties to a conflict each have their own history, and people do not relinquish their collective memory easily, as it invariably constitutes a key component of their collective identity' (2000: 190). This is certainly the case with China and Japan where official and unofficial, public and private narratives of the Second World War have become deeply embedded. Needless to say there is, as yet, little convergence between the various narratives. Debates about the Nanjing Massacre which re-surfaced in the 1990s illustrated the urgent need for an agreed truth. Chinese leaders frequently urged the Japanese to 'adopt a correct view of history'. It seemed that the Chinese and Japanese remained poles apart on their interpretation of the events of, and rationale for, the war, but the developments of recent years offer some hope that 'the struggle to broaden and deepen the parameters of publicly acknowledged truth' is gaining ground (ibid.: 187), and this will be considered in more detail in the next chapter.

The politics of reparations

Reparations, a further stage in the reconciliation process, can help two former enemies reconcile their differences in the form of material (for example, cash payments, provision of health care, etc.) or symbolic (for example, apologies, construction of memorials, etc.) measures. It is often the acknowledgement by the perpetrators of their former wrongdoings which is as important as the material compensation offered in these cases. In the 1970s, the negotiations on normalisation between Japan and China ostensibly dealt with the reparations issue at the level of the state, and it was only in the late 1980s that the question of individual compensation emerged. Some background to the Joint Statement is necessary here to find out why the settlement has since come to be perceived by some as unsatisfactory in terms of material and symbolic compensation.

Reparations claims in the immediate post-war period

Discussions between the Allied powers about the nature of a post-war settlement were underway even before the Japanese surrender[13] and promised favourable outcomes for China in terms of reparations. Under the Potsdam declaration, Japan would be obliged to pay reparations in kind (*jitsumono baishō*), and according to the 'Initial Post-Surrender Policy on Japan' produced by the Americans in September 1945, Japan would hand over assets and capital which would be dispersed by the Allied powers as reparations. The Chinese (GMD) government had produced a statement in March 1945 to clarify its position that, as the country that suffered the most at the hands of the Japanese military, China had a keen interest in reparations from Japan. In fact, the Chinese argued that they should claim at least 50 per cent of the total value of Japan's capital and assets.[14] By October 1946, the Chinese government had calculated an estimated sum of deaths and damages inflicted by the Japanese on China between 1937–45 (excluding North-east China and Taiwan) amounting to $31.3 billion in direct damages (public and private property), $20.4 billion in indirect damages, and 10.4 million military and civilian deaths or injuries (Zhu 1992: 28).

Edwin W. Pauley was appointed by President Truman to produce a reparations policy for Japan (he had carried out the same task for Germany). His interim report was announced in December 1945. The main objectives of his recommended programme were to prevent another build-up of Japanese industrial power (and therefore a revival of an imbalance of economic power

in Asia with Japan dominating the region) by moving most of Japan's plant
and machinery to Asian countries as reparations (Borden 1984: 66). Both the
Far Eastern Commission and GHQ accepted the plan initially, and work
began on designation of factories to be made available for transfer. By March
1947 one-third of the plants had been designated, but there were conflicts
between the recipients as to how the spoils would be divided. In April 1947
the interim report announced that an initial 30 per cent of the total reparations claim would be disbursed. China would receive 15 per cent, with the
Philippines, Britain, and Holland each receiving 5 per cent. It remained then
for the materials to be transferred. As part of a programme of advance
transfers, some reparations were made to China between January 1948 and
September 1949. China received approximately 22 shipments of machinery
and equipment worth $22.5 million (Tian 2002: 69). In addition, $18.1
million-worth of stolen property was returned to China. But in 1947 Pauley's
plan was already being questioned by some in the US government who
thought that the reparations programme would hold back Japan's economic
growth for too long, thereby imposing greater Occupation costs. By 1948,
SCAP policy on Japan and its economic and political rehabilitation was
beginning to shift as Cold War tensions began to rise. As the policy of con-
tainment emerged in the face of the perceived communist threat from the
Soviet Union, China and Korea, the US government began to identify Japan
as an ally in the region and started to reverse some of its earlier policies. By
May 1949 Pauley's reparations plan was cancelled and the issue of Japan's
reparations was put on hold. By November 1950, as part of the US government's plans for a peace treaty with Japan, it was suggested that reparations
be waived (Yamagiwa 1991).

The cancellation of the reparations plan did not put a stop to the requests
of the governments of the People's Republic of China (PRC) and the Republic of China (RoC) in the early 1950s. The RoC's ambassador in Washington,
Wellington Koo, told John Foster Dulles (special envoy to President Truman
charged with the task of drawing up a peace treaty with Japan) in 1950 that
'China anticipated reparations from Japan in any peace treaty' (Price 2001:
5). In the PRC's case, in response to the proposed San Francisco Peace Treaty
(SFPT), Zhou Enlai stated on 15 August 1951 that 'it is essential that countries occupied by Japan and having suffered great losses, . . . must reserve the
right to claim compensation' (Zhu 1992: 29). According to figures produced
by the PRC in 1951 these losses amounted to 10 million killed, and $50 billion
in economic damages (ibid.: 28).[15] Yet by 1952 Taiwan had agreed to waive
reparations in the Peace Treaty signed between Japan and Taiwan, and in
1972 the PRC did the same in the Joint Statement signed with Japan. Furthermore, no 'special' economic package was arranged with either country in
place of reparations as was the case with Korea or Burma.[16] The reasons for
this are linked to the SFPT.

The San Francisco Peace Treaty

Amidst the Cold War climate of the early 1950s, 48 countries signed the SFPT in 1951, but, ironically, this did not include those countries which had suffered the most at the hands of Japanese aggression, or who were the most resistant to the evolving US-centred security architecture of the region, that is China, Korea (to a lesser extent) and the Soviet Union. Neither the government of the PRC nor that of the RoC was invited to the peace conference due to a difference of opinion between the British government (which wanted to recognise the PRC) and the American government (which favoured recognition of the RoC). In the end it was agreed that the Japanese government would be allowed to sign a separate treaty with whichever of the two governments it chose – although, as is well known, there was to be very little choice in the matter.

Part of the US plans to make Japan an ally in the region included the need to revitalise the economy. This impacted upon the issue of reparations. The USA was insistent that the signatories to the peace treaty should waive their claims to reparations since Japan was not in a position to pay full damages, and that providing 'full reparations would harm Japan's economy and create a breeding ground for communism' (Price 2001: 2). Not all the parties welcomed the suggestion. The Philippine government was the most vocal in its protest, demanding compensation for $8 billion in damages. It failed to secure this amount, but it did manage to get the inclusion of clause 14 (a) into the treaty which had the effect of relegating reparations to a post-treaty process, limiting claims to states, not nationals (i.e., individuals), and allowing for reparations to be in kind (e.g., through the provision of services), therefore easing the strain on the Japanese economy (Price 2001: 8).[17]

Other dissatisfied Asian governments also made their feelings known by refusing to attend the conference (e.g., India and Burma), or ratify the treaty (Indonesia), preferring instead to deal directly with Japan in the 1950s and 1960s (Price 2001). As a result, only four countries were paid reparations in the form of cash settlements (Philippines, Vietnam, Burma, Indonesia). Other countries – Cambodia and Laos (1959), Korea (1965), Malaysia and Singapore (1968) – were offered economic cooperation in return for their renunciation of demands for reparations (Ts'ai 2001: 209).

The Treaty of Peace between Japan and the Republic of China: negotiations and resolutions

While the peace treaty awaited ratification in Congress, talks between the Japanese and Americans took place on the subject of Taiwan and China. Prime Minister Yoshida Shigeru and others in the Japanese elite had been very keen to restore links with the mainland in spite of the ideological stance of the government there, and were not well disposed to the notion of isolating China. But the evolving political situation in the region dictated otherwise. It was under considerable US pressure, not least the threat of non-ratification of the treaty in the USA, that Yoshida agreed to recognise the RoC. Nonetheless, the Japanese initially took pains to avoid designating the treaty with Taiwan a *peace* treaty, preferring instead to regard it as a treaty to end the state of war and normalise relations as well as a commercial agreement. Yoshida regarded the treaty with Taiwan as a stop-gap until such time as political and economic relations with the mainland could be restored (Yin 1996: 307–8).

The GMD had always been somewhat ambiguous on the issue of reparations. In August 1945 Jiang Jieshi had stated that China intended to adopt a 'magnanimous policy' (*kuanda zhengce*) towards Japan and 'return good for evil' (*yi de baoyuan*). This was not intended to mean a renunciation of reparations, but it did mean that China would not seek revenge and would not demand *cash* reparations or *unreasonable* reparations (Yin 1996: 324). In 1949, Jiang Jieshi (now in Taiwan) is reported to have mentioned to the Philippine president that it would be unfair to punish the Japanese people by demanding reparations, since it was the Japanese army, not the Japanese people who waged war (Tian 2002: 68). Tian considers this a move on Jiang's part to garner support from Japan to jointly combat communism, but by October 1950 this policy appeared to have changed when, during a meeting between Dulles and Ambassador Koo, the latter indicated that China would like to request some level of reparations. Another u-turn occurred in early 1951 which saw the RoC agree to the '7 principles for peace with Japan' proposed (by the USA) in November 1950, one of which was to waive the right to claim reparations, albeit with conditions (for example, that items stolen by the Japanese be returned, or that other countries also agreed to waive their right to claim reparations) (Yin 1996: 226–8). But once the SFPT had been signed, the RoC government started to reconsider its reparations policy once again, and resolved to seek reparations during the negotiations with Japan.

When Japan and Taiwan came to the negotiating table in February 1952, it took over two months and 12 rounds of meetings to reach an agreement on the wording of the treaty. The two major sticking points were the territories the treaty was to apply to (i.e., Taiwan and Pescadores and/or other territories under Taiwanese rule) and reparations. The draft treaty produced by the Taiwanese side was based largely on the wording of the SFPT, particularly Article 12 (which was a virtual copy of Article 14 of the SFPT). The Japanese side immediately protested the inclusion of this article, arguing, among other things, that it would not be acceptable to the Japanese people and that the Taiwanese draft exceeded Article 26 of the SFPT, which stated that Japan would be able to negotiate the same terms as those of the SFPT in any peace treaty signed within three years.[18] The Japanese side consistently pushed Taiwan to waive reparations. In one of the early rounds of unofficial talks, the Japanese delegates urged the Taiwanese side to dispense with the reparations clause altogether arguing that since it had been included in the SFPT it did not need to be re-stated in the Japan–Taiwan Treaty. The Japanese side also argued that Taiwan had already received reparations in the form of Japanese assets left in China at the time of surrender. This, according to the Japanese negotiators, made up 70–80 per cent of Japan's overseas assets and was worth 'several tens of billion' dollars. (This is in contrast to Pauley's estimate of $4 billion).[19]

The Taiwanese government, in turn, stood firm arguing that as Taiwan had not been a signatory to the SFPT and as China suffered the most during the China–Japan war, then the Taiwanese people would not allow its government to waive reparations. The talks often ended in stalemate. The negotiations continued in a similar manner until mid-April when, after a series of concessions from the Taiwanese side, the Taiwanese ceded to Japan completely, agreeing to waive the claim for all reparations as the Japanese negotiators had asked (Yin 1996: 277).[20] The treaty was signed on 28 April 1952. There are a number of explanations for the Taiwanese decision. Yin argues, for example, that the reparations waiver was always considered by the Taiwanese side to be their 'trump card', i.e., they were not so much interested in the value of reparations *per se* as how they could use it as a lever to get Japan to concede on matters more important, such as recognition that Taiwan was the sole legitimate government of China, thereby giving Taiwan some legitimacy and international standing. Yamagiwa (1991) suggests that the reasons were probably twofold – that the Taiwanese government felt it was unreasonable for Taiwan to claim compensation on behalf of the rest of China, and that it had always been very keen to be a signatory to the SFPT as a member of the Allied camp, with Jiang Jieshi himself indicating a wish to sign the treaty. The agreement reached between Taiwan and Japan on the issues of reparations was to impact upon the later agreement between Japan and the PRC.

The Japan–China Joint Statement (1972): upholding the reparations waiver

The conclusion of the SFPT and subsequently the Japan–Taiwan Treaty did not put an immediate stop to the PRC's insistence on its right to claim reparations (Himeda 1994: 150–5; Price 2001: 3). By 1955, however, it appeared that the Chinese government was changing its stance as relations between Japan and China improved. Although no official policy was enunciated, Zhou Enlai hinted that while China maintained the right to claim reparations, it depended on how the situation between China and Japan developed (that is, whether normalisation would take place or not). In the early 1960s the reparations issue was rarely raised by China, and by 1964 it became apparent that the Chinese leadership had reached a decision not to seek compensation from the Japanese. Echoing the 'generous' stance adopted by Jiang Jieshi, it is said that Mao did not want to inflict what would be considerable costs of compensation on to a generation of Japanese who were not responsible for Japanese militarism, and that he did not want the Chinese socialist economy to be built on the basis of compensation. In meetings between Chinese and Japanese friendship delegations in 1964 and 1965, and in statements made by Foreign Minister Chen Yi in 1965, it became clear to the Japanese side that the Chinese were not contemplating compensation claims, even as the Japanese were negotiating an economic cooperation package with South Korea as part of the normalisation process (Shimida and Tian 1997: 315–21; Zhu 1992: 30–1). Nonetheless, as the prospects for normalisation became increasingly likely after Nixon's shock announcement that he intended to seek a rapprochement with China, a key concern for the Japanese government was whether the Chinese side would demand that the Japan–Taiwan peace treaty be deemed illegal, raising the question of reparations perhaps to the tune of the $50 billion estimated by the Chinese in 1951. The Chinese side, however, did not appear to have the question of reparations at the top of their agenda.[21]

Tian (2002: 259) points out that despite Japanese concerns about the issue of compensation, the Chinese side maintained a relative silence on the issue. On his return from a visit to China in spring 1971, Fujiyama Aichirō (head of the DietMembers' League for Promotion of Sino-Japanese Normalisation, and former foreign minister) confirmed that the Chinese side were not thinking about compensation (Zhu 1992: 31). When Takeiri Yoshikatsu, Chairman of the Kōmeitō (Clean Government Party), visited Beijing on 27 and 28 July to discuss normalisation, 'the PRC leaders made it clear that China was willing to waive its claim of war reparations against Japan' (Ijiri 1987: 229). Takeiri was presented with the first draft of the Chinese version of the expected Zhou-Tanaka communiqué, point 7 of which referred to reparations: 'For the friendship between the People's Republic of China and Japan, the People's Republic of China renounces its right to demand war indemnities' (cited in Ijiri, 1987: 226). In response to the wording of this clause, the Japanese side argued that because the RoC had already renounced the *right* to demand war indemnities, then it would be more suitable if the word 'right' was removed. The Chinese agreed to this suggestion (ibid.: 292). In August 1972 Zhou Enlai reiterated that China would waive any claim against Japan for war reparations, explaining that the reason was an unwillingness to inflict upon the Japanese people the sort of suffering experienced by the Chinese people when China had been forced to pay large indemnities as a result of the (1st) Sino-Japanese war (Hsiao 1974: 110; Yamagiwa 1991: 20). In fact, the decision to waive reparations had a more tactical side to it, as Zhou Enlai considered it a potentially useful bargaining chip to get the Japanese side to compromise on other aspects of the negotiations (for example, Taiwan) (Zhu 1992: 32). The Chinese favoured a quick normalisation. Ijiri describes the process as one where 'ultimately it was the Chinese who were in a hurry and the Japanese who were rushed' (1987: 40). Ogata ascribes the speed with which the Joint Statement was formulated and agreed upon to China's 'haste to strengthen their strategic position *vis-à-vis* the Soviet Union', but also to Tanaka Kakuei's rush 'to forestall the possibility of intervention by the pro-Taiwan group' in the Liberal Democratic Party (1988: 55).

Thus, when Japan normalised relations with the PRC, the issue of reparations appeared to be resolved. Clause 5 of the 1972 Joint Statement states that 'the Government of the People's Republic of China declares that in the interest of the friendship between the People's Republic of China and Japan, it renounces its demand for war indemnities from Japan'. This wording is important, and, significantly, stands in stark contrast to the SFPT and other treaties signed between Japan and Korea, and Japan and the Soviet Union, since in the comparable clauses of these treaties, reference is made to relinquishing the *right* to claim by the government *and people* (Tanaka 1994b: 130; 1996: 6). That the words 'right' and 'people' were missing in the Joint Statement, it is argued, left the way open for Chinese citizens to make private claims in future years. Yamagiwa (1991: 20) suggests that the reason for the relative lack of interest in the reparations issue between China and Japan is related to the way the concept was viewed in the 1960s and 1970s as opposed to the way it has come to be understood in the 1990s in terms of compensation, apology and reflection. In addition, as we have seen, agreements on the nature and amount of reparations are the product of political situations and judgement of the time, and are open to manipulation or bargaining. This certainly applies to the agreements reached between Japan and Taiwan and Japan and China where the *realpolitik* of the day put greater importance on securing alliances, achieving international recognition, or striking a bargain than it did on settling issues to do with the past. Tanaka (1994b) notes, for example, that the negotiations for the Japan–Taiwan Treaty of 1952 were largely influenced by the conflict between the USA and the USSR (as played out in the Korean War), while the negotiations for the Japan–China Joint Statement 1972 were affected by the Vietnam War, the Soviet–US conflict and Sino-US rapprochement.

Ultimately China, the country most affected by Japan's aggression during the war, gained the least in terms of post-war settlements, due to the East–West tension of the late 1940s and 1950s, while Japan 'got off lightly' (ibid.: 130). Tanaka is not the only commentator to suggest that the Allied powers – mostly the USA – are to blame for the failure to deal properly with the reparations issue in the early post-war period, and that the Japanese benefited greatly from the provisions of the SFPT and subsequent bilateral agreements.[22] Tawara (1998: 126) argues that the USA let Japan 'off the hook' as far as reparations (to the signatories of the SFPT) were concerned in return for an agreement from Yoshida in 1952 to re-arm. Furthermore, the settlements made between Japan and the Allied nations are considered 'more equitable' than those agreed with Japan's former colonies or occupied territories. According to Nearey, 'Japan even accepted its responsibility to address personal injury claims from citizens of Allied powers, thus demonstrating the Japanese government's willingness to recognize its duty to the individuals of other nations' (2001: 137). This can be seen in the one-off payments made to

British former PoWs of £76.00.[23] The same willingness could not be seen in the case of agreements reached with other countries, notably the Republic of China and later the People's Republic of China. As a result, Japan is considered to have failed to compensate individual citizens with direct payments.[24]

Settling the past?

The third stage of the first phase of reconciliation between China and Japan concerns the expression of apology and regret. The processes that help two countries, peoples, cultural or ethnic groups to reconcile have changed over time. By the late twentieth century, the apology had become an important element of reconciliation in addition to reparations or material compensation. In Rigby's words:

> formal acknowledgements and apologies can act as powerful levers in the process of laying the past to rest . . . By acts of apology, opinion leaders can open up the symbolic space where victims and survivors can begin to cast the past in a new light.
>
> (2000: 188)

In this respect, Japanese governments are widely perceived as failing to fully reflect upon the past by openly acknowledging and apologising for the actions of the Japanese military during the war. If one considers the negotiations that took place in the run-up to normalisation between the two countries in 1972, however, it becomes clear that the Chinese government was not unhappy with the final wording of Japan's statement of regret.

Although the Chinese side did not seek reparations in 1972, they did, however, expect an acknowledgement of Japan's war responsibility. In the run-up to the negotiations it was not anticipated that the wording of an apology would be particularly contentious and little time was given over to discussions of the specific wording. Prior to Prime Minister Tanaka Kakuei's visit to China in September 1972, the Chinese showed little concern about the specific wording, given Tanaka's personal enthusiasm for normalisation with China and his earlier acknowledgement of the need for Japan to offer an official apology. In March 1972, for example, as Minister for International Trade and Industry, he stated in the Lower House Budget Committee that 'in my opinion, the first precondition for the normalization of diplomatic relations with China is our understanding that Japan caused China enormous trouble and that we truly want to offer an apology from the bottom of our hearts' (Wakamiya 1998: 25). For its part, the Japanese side had been keen to demonstrate its willingness to acknowledge the past throughout the negotiations. This resulted in a proposal to apologise to China for Japan's war crimes with the inclusion of a suitably worded clause in the preamble of the Joint Statement (Ijiri 1987: 248).

A verbal apology made by Kōsaka Zentarō (Chairman of the Council for the Normalisation of Japan–China Relations) to Zhou Enlai at a banquet held on 18 September 1972 seemed to bode well for the forthcoming visit of Prime Minister Tanaka, but the wording of Tanaka's attempted apology at the welcome banquet in Beijing on 25 September caused considerable upset. The Chinese side objected to Tanaka's reference to the war as 'causing trouble' (J: *go meiwaku o kakeshita*; C: *tian le mafan*). China's immediate and angry response was to stress the importance of the war responsibility issue to the Japanese side. Tanaka explained the next day that 'he meant to express his deep apology by the term as it is used in Japanese' (Ijiri 1987: 286). The Chinese accepted this explanation, but stressed the need for the inclusion of a phrase which would fully reflect Japan's acknowledgement of the events of the war. They agreed to the final wording of the 1972 Joint Statement which reads: 'The Japanese side is keenly conscious of the responsibility for the serious damage that Japan caused in the past to the Chinese people through war, and deeply reproaches itself' (Wakamiya 1998: 252; Zhu 1992: 37). This episode was perhaps the earliest indication of a dissonance between the Japanese and Chinese sides on the issue of Japan's sincerity and ability to fully acknowledge the view of the victim. As Chapter 5 will show, problems surrounding the wording of official apologies emerged in the 1990s, and continue to plague the relationship, casting serious doubt on the ability of the two sides to move ahead.

This chapter has described the first phase of reconciliation between China and Japan, highlighting the apparent settlement of the past through trials, treaties, and agreements on reparations at a government level in the early post-war period. As the remainder of this book shows, however, problems emerged in the 1980s, revealing the flaws in this settlement. Chapters 3, 4 and 5 deal with the second cycle of reconciliation, and consider the tensions that developed between China and Japan over the interpretation of the history of the war in the 1980s and 1990s, followed by the struggles over civil compensation in the 1990s, and, finally, the problems associated with apologising for and commemorating the war.

3   Uncovering the truth

Textbook issues and historical revisionism

This chapter considers the way in which the differences between Chinese and Japanese interpretations of the Second World War, which developed during the Cold War, emerged as a problem on the bilateral political agenda in the 1980s, and remained a problem at the beginning of the twenty-first century. In particular, it will focus on disputes over the content of Japanese history textbooks – not a new issue by any means, but one which exemplifies the clash not only between various parties in Japan who are seeking control over, or mastery of, the past, but also between Chinese and Japanese state and sub-state narratives of the war.

Textbook-related problems between China and Japan began in 1982, highlighting for the first time the very different ways in which the war was remembered and recorded in each country. They re-appeared in the mid-1980s and again in the late 1990s, and their recurrence sums up the very difficult challenge faced by both sides in attempting to move beyond this 'seeking the truth'-stage of the reconciliation process. While it is clearly unrealistic to expect both sides to be able to agree on one narrative, Maier suggests that historical controversies can 'end where clarification is reached on two or perhaps three basic stories, whose representatives understand the issues that separate them (which is itself difficult) and agree to live, so to speak, side by side' (2003: 302). As this chapter will demonstrate, there are now signs that what Maier describes as 'contrapuntal narratives' are beginning to emerge between China and Japan, facilitated by joint history projects, conferences and workshops, and much greater exchange between academics, students, and cultural groups. In this respect, then, recent developments suggest that what Torpey described as the pursuit of a communicative history is underway. Nonetheless, many problems remain, and these are largely due to the domestic problems associated with the interpretation of the war in both countries.

Chapter 2 referred to Chinese and Japanese 'collective amnesia' – the way in which the China–Japan war was temporarily 'forgotten' in both China and Japan in the early post-war period. Rigby notes (in reference to Cambodia) that the collective amnesia of a generation that perpetrated crimes or suffered them tends not to carry on into the next generation, and this can be seen in the case of China and Japan. With the memory boom of the 1980s and 1990s, the war was being remembered and reconstructed at different levels in both countries through various media: research monographs, oral testimonies, television documentaries, exhibitions, and museums. Readers and audiences in China and Japan began to question previous practices of forgetting, seeking instead actively to remember what 'really' happened, and to uncover the truth. But as Zolberg points out:

> the problem of knowing what 'really' happened becomes more complex the more we know, the more viewpoints expressed, the thicker the description. Indeed, a nation's 'official history' conventionally highlights its glories. But this idea is increasingly being subjected to 'readers' who wish to know what *really* happened.
>
> (1996: 79)

The process of finding out 'what really happened' is, needless to say, far from straightforward, as different groups vie with each other to present *their* truth as *the* truth. This problem can be seen most clearly in China and Japan where a younger generation of teachers, academics, lawyers, and civil groups are now working, separately and together, to find out more about certain aspects of the war which have been obscured for so long. Academics in both countries (for example, Yoshimi Yoshiaki, Yoshida Takashi, Su Zhiliang, Bu Ping, and many more) are unearthing new documentary evidence or conducting research that serves to further discussion and analysis of the war and its legacy. Their progress, however, is slow and their activities are often overshadowed. In Japan, progressive academics and groups face stiff opposition from the neo-nationalist revisionist groups that have been gaining ground and popularity since the 1980s. In China, a renewed interest in history in the 1990s, attended also by a neo-nationalist, sometimes anti-Japanese trend, has created further problems for those seeking to bring China and Japan closer to an understanding of the past.

The next section describes the different views of the war that emerged in both countries in the 1990s, before providing some background to the long-running domestic problem of Japanese history textbooks. The chapter then focuses on what is known in Japan as the 'third textbook offensive', which emerged in the late 1990s and gave rise to protests from the Chinese and Korean governments about the state of history education in Japan. Finally it explores the potential for China and Japan to 'get the history straight' (Torpey 2003: 7) and reach some agreement on a common interpretation of events.

The clash of histories: the widening gap between Chinese and Japanese views of history in the 1990s

In China's early Communist period, the party had a firm grip on historical output. In particular, the history of the War of Resistance against Japan was carefully controlled for political reasons. After the death of Mao Zedong, however, the government started to 'restore' the history of the war with commemorations of the war itself, reinterpretations of the role of both Communists and Nationalists, funding for new museums or memorials, and so on. Waldron attributes this movement to a 'craving for truth' and an 'awareness that it would be good politics finally to recognize the wartime sufferings of the Chinese people', but he also suggests a political rationale – that

> the new remembering of the Second World War in China is part of a general recasting of Chinese history, culture, and memory, both popular and official, that attempts to cope with the failure of the communist state to create a culture and patriotism of its own.
>
> (Waldron 1996: 951)

As Waldron points out, there have been various manifestations of this trend including the patriotic education campaigns (launched by Deng Xiaoping in the 1980s and then re-launched in 1994 by Jiang Zemin), the introduction of *guoxue* (national studies) in the school curriculum, and the implementation of a flag-raising ceremony in Tiananmen Square (ibid.: 977), all of which were aimed at reinforcing a sense of national identity, continuity, loyalty and patriotism. This was also reflected in intellectual and popular discourses of the 1980s and 1990s. In the 1980s, academic histories of Sino-Japanese relations were published which tended to stress Japan's aggression during the war, and warned against a revival of militarism in Japan, while at the same time reassuring readers that if Chinese and Japanese remain vigilant, then history need not repeat itself. Stories of heroism and references to patriotism were aimed at developing an awareness of and national pride in China's history. This trend continued into the 1990s, developing a neo-conservative element which enjoyed a degree of (tacit) official support because of its convergence with the official line (Louie and Cheung 1998: 559). Zhao explains, for example, that the intellectual discourse:

> supported the official version of state nationalism by arguing that a centralized power structure must be strengthened in order to maintain social stability and economic development. It also vocally promoted cultural nationalism or an 'anti-Westernism' movement by advocating a nativist value system and exploring Western mistreatment of China in modern history and the contemporary era.
>
> (1997: 732)

The same sort of approach was evident in popular literature on China–Japan relations, suggesting, as Whiting argues, 'the official approval of this theme' (1989: 45–6). Anti-Westernism includes anti-Japanism – a theme which appeared with regularity in books such as *A China that Can Say No* and others of the same genre (Song *et al.* 1996). They depicted the Japanese as either weak (because of economic difficulties, or an inability to stand up to the USA) or dangerous (strengthening their military power and the alliance with the USA) (Hughes 1997: 118). Historical novels dealing with the War of Resistance against Japan increased in volume and popularity, read mainly by the younger generation (Guo 1998: 170–84). The Nanjing Massacre was the focus of much attention and a series of books was published on the subject for both academic and mass audiences (Eykholt 2000: 46–7). Films and documentaries also tackled this and other events of the war (see Berry 2003), reinforcing an image of the Japanese military as particularly brutal and warning of the possibility of a revival of militarism in Japan.

In Japan, topics such as the war and war responsibility, culture and civilisation, values, identity, and Japan's international role were revitalised and debated in television programmes, journals and current affairs magazines, newspapers and *manga* from the late 1980s. That there was more open and frank discussion of such sensitive topics as war responsibility, history and nationalism was welcomed by some as a potentially positive step forward for Japan in its search for a new national identity. But in the 1990s, there were growing concerns about where this debate was heading when Liberal Democratic Party (LDP) politicians began to call for a more patriotic awareness of Japan's past, and revisionist history became increasingly popular. In August 1993 a group within the LDP called the Committee on History and Screening (Rekishi kentō iinkai) was formed. The 105-strong membership included senior members of the LDP such as Hashimoto Ryūtarō, Mori Yoshirō, and Nakayama Tarō. Their aim was to produce a summary of Japan's war in Asia, and their findings were published in book form (*Daitōa sensō no sōkatsu*) on 15 August 1995 to coincide with the 50th anniversary of Japan's defeat in WWII.[1] The summary had four main points: that the Greater East Asia War (GEAW) was one of self-defence and liberation; that the Nanjing Massacre and stories about comfort women were fabrications; that a new textbook battle was necessary in light of the emphasis on damage and invasion in recent textbooks; and that a national movement was needed to disseminate the historical view put forward in the first two points (Tawara 2001: 50–1). One of the aims of the publication was to demonstrate the group's dissatisfaction with the attempts of the Murayama administration to settle the past by offering a 'no war' resolution in the Diet (see Chapter 5).

Outside the political sphere, a similar trend was developing among 'neo-nationalists' (or new neo-nationalists) including, among others, Tokyo University professor Fujioka Nobukatsu, philosophy and German literature professor Nishio Kanji, historian Takahashi Shirō, and cartoonist Kobayashi Yoshinori. They established two main organisations in the 1990s, the Association for the Advancement of a Liberalist View of History (Jiyūshugi shikan kenkyūkai) and the Tsukuru kai. The overriding aim of these groups was to encourage in schoolchildren a 'healthy nationalism' (*kenzenna nashonarizumu*), and a sense of pride in their history. Echoing the efforts of the

Ministry of Education and LDP of the early 1980s (and prior to that the 1950s), the groups argued that children should no longer be taught what they saw as a 'masochistic' version of history, but should be told more about the heroes and heroines of Japan's past.

The campaign of the neo-nationalist groups went through various phases in the 1990s – from criticism of the government's handling of the comfort women, a questioning of the received wisdom on Japan's war responsibility and its effect on national identity, to the content of purportedly left-leaning, masochistic textbooks, and the weakness of the textbook screening system which allegedly pandered to the demands of foreign governments. Their protests also extended to peace museums, commemorative halls, and films tackling war-related issues (Tawara 2001: 52).[2] By the late 1990s they had produced hundreds of publications and held many hundreds of meetings and seminars throughout Japan. Hicks (1997) comments on the 'comparative sophistication and articulateness of some exponents of the revisionist view, as compared with Germany and other Western countries where the extreme right is generally marginalized'. The 'nationalist intellectuals', Hicks argues, have sometimes produced arguments plausible enough and with occasional factual basis to lend confidence to less sophisticated or cautious spokesmen or agitators (ibid.: 79).

Despite the fact that a strong counter-movement developed in Japan (discussed below), the support for the new revisionist groups seemed to expand rapidly. Particularly worrying was the fact that by the late 1990s neo-nationalist literature was popular among younger age groups – particularly university and schoolchildren who were the target audience of publications like Kobayashi Yoshinori's *Sensōron* (On war) or the *manga* version of Fujioka Nobukatsu's *Kyōkasho ga oshienai rekishi* (History the textbooks don't teach) (Oguma Eiji 1998: 94). While the neo-nationalists were self-proclaimed liberals, many of their critics saw them as no different from the traditional right-wing, and felt that the trend could be potentially 'disturbing' if they integrated with the established right-wing groups (McCormack 1998: 17). On the other hand, others dismissed the idea that the groups were a threat, given their emotional, incoherent arguments, lack of a sound intellectual basis, and inability to agree among themselves (see Rose 2000: 176). Nonetheless, the groups continued to produce a steady stream of articles and monographs, and by early 2001 the battle for history had gone one stage further as the Tsukuru kai sought, and gained, approval for a middle-school history textbook. Before considering the details of what was to become the third major diplomatic row between China and Japan over history textbooks, it is worth providing some background about the long-running domestic struggle in Japan over history education, and the ensuing tensions with China (and South Korea).

History battles in Japan, and their internationalisation

The content of Japanese history textbooks has been a controversial issue within Japan since the early post-war period, and continues to pit textbook writers, teachers and professors against the Ministry of Education and conservative forces within government, as well as right-wing groups, writers and journalists. The Japanese government's response to the internationalisation of the textbook issue since 1982 (when the Chinese and South Korean governments first lodged diplomatic protests) must be understood largely within the domestic context.

Domestic politics in Japan has, as in other countries, considerable impact on the writing and teaching of history. Contending approaches to the interpretation and explanations of Japan's history, both ancient and modern, were represented in the immediate post-war period by 'progressives' (teachers and academics, the Japanese Teacher's Union, socialists) and conservatives (the LDP, the Ministry of Education, right-leaning academics and groups). The struggle to record what each side viewed as the 'correct' version of history began in earnest in the 1950s which saw a conservative turn in educational policy, and the passing of a law in 1953 giving the Ministry of Education the authority to screen textbooks.[3]

The Ministry of Education maintains control over textbook content in a number of ways. First, it sets out Guidelines for Textbook Authorisation (*kyōkasho kentei kijun*) for textbook writers, which themselves conform to a national curriculum or Course of Study (*gakushū shidō yōryō*). Second, it has the authority to pass or fail textbooks through a system of textbook authorisation (*kyōkasho kentei*).[4] The nature of the textbook authorisation guidelines and the results of the triennial textbook authorisation process act as a measure of the climate of history education in Japan. The extent to which the Ministry of Education demands (and achieves) close adherence to the guidelines, for example, is often perceived as an indicator of its strength or weakness *vis-à-vis* the textbook publishers and writers. The results of each round of textbook authorisation are closely followed in the Japanese press, which carries regular reports about the extent to which textbook manuscripts are subject to Ministry 'opinions' (*kenkai*) (i.e., recommendations for change) in any particular year. The Ministry's preference for the inclusion of ever-greater levels of patriotic spirit in textbooks is a recurring theme in such press reports.

Once the Ministry of Education had regained its authority over textbook content in the 1950s (as the Occupation came to an end), the conservatives ran periodic campaigns against what they considered biased history textbooks, that is, those written by left-wing teachers and academics, which adopted too liberal a stance, particularly relating to descriptions of the war, or the emperor system. The first campaign was conducted in the mid-1950s, the second in the late 1970s/early 1980s. These campaigns, or 'offensives' sought to expose the 'deplorable' state of textbooks and promote (among other things) a more patriotic tone in history education. They were driven largely by groups within the LDP and the Ministry of Education, with some support from right-wing groups such as the National Committee for the Protection of Japan (Nihon o mamoru kokumin kaigi), later renamed the Japan Committee (Nihon kaigi). The campaigns also tended to occur when the LDP had re-gained political ground and had the confidence and power to follow policies through. For example, 1955 saw the merger of the Liberal and the Democratic parties and the subsequent election of the LDP to power, and the late 1970s saw a return to majority rule of the LDP in both houses of the Diet after a period of 'equality' (*hakuchū kokkai*) throughout the early 1970s. The third textbook offensive, discussed below, would emerge in the mid-to-late 1990s when there was a shift to the right after a brief period of non-LDP coalition governments in 1993–94.

The 'biased textbooks' campaign of the 1950s achieved the aim of tightening the Ministry of Education's control over history textbook content, resulting in the use of more ambiguous language in descriptions of Japan's war in China. But as a result of a partial ruling in favour of one of Ienaga Saburō's court cases in the early 1970s, the Ministry of Education relaxed its criteria for textbook authorisation, and authorised new or revised textbooks which contained a greater amount of information on Japanese wartime atrocities (Nozaki and Inokuchi 1998: 42).[5] For example, references to the Nanjing Massacre began to appear in high-school and middle-school history textbooks after 1974 (Tawara 2001: 49). By the early 1980s the LDP was seeking once again to clamp down on 'deplorable' textbooks, and there were fears that textbook content would suffer once more. This second textbook offensive had international repercussions. In 1982, the South Korean and Chinese governments complained about the lack of factual accuracy in Japanese high-school history textbooks and requested that some of the newly-authorised textbooks be revised. In particular, the Chinese government expressed its concern about the descriptions in the textbooks of the Nanjing Massacre, the Manchurian Incident, and the use of the word 'advance' (*shinshutsu*) instead of 'invade' (*shinryaku*) to describe Japan's actions in China.[6] The Chinese press launched an anti-Japanese campaign which acquired an increasingly hostile tone as the issue developed (see Rose 1998). The summer-long diplomatic row between Japan and its two closest neighbours resulted in a concession made by the Japanese government, announced by Chief Cabinet Secretary Miyazawa, that the Guidelines for Textbook Authorisation would be amended to include advice for authors to pay greater attention to the feelings of neighbouring countries when compiling history textbooks (see Appendix 3 for the full wording). By 1984 all middle-school textbooks (and 1985 for high-school texts) referred to the Nanjing Massacre, and some even included reference to Unit 731 (Tawara 2001: 50).[7]

The year 1986 saw the next major instalment of the textbook issue with the publication of a textbook *Shinpen Nihonshi* (A New History of Japan) produced by the right-wing group Nihon o mamoru kokumin kaigi. As with

Fujioka's group a decade later, the group was concerned that Japanese text-books were moving too far to the left (Yokoyama 1994: 45), and wanted 'to produce a textbook, written from a nationalist perspective that would affirm Japan's history and make "young people love their country's history"' (Whiting 1989: 56; Yokoyama 1994: 57). Having scrutinised the manuscript and requested approximately 800 changes in late 1985, the TARC announced its decision on 27 May 1986 to pass the revised text for publication (Whiting 1989: 56).

A South Korean protest was followed by complaints from China, Taiwan and South-east Asia. On 7 June, the Head of the Asia Bureau of the Chinese Foreign Ministry submitted a memorandum requesting that 'the erroneous content be corrected', but there followed no mass media campaign as there had been in 1982 (ibid.: 57). Nonetheless, China's official request put great pressure on Prime Minister Nakasone (and the Ministry of Foreign Affairs), and he promptly moved to contain the issue by directing the Ministry of Education to adjust the (offending) passages (Yokoyama 1994: 47–8). Irie states that the Prime Minister tried to halt publication of the textbook, but the Ministry of Education sought to proceed with it. Nakasone asked that the textbook undergo screening once more. After four rounds of recommendations for revision, the textbook was published (Irie 1997: 306–15). Yokoyama argues that it was due to Nakasone's 'view of history' (*rekishikan*) that the issue was solved so quickly – Nakasone had acknowledged on two occasions that the war was one of aggression and stated that history text-books had to reflect the truth (1994: 47–8). In addition, Nakasone, on the eve of a double election, no doubt wanted to avoid a diplomatic row. As with the 1982 textbook issue, the matter soon died down, but returned to the agenda a decade later.

The third textbook offensive

In Japan, the education system as a whole came under scrutiny in the 1990s as policy-makers attempted to devise a new type of education system that would place an emphasis on creativity, flexibility and a 'relaxed' approach to education (*yutori kyōiku*). Part of the reform package implemented during this period focused on history education, and new guidelines encouraged teachers to develop in schoolchildren a greater pride in their country. This element of the reform programme emerged as a reaction against what some in the LDP considered to be too moderate a stance on textbook screening which had taken hold in the 1980s and early 1990s. Tawara and Ishiyama (1995) attribute this development to the internationalisation of the textbook issue in 1982, and the impact of the Ienaga textbook trials, particularly the third trial (originally brought in 1984) which received a partial ruling from the Tokyo High Court in 1993 in Ienaga's favour. Other reasons include a series of diplomatic efforts made by the Japanese government in the early 1990s aimed at placing more stress on relations with Asian neighbours in modern history education and at improving relations with Asian countries (for example, apologies expressed during President Roh Taewoo's visit to Japan in 1990, and Prime Minister Kaifu's visit to the ASEAN countries in 1991 – see Table 5.1). Tawara and Ishiyama (ibid.: 67) further argue that with the government intending to send Japan's first PKO mission to Cambodia in 1992, the government had probably applied some political pressure on the Ministry of Education to tone down its directives to textbook writers so as not to raise the suspicions of Japan's neighbours.[8]

It should also be noted that, by the early 1990s there was also a great deal more information available to textbook writers about, for example, the comfort women system or forced labourers, due to the research activities of fellow academics. In addition, a number of compensation cases were being fought in the Japanese courts and attracted a great deal of media coverage. These topics found their way into textbooks by the mid-1990s. Tawara and Ishiyama's study of high-school history textbooks authorised in 1992 shows that a number of changes – for the better in the view of the progressives – had been made since the late 1980s. In general, the number of pages devoted to topics such as the war increased (which is all the more notable given that overall the textbooks were shorter), with more detail, and improved use of language and phraseology. Specifically, the word 'invasion' or 'aggression' (*shinryaku*) replaced advance or incident (*shinshutsu* or *jiken*), and phrases such as 'Chinese and Japanese troops clashed' were changed to 'Japanese troops fought with Chinese troops' so that in general Japanese behaviour was no longer using the passive voice, and responsibility was seen to lie with Japan. All the textbooks took up the Nanjing Massacre although they varied in their reference to the number of casualties. Some books moved this information up from the footnotes, and where previously texts had described the events as reported events, they were now described as fact. The word 'rape' was not always allowed by the Ministry of Education but on the issue of casualties it was acceptable to state the figures accepted at the Tokyo trial. Unit 731 was mentioned in most of the textbooks (previously references to this had not even been allowed in footnotes) and details of the sort of experiments that took place there appeared in most books. Reference to the use of forced labour and comfort women also began to appear in texts, as did the practice of forcing Koreans to change their names to Japanese names. The issue of post-war compensation appeared in some textbooks, comparing Japan's treatment of compensation cases with that of Germany (Tawara and Ishiyama 1995: 70–6).

The content of these textbooks soon met with criticism within Japan. Articles appeared in the right-wing press (*Sankei shinbun, Shokun, Seiron*) in 1993 and 1994, and some LDP Dietmembers began to ask questions in the Diet. By 1995 attention was being turned towards the state of middle school textbooks in particular, with, for example, right-wing groups sending faxes to publishing houses and ministries calling for better treatment of such issues as the emperor system, wartime 'personalities', Japan's defence and so on (ibid.:

68). But the third textbook offensive began in earnest when the results of the 1996 screening of middle-school history textbooks (for use in schools from 1997) were announced at the end of June, revealing that all seven textbooks contained some reference to the comfort women and post-war compensation (Bu 2000a: 169; Tawara 2001: 50).

The groups who were influential in launching the attacks on the textbooks had already begun to form in the early 1990s and involved a mix of LDP and former New Frontier Party politicians (Shinshintō),[9] academics, journalists, right-leaning media and publishing houses (for example, *Sankei shinbun*, *Bungei Shunjū*, Fusōsha – a subsidiary of Sankei), as well as pro-constitutional reform groups (in particular, the Nihon kaigi) and the more radical right-wing groups. The fundamental problem with the version of history in middle-school textbooks in the mid-1990s, according to these groups, was that it would be difficult for schoolchildren to take pride in their country. A central concern was the topic of the comfort women who, the groups argued, had not been forced into prostitution. Other disputed topics included the Nanjing Massacre, the Marco Polo Bridge incident, and the use of the term 'aggression' (Shuppan Rōren 1997: 4).

The most active group behind the campaign was the Tsukuru kai, but the LDP played an important supporting role. In June 1996 over 100 members of the LDP formed the DietMembers' Alliance for a Brighter Japan (Akarui Nihon kokkai giin renmei), headed by Ōkuno Seisuke (who had publicly denied in 1988 that the war was one of aggression). Upper House LDP Dietmen also formed a group to discuss the textbook problem, and called for some passages to be deleted from textbooks. The LDP General Council (Sōmukai) raised criticisms about the comfort women, the Nanjing Massacre and the Marco Polo Bridge incident, and the textbook problem was raised in Diet sessions on 11 and 18 December when there were calls for the Miyazawa statement of 1982 (see Appendix 3) to be removed from the Guidelines for Textbook Authorisation. Political activism was not restricted to the LDP. Some members of the Shinshintō formed their own group called the DietMembers' League for Teaching Correct History (Tadashii rekishi o tsutaeru kokkai giin renmei) which issued a statement on 20 December criticising the textbooks (Shuppan Rōren 1997: 5).

The LDP, in concert with right-wing groups and revisionist groups, were active at the local level too, launching campaigns to encourage local assemblies and councils to sign petitions calling for the deletion of passages about comfort women from textbooks or in favour of strengthening textbook authorisation. One such campaign was launched in September 1996 and targeted 31 prefectural assemblies and 339 town/city councils. Opposition, largely from the Japanese Communist Party (JCP), citizens' groups, women's groups and unions, meant that the campaign was not successful, with only 38 per cent of regional assemblies and 12 per cent of councils adopting the petition. Undeterred, the right-wing groups launched a second wave which called upon local governments to demand a strengthening of the textbook authorisation process (Tawara 1998: 206–8). Tawara comments on the unusual nature of these local campaigns in that they were highly organised and did seem to form a strong movement, uniting, for example, prefectural branches of groups such as Nihon kaigi, the Japan Association of War Bereaved Families (Izokukai), and National Association of Shinto Shrines (Jinja Honchō) into larger organisations such as the Council for Correcting Textbooks (Kyōkasho zesei kyōgikai) (ibid.: 209).

By the late 1990s, the government and Ministry of Education had embarked upon a patriotic education campaign reminiscent of the early 1980s. This coincided with a shift back to LDP dominance after a period of relative lack of power in 1993–96, when Prime Ministers Hosokawa and Murayama had attempted to settle the past in a more conciliatory way than the LDP and supporting groups would have liked. Chinese scholars identify the root of the third textbook offensive as this turn to the right, evidenced also by such developments as the revision of the guidelines for USA–Japan defence cooperation, Prime Minister Mori's 'divine country' speech, and the national anthem and flag issue.[10] As far as textbook authorisation was concerned, it seems that the Ministry of Education was keen to regain control over authors and publishers. In 1998 Education Minister Machimura Nobutaka stated that history textbooks lacked balance. In the following year, the Ministry of Education requested textbook publishers to ensure 'more balance' in textbooks, a policy line allegedly backed up by pressure (in the form of telephone calls) from the Prime Minister's Office. The Ministry also directed editors to place more emphasis on respect for national symbols, specifically the national flag and anthem (Negishi 1999).

The results of the campaign could be seen in the middle-school history textbooks screened in 2000, particularly in the descriptions of comfort women. Of the seven textbooks which had previously described the issue, only one textbook contained a more detailed discussion of the system, whereas the other six had either removed all references or had substantially reduced the length of the passages relating to the issue. Aside from the comfort women issue, other areas which had received attention from the Ministry of Education examiners during the authorisation process were the 'Three Alls Strategy'[11] (which was deleted), the term 'invade' (*shinryaku*) which was replaced by 'advance' (*shinshutsu*), Unit 731 (deleted), and the Nanjing Massacre (toned down to 'Nanjing Incident') (Inokuchi and Nozaki 2001; Tawara 2000). But the most controversial aspect of the authorisation of this batch of textbooks was the introduction of a new textbook, produced by the Tsukuru kai. The submission of the manuscript for *Atarashii rekishi kyōkasho* (New history textbook) was no surprise. The group had already produced a pilot version of the textbook for general consumption called *Kokumin no rekishi* (The history of a nation), and had, of course, always been explicit about its intention to produce a new Japanese history textbook which would 'portray Japan and the Japanese with dignity and balance in the context of world history' (Japanese Society for History Textbook Reform 1998: 32).

The progress of the manuscript through the screening process was closely followed by domestic and foreign observers. It was submitted in April 2000 and was strongly criticised by many Japanese historians from the outset, who publicly stated their objections. Problematic passages in the textbook included references to the 'foundation myths' of the Japanese nation (and the treatment of the Emperor Jimmu as a 'real' historical figure), the description of the Greater East Asian War, and its justification as a war of liberation.[12] In April 2001 the results of the screening were announced and the *Atarashii rekishi kyōkasho* was approved for use in schools from 2002. Academic and popular analyses of the textbook soon followed, and its publication (a commercial edition was published in June 2001) was roundly condemned by critics. Although the textbook itself was adopted for use in only a small percentage of schools in its first year and may not have achieved the success its authors had hoped for, the LDP, Tsukuru kai and affiliated groups had been successful in their aim of reducing the amount of attention devoted to the comfort women and other war-related topics in the other textbooks.[13] In so doing, however, the third textbook offensive also succeeded in attracting a huge amount of angry opposition, both at home and abroad.

The counter-offensive

The revisionist groups involved in the movement to correct what they saw as masochistic tendencies in Japanese history books faced fierce opposition at home, and one of the marked differences between the domestic textbook issue of the 1980s and that of the 1990s is the level of citizen activity seeking to raise awareness about the content of history textbooks and to protest against groups like the Jiyūshugi shikan kenkyūkai and Tsukuru kai. The 1990s saw tremendous growth in the number of organisations, led by academics, teachers, journalists, and union members, which launched a systematic and sustained counter-attack on what they saw as a dangerous and regressive trend in history education and historiography. The Children and Textbooks Japan Network 21 (Kodomo to kyōkasho zenkoku netto 21, hereafter Kyōkasho netto 21) is one of the leading organisations, headed by Tawara Yoshifumi.[14] One of its main functions is to disseminate information about the nature of the so-called liberal view of history, the content of the *Atarashii rekishi kyōkasho*, and debates about history education. Other organizations concerned specifically with the textbook issue and the problem of historical revisionism include the Committee for Truth and Freedom in Textbooks (Kyōkasho ni shinjitsu to jiyū o renrakukai) established by Ienaga Saburō and his supporters, the Advisory Committee for Discussing Social Studies Textbook Problems (Shakai kyōkasho kondankai sewaninkai), the Japanese Society for Democratic Education (Zenkoku minshushugi kyōiku kenkyūkai), and many more.[15] They publish pamphlets, books, journal articles and conference proceedings, and maintain websites on which they publicise workshops and other events. Just as the LDP, Tsukuru kai and other pro-revision groups lobbied local assemblies, so too did opposing groups organise their counter-offensive at the local level, gaining the backing of parents' groups, local schoolteachers, university professors, and lawyers. Local branches of the Committee for Truth and Freedom in Textbooks were set up around the country, for example, the Ibaraki branch was established in early 1997 with a membership of 80 in the initial stages (Kyōkasho ni shin-jitsu to jiyū o Ibarakiken renrakukai). Its goal, as with all the other groups mentioned above, was to raise awareness about the activities of groups such as the Tsukuru kai to put pressure on local education boards and schools not to adopt the new textbook.

When the *Atarashii rekishi kyōkasho* was going through the authorisation process, the groups lobbied central government, issuing an appeal in December 2000 which warned that 'the certification of such a textbook by the Japanese government and its adoption for use in history education will pave the way for the revival of chauvinistic history education of pre-war and wartime Japan'.[16] The appeal was initially signed by 60 Japanese historians, but the number of signatories soon increased as it was publicised domestically and abroad, reaching 899 in March 2001. A further appeal was made by concerned academics and writers in March 2001 who criticised the government's stance on the textbook problem, demanded that the government enhance the transparency of the textbook screening process, and called for an open debate on the reform of the textbook system as a whole.[17] The groups have gained the support of other organisations involved in the debate on the issue of war responsibility such as the Violence against Women in War – Network Japan and the Centre for Research and Documentation on Japan's War Responsibility (Nihon sensō sekinin shiryō senta), and through these links, they have been successful in internationalising their activities. In June 2001, for example, the Asian Solidarity Conference on Textbook Issues in Japan (Ajia rentai kinkyū kaigi) was held in Tokyo, bringing many of these groups together along with participants from Korea, China, Taiwan, the Philippines, Malaysia and Indonesia. The conference produced a 36-point action plan which aimed, broadly, to stop the adoption of the Tsukuru kai's *Atarashii rekishi kyōkasho* in schools, and 'to establish history education to create a common future of [sic] Asia'. Activities were planned at all levels, from community-level lobbying of local schools and education committees to international-level appeals to UN agencies and global NGO networks. Furthermore, the conference agreed to form an Asian Network on History Education (Rekishi kyōiku Ajia nettowāku) which has since launched a project aimed at developing a common history textbook/reader for use in China, Korea and Japan (see below).[18]

Needless to say, the publication of the *Atarashii rekishi kyōkasho* caused an outcry abroad. The most vocal protests came from South Korea and China, but many western academics, overseas Chinese groups, and NGOs have followed the issue closely and have become involved in the counter-offensive by signing petitions and raising awareness via e-mail circulation lists, discussion pages, the media, and so on.

The Chinese and Korean response

The official announcement that the *Atarashii rekishi kyōkasho* had been passed for approval came on 3 April 2001. The decision was soon met by protests from the Chinese and Korean governments. The Korean response was perhaps more forceful than that of the Chinese government. On 9 April the South Korean government temporarily recalled its ambassador from Japan to report on the situation, and on the 11th President Kim Daejung expressed his dissatisfaction with the Japanese government's actions. Both the Korean and Chinese governments raised the issue in the UN Commission on Human Rights on 10 and 11 April. The Korean government also suspended the import of Japanese cultural products (which had only been permitted from 1998), indicated that it would withdraw its support for Japan to gain a permanent seat on the United Nations Security Council (UNSC), and cancelled plans for joint naval exercises. There were also demonstrations in South Korean cities protesting against the new textbook (*People's Daily Online*, 8 May 2001). After studying the textbook, the Korean Education Department, along with the Foreign Ministry, and the Culture and Tourism Department produced a list of 35 items to be brought to the attention of the Japanese government for revision.

By contrast, the Chinese government did not demand as many specific changes to the textbook, or recall an ambassador, but it did call on the Japanese government to correct the errors in the text and cancelled the planned visit of Li Peng, National People's Congress (NPC) chairman (*People's Daily Online*, 3 April 2001, 10 May 2001).[19] The Chinese ambassador to Japan, Chen Jian, called a press conference on 3 April at which he condemned the way the textbook denied and beautified history (Su 2001a: 6). On the same day a spokesperson from the Chinese Ministry of Education also issued a statement on the new textbook, expressing deep consternation (ibid.: 133). A flurry of diplomatic activity ensued, starting with a meeting between Chinese Foreign Minister Tang Jiaxuan and Japanese ambassador Anami Koreshige on 4 April. On 11 April Ambassador Chen Jian asked Deputy Foreign Minister Kawashima Yudaka to correct the distorted history in the textbook and eradicate its 'pernicious tendencies', while in Beijing similar discussions took place between Vice-Foreign Minister Wang Yi and Japanese Ambassador Anami (*People's Daily Online*, 12 April 2001, 13 April 2001). On 16 April, Vice-Premier Wen Jiabao met a Japanese trade delegation and expressed his hopes that the Japanese government would deal with the problem properly (Xinhua, 16 April 2001). Apart from Li Peng's visit, a number of visits by other Chinese officials were cancelled, for example, that of Dai Bingguo, head of the CCP International Liaison Department, and Ma Hong, Director General of the State

Council Social Development Research Centre (*Daily Yomiuri*, 22 April 2001).

Although the textbook issue attracted a great deal of media attention in China, there was no sustained media campaign in China as there had been during the 1982 textbook issue when the *Renmin Ribao* carried a total of 232 articles relating to the problem in the space of two and half months (Rose 1998: 131). In 2001, although there was certainly a steady stream of articles on the subject in the *Renmin Ribao* from April to July, the issue did not dominate the press coverage in the same way as in 1982, and the tone of the articles was not quite as hostile.[20] China's specific problems with the textbook were clarified on 16 May when the Deputy Head of the Asia Bureau of the Chinese Ministry of Foreign Affairs met the Japanese ambassador and handed over a memorandum which contained a list of the sections of the textbook to which the Chinese objected. These were: the 1920s' anti-Japanese movement and boycotts in China; Manchuria; the occupation of Nanjing; the Nanjing 'incident' and the numbers killed; the nature of GMD and CCP resistance to Japan; the Marco Polo Bridge incident; the Greater East Asia declaration of 1943; resistance under the Greater East Asia Co-Prosperity Sphere, and the Tokyo trial. In all cases, the Chinese side was concerned about the lack of detail contained in the textbook, or the amount of inaccurate or misleading information, which, it was argued, could misinform readers about Japan's aggression in China and Asia (Su 2001a: 194–9).

The Japanese government's response to China's protestations was mixed: on the one hand, there was a willingness to explain the situation and reassure Chinese leaders that there was no change in the Japanese government's attitude towards China, but, on the other, the government reiterated that the views expressed in the textbook did not represent the government view and that the government was not willing to make any 'corrections'. Part of the ambiguity came from the very different responses of Prime Minister Koizumi and newly appointed Foreign Minister Tanaka Makiko (daughter of Prime Minister Tanaka Kakuei who had secured Japan's diplomatic normalisation with China in 1972). Koizumi's reaction to the Chinese and South Korean protests was, from the outset, that nothing could or would be done to revise the textbook (ibid.: 138). Foreign Minister Tanaka appeared to take a more conciliatory stance. In a telephone call to her Chinese counterpart, Tang Jiaxuan, on 7 May, she stated that Japan's relationship with China was considered one of the most important and that the government continued to stand by the sentiments expressed in the Joint Statement of 1972 and former Prime Minister Murayama's statement of 1995. She also took the opportunity to reassure the Chinese that Japan was not seeking to create two Chinas and did not support an independent Taiwan (this was in the wake of the decision to allow Li Denghui to visit Japan at the end of April for medical purposes). Tang Jiaxuan's view was that a series of recent events had caused a great deal of harm to the relationship between China and Japan (*People's Daily Online*, 7 May 2001).

The dispute continued until early July by which time the commercial version of the textbook had been published and was on sale, albeit carrying minor changes in response to some of the South Korean demands.[21] The Japanese government decision, announced on 8 July, was that 'it could not satisfy China's demands for making further revision of the history textbook because there is no obvious deviation from historic fact in the book and different opinions exist among Japanese historians'. The decision was 'unacceptable' to the Chinese government, which expressed its 'utmost regret and strong indignation' (*People's Daily Online*, 9 July 2001), but it is worth noting that it did not take the matter further at a diplomatic level and the issue did not seem to have a long-term, adverse effect on other aspects of the relationship. Yang Jian observes in this a more pragmatic stance from China on the history problem, suggesting that 'China's reaction was more restrained than that of South Korea and economic relations have not been seriously affected' (Beal *et al.* 2001: 183). Yang Daqing (2002) also remarks on China's more restrained approach to the history problem in the late 1990s. Similarly, studies of some of the other sensitive issues in Sino-Japanese relations, such as disputes over the Diaoyu/Senkaku islands, reveal the same sort of pragmatic response from the Chinese government, perhaps in the interests of maintaining the economic relationship (see, for example, Downs and Saunders 1998: 135–7). In fact, the Chinese government appears to be keen to play down some of these issues by toning down reports in the Chinese media, clamping down on student protests, and tightening control over anti-Japanese Internet sites and discussion boards. While it is impossible to know what is said between diplomats and political leaders behind closed doors, it would seem that the Chinese response to the latest instalment of the textbook issue fits with the official line of taking a more conciliatory stance in public in an attempt to settle the past, and avoid whipping up anti-Japanese (and potentially anti-government) sentiment at home.

This more pragmatic response may be having a trickle-down effect, and it is worth considering the response of Chinese academics to the textbook issue, in addition to some of the initiatives being implemented at grass-roots level, some a result of government schemes to promote greater exchange and understanding between the Chinese and Japanese peoples.

Towards a common understanding?

Chinese scholars viewed the textbook issue with concern, and a number of workshops took place in China in early 2001 to discuss the issue of the *Atarashii rekishi kyōkasho*. Participants often warned of a 'dangerous trend' in Japan, a 'new-style militarism', and talked of the need to enter into a long-term battle with Japanese right-wing forces by exposing their lies.[22] Analysis of Japan's third textbook offensive reached a consensus that it was a politically-driven movement, with LDP politicians setting in motion a drive against what they saw as masochistic textbooks. Bu Ping argues that a group of LDP politicians (the Rekishi kentō iinkai) encouraged right-wing academics to put pressure on the Ministry of Education and the progressives, and created a 'a social movement with widespread support' (Bu 2000b: 176, see also Wang 2001, and Bian 2001). The Chinese academic community continues to follow the history debate in Japan, perceiving historical revisionism as a particularly dangerous trend in Japan that is no longer confined to a small handful of right-wing elements, as editorials in the *Renmin Ribao* would suggest. On the other hand, there is an awareness, and appreciation, of what the progressive groups in Japan are trying to do, and Chinese academics urge their colleagues to become more familiar with the work of Japanese academics and activists (Bu 2000b: 179). Su Zhiliang, for example, provides a detailed overview of the various progressive groups in Japan and their influence on the textbook issue, stressing the role that Chinese can play in helping their cause by forming private or scholarly links, publicising their work or holding exhibitions and so on (Su 2001a: 164).

Joint activities of this nature got underway in the 1980s but proliferated in the 1990s and early 2000s. The Institutes of History, Japanese Studies and Asia Pacific Studies in Beijing, Shanghai and Nanjing host numerous joint workshops and conferences every year. Chinese academics are also involved in the Asia-wide non-governmental movement which grew out of the Asian Solidarity Conference held in Tokyo in June 2001. The Asian Network for History Education (Rekishi kyōiku Ajia nettowāku), which was established after the conference, has held a number of meetings to discuss the development of a joint Japan–China–Korea history reader, designed to supplement existing middle school history textbooks in all three countries. The project was launched at a workshop held in Nanjing in 2002, and the group has since met in Tokyo and Seoul in 2003. Joint historical research has a chequered past between Japan and Korea, and previous efforts have not been successful in terms of producing a common textbook,[23] but there are hopes that the Japan–China–Korea project will have greater success. The *South China Morning Post* described it as 'a step towards a new era of mutual reconciliation' (22 March 2003: 16), and those involved in the initiative are extremely positive about its prospects.[24]

Other activities are taking place elsewhere within the sphere of school and university history education. This has been in the form of exchanges of Japanese and Chinese history teachers, visits of Japanese teachers to North-east China to visit historical sites, joint publications and conferences, and cooperation in gathering oral testimonies.[25] It must be stressed that such exchanges have come about partly due to Japanese and Chinese government initiatives and agreements. For example the 'Peace, Friendship, and Exchange Initiative' announced by the Japanese government in 1995 provided support for historical research and exchange programmes.[26] In addition, however, a number of projects have come about as a result of individual initiatives by school teachers or university lecturers. One such project involved a study visit of Japanese high school students from Saitama to Harbin and Shenyang where they met and discussed chemical warfare and Unit 731 with Chinese students.[27] While many of these exchanges involve relatively small numbers of people, they are nonetheless important in the development of a common understanding of the past, and are an essential step in the reconciliation process. As Montville suggests, joint analysis of the history of a conflict is one important element of 'a process of transactional contrition and forgiveness between aggressors and victims which is indispensable to the establishment of a new relationship based on mutual acceptance and reasonable trust' (cited in Fisher 1999:85).

Conclusion

The textbook issue of the late 1990s/early 2000s resembled those of the 1980s in a number of ways. The issue began as a domestic problem in Japan, with criticisms of the state of history education coming from LDP politicians and pressure groups seeking a greater sense of patriotism in textbooks. A perceived shift to the right in the content of history textbooks was greeted by a backlash in Japan from progressive groups, which was then joined by external pressure on the Japanese government from foreign governments. As in 1982, the response of the Chinese government in the third textbook issue was expressed through diplomatic channels, and consisted of a list of demands for amendments to the problematic textbook. The wording of China's various representations, along with the media coverage, consisted of formulaic criticisms of the 'handful of Japanese militarists' who continue to distort historical facts and hurt the feelings of the Chinese people. Despite the fact that no changes were made to the textbook in accordance with the Chinese requests, the issue was nonetheless dropped, albeit with a warning that the Chinese government would continue to monitor the situation.

But there were also a number of differences in the 1990s. Japanese academics and the citizens' groups that formed in opposition to the neo-nationalist groups helped to maintain a very high level of awareness of the issue. They applied pressure at national and local government level to ensure that the textbook was not adopted widely, and worked hard to discredit the Tsukuru kai and similar groups. In addition, these groups were active in presenting a more balanced version of the history of the Sino-Japanese war at academic conferences and workshops, and through publications and Internet activism. Parents, teachers, academics, and the media all played a key role in raising awareness of the ongoing textbook problem. In addition, the active involvement of scholars outside China and Japan has been crucial to a broadening of the issues involved in the debate. Numerous international conferences have taken place either devoted entirely to the study of Sino-Japanese war issues, or at least with panels on the textbook issue, or specific topics such as Nanjing, and the compensation movement. Overseas Chinese groups, Chinese Americans, and NGOs have taken up the issue of the content of Japanese textbooks (and the issue of the war's interpretation as a whole), and publicized it on websites.[28]

The activities of these groups are important because they highlight the depth and breadth of the debate. Their output helps to shift the view of history away from something purely Japanese or purely Chinese to something more inclusive, something which approximates a transnational collective memory, or at least a collective memory which allows the Japanese to see the past not in terms of the victim, but in the broader context of human rights, and gender issues. By contrast, the Tsukuru kai's struggle is all about preserving the nation and the nation's history, on which there is no room for compromise. Its 1998 'Declaration' states that:

> It is impossible for nations to share historical perceptions. Japan has progressed far beyond the early stage of nationalism, while our Asian neighbours are just arriving, and explosively so, at that point. If we were to make compromises with other Asian nations regarding our perception of history, and vice versa, that would amount to an *act of submission on the part of Japan*. Such an act would only aggravate the system that has already presented itself, i.e., the *loss of a national history*.
>
> (Japanese Society for History Textbook Reform 1998: 3, italics added)

Yoneyama suggests that, in contrast to the proponents of the so-called liberal view of history, the Japanese groups and individuals involved in counteramnesic practices move beyond the national boundary in their view of the past, present and future. In so doing they have become involved in the 'transnationalization of mnemonic communities', and their struggles have broadened to include debates about gender, class, ethnicity, sexuality and so on:

> Thus the recent debates on the nation's historical amnesia do not simply revolve around the recovery and suppression of facts in national history. Rather, they are more than ever concerned with problematizing the very subject of remembering – that is, with analyzing from whose perspective and for whom remembering is urgently required.
>
> (1999: 216)

The need for this 'transnationalization of mnemonic communities' is discussed by Su Zhiliang who sees the emergence of a wider, more active, set of institutions and organizations involved in the textbook issue as an encouraging sign that Japan (and China) could be coming to terms with the past. But he argues that more political pressure should be applied on the Japanese government to deal with the history problem, perhaps in the form of a united front of Asian governments or by continuing to raise the issue in global organizations (such as the UN Commission on Human Rights, or the World Conference against Racism) (Su 2001a: 166). Given the lack of direct political pressure from the Chinese government on the Japanese government to deal with the textbook problem, transnational civil society may be one means of achieving a greater understanding and cooperation between the two sides.

4 The search for justice

The 1990s' compensation movement

Having considered the difficulties experienced at the 'seeking the truth' stage of the reconciliation process between China and Japan in the 1980s and 1990s, this chapter focuses on the renewed search for justice which started in the late 1980s when former victims of Japanese aggression during the war began to speak out about their experiences and sought redress in the form of civil compensation and apologies. As with the textbook issue, civil society in both countries, and the growing networks of transnational civil society interested in human rights and gender issues, have played a pivotal role in bringing many of the cases to light.

As we saw in the description of patterns of reconciliation in Chapter 1, agreements on war reparations between two (or more) states form one aspect of the process and help to 'repair history', but in the 1990s, civil compensation emerged as a means for individuals or groups of victims of war crimes or crimes against humanity to seek justice. This chapter considers a small sample of lawsuits brought on behalf of a number of Chinese victims of Japanese aggression during the Second World War and explores the reasons for their success or failure. In particular, it will focus on cases brought by (1) former forced labourers; (2) comfort women; and (3) victims of biological and chemical warfare and experimentation and those injured by abandoned chemical weapons. Over 60 lawsuits have been lodged in district courts and higher throughout Japan, and a further 15–20 have been fought in US courts. Only a small number of cases have resulted in the plaintiffs being awarded compensation. The majority of the cases have been dismissed, are pending a verdict, or have gone to appeal. Successful cases tend to be those where the complaint is against Japanese companies rather than the state. To date, although a number of judges have acknowledged the suffering of the plaintiffs, they have never ruled that the Japanese state should take legal responsibility.

Despite the poor success rate, the compensation cases are worth considering in detail because the efforts of Chinese, Japanese, and American scholars and lawyers who have helped to bring them about provide evidence of the growing power of transnational movements. More importantly, perhaps, they offer some hope for a grass-roots-led process of reconciliation between the Chinese and Japanese as described in Chapter 1. The key point of this chapter then is not to highlight the failure of the court cases (although this is significant because it shows (1) the continued reluctance of LDP-dominated governments to accept war responsibility; and (2) the working of Japanese courts and the interference of politics in the judicial system), but to emphasise the successes of the citizens' groups, lawyers' associations, and academic communities in bringing to light issues that had largely been 'forgotten' or suppressed during the trials which took place in the first phase of reconciliation, and in gaining some justice for the victims who have otherwise been ignored. Before considering the details of the compensation cases brought by China's Second World War victims, it is useful to provide some background to the development of the Chinese movement for compensation in the 1990s.

The international, regional and domestic settings

Although the 1972 Joint Statement had apparently resolved the issue of state-to-state reparations, by the late 1980s a number of Chinese groups, with the backing of Japanese human rights lawyers and citizens' groups, began to call for individual compensation. The Chinese 'movement' for compensation (*suopei yundong*) should be seen as part of a burgeoning trend in Asia for compensation from Japan which began in the 1970s and 1980s with claims for the repayment of salaries, military postal savings, and pensions from Taiwanese veterans who had fought for the Japanese army during the war.[1] The Asian compensation movement gathered pace in the late 1980s as the international and regional political climate changed. Under the international structure of the Cold War and the domination of authoritarian governments, many of the people living in countries which suffered the most during the war with Japan had been unable or unwilling to speak out. After the end of the Cold War, however, rapid economic growth, democratisation, and the growth of civil society paved the way for conditions in which former victims or their families could pursue the issue of war responsibility and seek compensation and justice for past wrongs.[2] By the mid-1990s compensation claims had been brought by Koreans who had been abandoned in Sakhalin, former Korean and Taiwanese B/C war criminals, Korean and Chinese forced labourers, Korean comfort women, and many more. The main characteristic of these various cases was that they were brought by individuals (or groups) against the Japanese state and companies, and the home governments rarely provided support for their efforts. To date, few cases have been resolved to the satisfaction of the claimants. Indeed, in the cases of the complaints brought against the Japanese government by groups of Korean comfort women and British prisoners of war, it was the home governments which, for various reasons, eventually produced compensation packages for the victims (Barkan 2000; Preece 2001; Soh 1996).

The Korean comfort women movement: a model for China?

The compensation movement for Korean comfort women has attracted a great deal of academic attention, and is worth reviewing here for its parallels with, or lessons for, China's compensation movement.[3] A more relaxed environment politically in Korea at the end of the 1980s and a rapidly growing feminist movement helped to encourage former sex slaves to come forward. In 1990, the Korean Council for the Women Drafted for Military Sexual Slavery by Japan (Han'guk Chongsindaemunje Taech'aek Hyopuihoe, hereafter Korean Council) called for an apology and compensation from the Japanese government, but the issue was really brought to the region's attention when, in 1991, Kim Haksun, a former comfort woman, came forward to tell her story. Testimonies from other former comfort women ensued, and prompted Japanese academics to conduct research into the issue. Chūō University professor Yoshimi Yoshiaki played a key role in discovering evidence of the Japanese military's involvement in the establishment of comfort stations and his research forced the Japanese government to acknowledge the state's involvement in the system.

Although the Japanese government acknowledged its responsibility and issued an apology in 1993 (see Appendix 3), this was not considered adequate. In response to the demands for compensation, the Japanese government established a relief fund called the Asia Peace and Friendship Fund for Women (*Josei no tame no Ajia heiwa yūkō kikin*), hereafter Asian Women's Fund (AWF).[4] The government pledged ¥500 million (for fiscal year 1995) to which would be added private donations. The government made it clear that this was not to be considered direct reparations, and that the money should be used to pay for medical and welfare support for former comfort women. In addition, a personal letter from the incumbent prime minister expressing his heartfelt apology would be sent to those women who accepted support from the fund. Here the contradiction between acknowledgement of a moral responsibility on the one hand, and the abdication of a legal responsibility, on the other, is clear (Bu Ping 2000a: 167; Hayashi 2001: 58), and only added fuel to the fire. The AWF received smaller donations from the private sector than the Japanese government had anticipated, but this was irrelevant since many women refused to accept any money which was not fully funded by the Japanese government, nor did they accept the personal, written apology from the Japanese prime minister. In fact, the establishment of the AWF caused divisions within those very groups that had worked so hard to produce a response from the Japanese government. Soh (2001), for example, describes how seven Korean women who chose to accept the money offered by the AWF were sharply criticised by Korean activists, and how the Korean survivors were instead provided with Korean government (and private) funding, on the condition that they would not accept AWF money.

The Korean Council, Japanese progressive academics and other NGOs were hindered in their struggle by the reluctance of the Japanese (and initially the Korean) government, but were helped by a burgeoning worldwide gender and human rights movement, itself facilitated by the development of international laws on human rights since the end of the Second World War. There was a growing international consensus that war crimes have no time limit, and that states have the responsibility to claim compensation for *individual* victims of war crimes (Matsuo 1998: 13). In addition, Murayama cites the growing expectation of international public opinion for individual post-war compensation as a result of the German 'model' (1993: 135). Thus, what began as a domestic movement in Korea soon developed into an international women's and human rights movement (see Piper 2001). In Japan, a number of NGOs provided support and assistance to the comfort women's struggle. The Centre for Research and Documentation on Japan's War Responsibility (Nihon no sensō sekinin shiryō sentā), formed in 1993 by historians and legal experts, performs a central role in collecting and disseminating information about Japan's wartime activities and their repercussions, and has published frequently on the comfort women issue. Another important organisation which became actively involved in the comfort women issue and war responsibility debate is the Violence against Women in War Network, Japan (VAWW–NET Japan) which was formed in 1998 and was responsible for setting up the Women's International War Crimes Tribunal, held in Tokyo in December 2000. Other groups include the Association to Clarify Post-war Responsibility of Japan (Nihon no sengo sekinin o hakkiri saseru kai), the Taiwan Comfort Women Legal Support Group (Taiwan no moto ianfu saiban o shi'en suru kai) and many others.[5]

As former comfort women from Korea, the Philippines and other Asian countries began to launch lawsuits against the Japanese government, the UN Commission on Human Rights took up the issue of the comfort women in 1992 at the behest of the Korean Council. The (interim) report submitted by Rhadika Coomaraswamy to the UN in 1996 (on Japan's military sexual slavery against Korea), and the final report produced by Gay McDougall in 1998 entitled 'Systematic rape, sexual slavery and slavery-like practices during armed conflict' supported the demands of the Korean, Taiwanese, Filipina and other groups in their struggle to bring to light the scale of sexual slavery during the war and to force the Japanese government to deal with the issue fully.[6] The formation of a collective identity and attendant political activism were important elements of the comfort women movement. Although they were unsuccessful in their attempts to wrest compensation and an apology from the Japanese state in the way they had envisaged, the movement achieved a great deal in terms of consciousness-raising and recognition of their years of suffering (Piper 2001: 133). As the previous chapter showed, the topic of comfort women was introduced into Japanese middle- and high-school textbooks by the mid-1990s. Another successful element of the movement was the sense of 'international solidarity achieved among women in victimized countries and Japan' which helped them to pursue their goals of redressing war crimes, sexual violence and discrimination (Hayashi 2001:

576). As the remainder of this chapter will show, there are a number of parallels between the development of the (Korean) comfort women movement and the development of a Chinese movement for compensation for former forced labourers and other victims of Japanese atrocities. For instance, the creation of Chinese civil groups was accompanied, or in some cases preceded, by the creation of support groups in Japan which sought to publicise the efforts of the Chinese groups, publish accounts of victims, raise funds and help launch the lawsuits. By raising the profile of individual Chinese victims and publicising their experiences, these groups together managed to create a collective identity which in turn helped to raise national and international consciousness and lent a mood of political activism to the whole movement.

The origins of the Chinese compensation movement

In addition to the changing international and regional political and legal environment in the 1990s, the combination of social, political and economic changes in both China and Japan also contributed in some measure to the emergence of the compensation movement.

The first set of factors relates to the need to counteract the failure of the Japanese to deal with the issue of war responsibility in the aftermath of the war, as discussed in Chapter 2. The problems that were brought about by the omissions of the Tokyo trial were exacerbated by subsequent denials by Japanese of wartime aggression, frequent remarks ('slips of the tongue' (*mōgen*)) made by politicians in the 1980s and 1990s, and attempts to 'beautify' and re-affirm the Greater East Asia War. All pointed to a continued avoidance of war responsibility, and an inability to acknowledge the suffering of Japan's victims (Tawara 1998: 124–5). A perceived shift to the right in the 1990s, evidenced by the third textbook offensive, the legalisation of the national flag and anthem, the strengthening of the USA–Japan security alliance, and the emergence of a new generation of neo-nationalist politicians, academics and commentators, were further causes for concern and provided an impetus for groups in Japan who sought to thwart this trend. The proactive stance of progressive Japanese groups involved in trying to refute the neo-nationalist view of history, acknowledging Japan's war responsibility, and supporting global gender and human rights movements was essential to the development of the movement. Beginning in 1991, the International Forum for Post-war Compensation in the Asia Pacific (Sengo hoshō kokusai fōramu), a voluntary group made up of lawyers (such as Takagi Ken'ichi), experts and citizens, organised a number of conferences at which victims were able to voice their stories and international panels discussed the means by which justice could be sought. Many other groups have since emerged to take up the cases of particular groups of victims, and their activities are discussed below.

The second set of factors is connected to the changes which have taken place in Chinese society since Deng Xiaoping's reform policies of the 1980s. These include the proliferation of Chinese social organisations, a greater awareness of human rights, and an environment in which Chinese people were able, indeed encouraged, to speak out about their experiences of the War of Resistance against Japan. The movement for compensation in China began in the late 1980s and was perhaps spurred on by such officially sanctioned events as, for example, the opening of the Memorial Hall for the Victims of the Nanjing Massacre in 1985 and the 50th anniversary of the start of the Sino-Japanese War in 1987 (Itō 1991: 8).

Matsuo (1998: 9) argues that the Chinese government had always held the view that although the PRC government had waived compensation in 1972, this did not preclude claims from private citizens. The Vice-President of the Japan–China Friendship Group referred to this point in a speech made in November 1990 to a delegation from the Japanese Committee on Chinese forced labour (Chūgoku kyōsei renkō o kangaeru kai) (Tanaka 1991: 50). It was at grass-roots level that the movement for compensation began to take off in the late 1980s and early 1990s. Li refers to a number of individuals who became actively involved in the move for compensation. Two in particular, Li Guping from Renmin University, and Tong Zeng, a Beijing University graduate, took separate measures to raise awareness about compensation. In August 1987, the same year in which Deng Xiaoping had stated that Japan owed more to China than to any other country, Li sent letters to members of the National People's Congress (NPC) about the issue of private compensation, carried out an opinion poll, and met with Nanjing Massacre survivors (Li 1999: 66–8). In March 1991 Tong Zeng began to canvass members of the People's Congress for their opinion, and in the following year he, along with other representatives, submitted a formal proposal for compensation to the joint Chinese People's Political Consultative Conference (CPPCC) and NPC (Su 2000b: 170–1).[7] It charged that $18 billion was due from the Japanese government to the Chinese people as private compensation for the killing of 10 million civilians, the wounding and forced labour of 300,000 (this included the 40,000 labourers taken to Japan), the suffering of citizens by chemical weapons and poisoned gas, and the destruction and pillage of public and private property. Tong Zeng's main argument was that a distinction should be made between reparations for war and compensation for damages. The former (amounting to $12 billion) was settled between the two states after the war (i.e., with China waiving its claim), but the latter ($18 billion) was not (Tanaka 1994a: 17).[8]

The content of the proposal is worth outlining in more detail. It begins with a brief outline of the suffering caused by Japanese aggression in China and then discusses the changing nature of compensation in an international, historical context (from indemnities to 'damages'). It details the Yalta Agreement, and the Cairo and Potsdam declarations and compares the amount of compensation paid by West Germany with that of Japan. The next section then provides considerable detail on Japan's violation of international laws during the Second World War (for example, in the treatment of PoWs, the massacre of civilians, and the use of slavery and forced labour). Tong Zeng recommended that a law be passed enabling organisations such as the Overseas Chinese Association or the Chinese Red Cross to gather information on Chinese victims of Japanese aggression and prepare a case for compensation which could then be presented to the Japanese government by the Chinese government 'at a suitable time'. This, he argued, would be in keeping with international law and customs. By seeking compensation from Japan, Tong Zeng hoped to achieve two aims: to get the Japanese side to fulfil their duty and to enable China to use 'normal' international channels to get compensation. The proposal emphasised the importance of non-governmental channels in seeking compensation, citing the success of citizens' groups in other countries, for example the Canadian Japanese Association (see Chūgoku kenkyūjo (ed.) 1991: 89–106).

The aim of the proposal was to try to establish a bill on civil compensation from Japan (*minjian duiri suopeifa*), and it caught the attention of Japanese journalists in China who were keen to find out the Chinese government stance. In response to a question from one Japanese journalist, Vice-Foreign Minister Qian Qichen stated that although people's representatives have the right to submit proposals, there was no change in the Chinese government position on reparations as expressed in the 1972 Joint Statement. He did state, however, that the Japanese government should respond appropriately to the complex problems thrown up by the invasion of China (Matsuo 1998: 12; Shi 2000: 121). On 11 March a Foreign Ministry spokesman said that the Chinese government had already resolved the issue of reparations, but that the government would not disrupt any direct contact between Chinese victims and Japanese authorities. Thus, the position of the Chinese government was clear from the start, and has not changed since. Jiang Zemin took up the issue on 1 April 1992 during a press conference for Japanese reporters, reiterating the stance that the Chinese government's position had not changed (Shi 2000: 122). In 1995 the Chinese Foreign Ministry urged the Japanese to 'take a responsible attitude' and 'respond appropriately' to the lawsuit brought against Kajima Construction, but did not attempt to intervene (Tanaka 1996: 6; see also Su 2000b: 170–1). Although the NPC did not adopt the proposal in 1992, this was the first time since normalisation that the issue of compensation had been publicly discussed (Matsuo 1998: 12) and the movement for compensation soon gathered speed, particularly when Chinese and Japanese groups began to work together.

Sino-Japanese cooperation on compensation cases

The exhaustive activities of Japanese and Chinese lawyers and academics and their support groups have played a crucial role in helping to raise awareness and bring about lawsuits. The number of Japanese lawyers' associations, civil groups, and academic conferences concerned with the compensation issue started to increase in the 1990s. Japanese lawyers and activists have been particularly pro-active, and have played a key role in helping to launch research projects or law cases. Chinese civil groups tend to be small in terms of membership and are described by Chinese academics as spontaneous groups (*zifa de*) – rather than social organisations (*shehui tuanti*) – since they do not have official backing and are not registered. Representatives of the groups are quick to point out they are merely 'groups of volunteers', not members of a non-governmental organisation. Indeed, it seems that attempts by some individual activists to broaden the campaign too far were treated with suspicion by the government in the mid-1990s.[9] While the Chinese government appeared to be taking a more tolerant attitude to 'reparations campaigners' by the late 1990s, the groups were still fairly small and limited their activities to holding small meetings or study groups. Nonetheless the Chinese groups have been an essential link between Japanese organisations and the people they hope to support and represent.

Lawyers' groups

In May and July 1994 a group of Japanese lawyers, the Research Committee on the Chinese Judicial System (Chūgoku shihō seido chōsadan), visited China. At about the same time, then Japanese Justice Minister Nagano Shigeto enraged the region by announcing that the Nanjing Massacre was a fabrication. The lawyers' group immediately lodged complaints with Prime Minister Hata Tsutomu and with the Japanese Ambassador in China. This event apparently spurred a group of Chinese to ask the lawyers for help in their legal battles for compensation (Matsuo 1998: 15). By October 1994, the lawyers had formed the Chinese War Victims Lawyers' Research Committee (Chūgokujin sensō higai hōrikuka chōsadan), led by Ōyama Hiroshi and Onodera Toshitaka, with a membership of 280 lawyers willing to represent Chinese victims. The committee made a number of fact-finding visits to China between 1994 and 1995 to gather statements from survivors (or their relatives) of the Nanjing Massacre, Unit 731, indiscriminate bombing campaigns, and forced labour camps (Matsuo 1998: 15–16; Okuda and Kawashima 2000: 226). In 1995 the group, now renamed the Chinese War Victims' Compensation Claim Group (Chūgokujin sensō higai baishō seikyū bengodan), brought its first case against the Japanese government on behalf of four Chinese comfort women. Other lawyers' groups also coalesced around compensation cases for forced labourers, chemical warfare, and so on. Chinese lawyers played an increasingly important role in fact-finding and information gathering and in the court cases themselves, and representatives of the All China Lawyers' Association (ACLA) called for a more standard, coherent approach to civil actions (*People's Daily Online*, 15 January 2002). In terms of joint activities, between 1996 and 1998, a series of joint symposia arranged by the Chinese Academy of Social Sciences and the Japan Democratic Lawyers' Association (Nihon minshu hōritsuka kyōkai) was held in Beijing to discuss compensation and war responsibility (Matsuo 1998: 18–19).

Academic and citizens' groups

Academics in both countries have played an important role in the compensation movement providing evidence in court and unearthing archival material in support of the claims. Chinese academics have been called as expert witnesses in a number of court cases, providing documentary evidence from Chinese archives and supporting oral testimonies made by Chinese victims. Joint Chinese-Japanese conferences and workshops on compensation started to take place on a regular basis in the early 1990s. As public awareness was raised about the issues, citizens' groups started to form in Japan and provided an even greater impetus to the movement. For example, to support the activities of the Chūgokujin sensō higai baishō seikyū bengodan mentioned above, a group of academics and activists held a conference in May 1995. By August it had developed into a fund-raising and campaign group called the Society to Support the Demands of Chinese War Victims (Chūgokujin sensō higaisha yōkyū o sasaeru kai, or Suopei).[10] Suopei has since become one of the most active groups in the compensation movement, collating material, raising funds, and reporting on the progress of various lawsuits (http://www.suopei.org/index.html). As of February 2001 it enjoyed a membership of approximately 2,000 people, including Ienaga Saburō (now deceased), Fujiwara Akira, Honda Katsuichi, Matsui Yayori (journalist and head of VAWW-NET Japan, now deceased), Morimura Seiichi and many other well-known academics and writers (Matsuo 1998: 16). In addition, a number of legal experts are attached to the support group and are often asked to provide expert testimony during court hearings, as are foreign experts (such as Sheldon Harris, author of *Factories of Death*). The growth of the Internet has undoubtedly helped Suopei and other support groups to disseminate information about their activities. Most maintain websites, providing further information about particular groups of victims or court cases in progress. The Japanese groups canvass for support, financial and otherwise, from the local and foreign communities. The content and slant of each website are clearly diverse – some are more objective than others – but nonetheless they demonstrate the interest such issues have generated, and help to maintain a high level of awareness.

Compensation cases in the 1990s, the fight for justice

According to Brooks (1999), a number of criteria are needed for civil redress to be successful: claims must be in the hands of legislators, not the judiciary – that is those who have the power to create new laws, not those whose can only act according to existing laws; claims must be supported by as large a group as possible in order to apply political pressure on the legislators; internal solidarity and support are essential; and claims must have merit, that is, there must be well-documented proof that a human injustice was committed, and that the victims are 'identifiable as a distinct group' and continue to suffer harm as a direct result of the injustice (ibid.: 7). As this section points out, the success rate of the Chinese compensation claims in the Japanese courts has been relatively low, suggesting that one or more of the criteria is lacking in the Chinese–Japanese compensation movement. This section will consider some of the lawsuits brought by Chinese victims to assess the extent to which they have achieved their aims. Most of the cases described have been brought in Japanese courts, but some of the US-based cases are included in order to highlight the level of interest that such cases have attracted. Table 4.1 provides a list of some of the cases described in this chapter, but a great many more have been brought since the mid-1990s.[11]

Former forced labourers

Approximately 40,000 Chinese were taken forcibly to Japan in the periods April–November 1943 and March 1944–May 1945 to work in 135 construction and mining companies. Their treatment was brutal, and an estimated 7,000 lost their lives.[12] In the early 1990s, the Japanese Ministry of Foreign Affairs (MoFA) claimed that all documentation relating to former forced labourers had been destroyed after the war. But a series of reports, originally produced in 1946 for the MoFA based on information received from the 135 companies which had 'employed' the labourers, was discovered in 1993 in the Tokyo headquarters of the Overseas Chinese Association.[13] The existence of these reports was certainly known about in the 1950s and even referred to in a document produced by the Committee to Repatriate the Souls of Chinese Prisoners of War (Chūgokujin furyo junnansha eirei jikkō iinkai) formed by the Japanese Red Cross Society and the Japan–China Friendship Association (NHK 1994: 10). But it was only after the issue was taken up in the Lower House Budget Committee on 21 May 1993 that the MoFA undertook investigations into the whereabouts of this 'missing' report on forced labourers (ibid.: 220). The reports and supporting data have since been published in Japanese (Tanaka and Matsuzawa 1995) and, as with Yoshimi Yoshiaki's data on the comfort women system, provide essential information about the nature and extent of the forced labour system.

A number of Japanese companies, including NKK, Mitsubishi Heavy Industries, Nachi-Fujikoshi, Nippon Steel, Kajima, and Nishimatsu Construction have had cases brought against them in Japanese courts by Taiwanese, Koreans, Filipino and Chinese plaintiffs. In most cases, the plaintiffs have demanded compensation for harsh treatment and/or reimbursement of unpaid wages from the companies, in addition to an official apology from the company and the Japanese government. A number of cases have been brought against Japanese companies by American law firms in US courts.

Table 4.1 List of compensation cases

Date	Name of case	Plaintiffs	Seeking	Support group(s)	Outcome
1989–2002	Hanaoka vs Kajima Corp.	10 claimants on behalf of 986 forced labourers	¥5 million each, plus apology and memorial	Hanaoka Trial Support Committee; Committee on Chinese Forced Labourers	1990 Joint Statement (apology from Kajima) 2000 Out of court settlement of ¥500 million (total) paid into the 'Hanaoka fund'
2000–2003	Forced labourers vs Mitsui Mining	15 former forced labourers	¥23 million each plus apology	Suopei	2003 Fukuoka District Court orders Mitsui to pay ¥11 million to each plaintiff
1995/6– ongoing	Former comfort women vs Japanese state	First case: Li Xiumei et al. Second case: Wan Aihua et al.	¥20m each, plus apology	Suopei; Japan Democratic Lawyers' Association and Chinese lawyers	2001 and 2002 Tokyo District Court dismissed cases; cases taken to appeal
1997–2002	Unit 731 lawsuit	180 victims of Unit 731 biological warfare	¥10m each plus apology	Lawsuit for compensation for 731 Biological Warfare; Chinese and Japanese lawyers	2002 case dismissed
1996/1997– 2003	Abandoned chemical weapons cases	Case 1. Thirteen people involved in three accidents since 1974 Case 2. Five people involved in four accidents between 1950–1987	Case 1. ¥200 million in total Case 2. ¥80 million yen in total	Both cases supported by Suopei; Japanese and Chinese lawyers	Case 1. Sep. 2003. Court orders government to pay ¥190 million Case 2. May 2003 case dismissed

Source: Matsuo (1998), Tawara (1999), various press articles and court proceedings.

Cooperation between Chinese, Japanese, American, and Chinese-American lawyers has helped to bring the lawsuits to fruition.[14]

US-based cases

In the early 1990s, hopes were high that cases brought by American and Asian former PoWs, forced labourers and comfort women would be won in US lawcourts because of the success of US law firms in Holocaust restitution cases:

> Without a doubt, the claims against the Japanese multinationals are a direct result of the earlier litigation brought against their European counterparts. Aging victims of Japan's wartime activities began filing their lawsuits in American courts only after seeing the successes achieved by their counterparts in the Holocaust litigation.
>
> (Bazyler 2001: 71)

Another reason can be attributed to changes in the statute of limitations on matters relating to the Second World War, which, due to a law enacted in July 1999 (California Code of Civil Procedure Section 354.6), extended the period within which claims could be made to 2010. By contrast, Japan's statute of limitations was (and remains) twenty years after the event. In California, over 30 cases were lodged in 1999–2000, but here a few examples will suffice (Bazyler 2001; *The Economist* 2000).

In February 2000, the law firm Milberg Weiss brought two lawsuits against Mitsubishi Corp., Mitsui and Co., and their subsidiaries seeking recovery of unpaid wages.[15] In summer 2000, Barry Fisher (well known for his work on human rights law) brought two suits against the Japanese government and companies, one on behalf of fifteen Asian former 'comfort women' (the first of its kind for comfort women), and the other on behalf of nine Chinese forced labourers.[16] By this time at least ten cases against Japan or Japanese companies were pending in the USA, three of which were on behalf of Chinese claimants (Bazyler 2001; *Kyodo News*, 18 October 2000).

Despite high hopes for these lawsuits, however, their success rate has been disappointing. Many of the cases have been dismissed, though some have gone to appeal. Reasons for the dismissals are varied: cases brought against Japanese companies on behalf of American or Allied former PoWs have been dismissed on the grounds that signatories to the San Francisco Peace Treaty are not allowed to claim compensation. Those brought on behalf of non-US, non-Allied Power victims (e.g., Koreans and Chinese) against Japanese companies have been dismissed for a number of other reasons. One judge, for example, found that the California law 345.6 was unconstitutional, while, in other cases, 'pressure' from the US government via its statements of interest prevented the cases from proceeding.[17] Finally, those cases brought against the Japanese government on behalf of former comfort women have failed, also because of the US government stance which has not been supportive of the plaintiffs' claims. The influence of the US government in these lawsuits is worth noting, and Bazyler puts the failure of the court cases down to the government's pro-Japan stance and its willingness to side with Japanese companies. The defence lawyers acting on behalf of one group of Korean and Chinese comfort women protested against the US government's statement of interest, arguing that the position adopted by the Department of State was 'a strategic one, rather than a legal one' aimed at maintaining the status quo in USA–Japan relations.[18] The pro-Japan stance of the US government has been contrasted with its position on the issue of German compensation where the government played an active role in encouraging Germany to set up a compensation fund, and some US judges were willing to uphold claims for compensation brought in US courts when it appeared that Germany was not keeping to 'its part of the bargain' (Bazyler 2001; Niven 2002: 234). It seems, therefore, that the political pressure brought to bear by the US government on compensation cases relating to the Japanese state or companies has stymied the chances of success for the plaintiffs.

Japan-based cases

In contrast to the poor record of the US-based lawsuits, in Japan there have been some successes for former forced labourers. By 2002, 40 to 50 cases had been filed in Japanese courts. The majority of them had been dismissed, were on appeal, or pending, but a small number of cases achieved some of their aims: the Liu Lianren case, the Hanaoka vs. Kajima case, and the Mitsui Mining case.

THE LIU LIANREN CASE

In September 1991, and again in 1993, a Chinese man in his seventies, Liu Lianren, visited Japan to seek an apology and compensation from the Japanese government. Liu was a former forced labourer, but his case was particularly remarkable. Along with other people from his own and surrounding villages in Shandong, Liu had been forcibly removed to Hokkaido in 1944 to work in a coal mine run by the Meiji Mining Company. He managed to escape the mine with two other comrades but only he remained uncaptured, staying undetected for thirteen years. Liu was discovered in 1958 hiding in a cave in Hokkaido, unaware that the war had ended. Once found, he was expelled from Japan as an illegal immigrant by Prime Minister Kishi (who, ironically, had implemented the forced labour policy during his tenure as Minister of Commerce and Industry during the war). Liu's return to China was widely covered in the press at the time, and he became a national hero in China. When he launched his court case, he again attracted much publicity and the case was followed closely in the press in both China and Japan, with his story being re-told to a new generation. Although Liu's experience is somewhat extraordinary, he is just one of many Chinese victims of Japanese wartime abuses who started to come forward in the early 1990s to tell their stories and seek recognition of, and compensation for, their suffering (Matsuo 1998; Nozoe 1995).

Both of Liu's visits in the early 1990s met with little success and his court case was dismissed. In 1996 Liu appealed to the Tokyo District Court and the case was still ongoing when the news of Liu's death was announced in September 2000 (Matsuo 1998). The final judgment of the Tokyo District Court was made in July 2001 with an order to the state to pay ¥20 million to Liu's next of kin for his suffering. Although the verdict was hailed as a landmark by the Japanese and Chinese media, it is important to note that the judge (Nishioka Seiichirō) clearly stated that the state was *not* liable to compensate Liu for his abduction and subjection to forced labour. Rather the compensation was for the thirteen years Liu spent in the hills of Hokkaido as a 'fugitive' (*Japan Times Online*, 13 July 2001).

HANAOKA LABOURERS VS. KAJIMA CORPORATION

One of the more high-profile cases brought by former forced labourers involves claims against Kajima Corporation, a construction company which ran the forced labour camp at Hanaoka – the setting of the 'famous' Hanaoka uprising or incident (*Hanaoka jiken*) of June 1945.[19] Some 986 Chinese were taken to Hanaoka town (now Ōdate city) in Akita prefecture in northern Japan in the latter stages of the war (from August 1944 onwards), but 418 died there. According to NHK, in 1984, two Hanaoka survivors who had remained in Japan after the war demanded the wartime wages that were due to them. This news reached China and three years later one of the survivors of the Hanaoka incident, Geng Zhun, was invited to Japan where he visited Ōdate and participated in a memorial ceremony. On his return to China, Geng Zhun, along with three other survivors, Wang Min, Zhang Zhaoguo and Li Jiasheng, formed a group for Hanaoka survivors and their relatives called the Hanaoka Victims' Group (Huagang shounanzhe lianyi-hui). In December 1989 the group announced their decision to seek compensation of ¥5 million per survivor or relative (which would total nearly ¥5 billion), in addition to a formal apology and the erection of memorial museums in Beijing and Ōdate. Geng Zhun and five other members of the group travelled to Ōdate in June 1990 to enter into direct negotiations with the company, accompanied by Japanese lawyer Niimi Takashi. As a result of these talks, the company and the group agreed on a joint statement, issued in July 1990, in which the company acknowledged that Chinese labourers had been forced to work in the mine, accepted corporate responsibility, and expressed its 'profound apology' (*shinjinna shazai no i o hyōmei*) to the survivors and families (NHK 1994: 217; Uchida 2001). But the issue of compensation was not resolved. Instead the company indicated that it was willing to enter into talks with a representative of the group in order to resolve the issue as quickly as possible. In reality, negotiations were very slow (Li 1999: 41). In 1993 and 1994 members of the group returned to Japan and reiterated their demands, but by May 1995 the direct negotiations had broken down. In June 1995, eleven members of the survivors' group subsequently filed a lawsuit in Japan (Macintyre 1996; Tanaka 1992:19).

The case started in the Tokyo District Court in June 1995, but by December 1997 had been dismissed on the grounds that claims could not be made beyond the twenty-year statute of limitations. The case was then taken to the High Court which advised in September 1999 that it would be better to effect a mediated resolution rather than settling the matter in court. After a number of further meetings between Kajima, the Huagang shounanzhe lianyihui, and the Chinese Red Cross, the High Court produced a draft resolution in April 2000 which reiterated the main points of the joint statement of 1990 and suggested compensation of ¥500 million. On 29 November 2000 Kajima eventually, and it appears somewhat reluctantly, agreed to set up the Hanaoka Fund for Peace and Friendship (*Hanaoka Heiwa Yukōkin*) amounting to ¥500 million.[20] The initial reaction from the Huagang shounanzhe lianyihui, other support groups, and the press was very positive, and the settlement seemed to offer hope for future claims.

The role of a number of groups in this case is notable. As with the other cases considered in this chapter, the activities of grass-roots organisations in China and Japan, and the cooperation between these groups were crucial to maintaining pressure on the company to produce a settlement. Niimi Takashi, one of the Japanese lawyers representing the Huagang shounanzhe lianyihui, stated that one of the reasons that the case was able to be brought was precisely the cooperative efforts of scholars, citizens and organisations, and that this sort of collaboration would form the basis of Sino-Japanese friendship in the future (Niimi 1998: 2–7). The Huagang shounanzhe lianyihui found support from a number of domestic Japanese groups: the Hanaoka Trial Support Committee (Hanaoka saiban shi'en renrakukai), and the Committee on Chinese Forced Labour (Chūgokujin kyōsei renkō o kangaeru kai),[21] as well as US groups such as Nikkei for Civil Rights Redress (NCRR). The evidence upon which the court case was built, as with the other cases, also came from research carried out by academics. NHK (1994) remarked upon the efforts made by academics in gathering documentation on former forced labourers. Hebei University professor Liu Baozhan, for example, carried out surveys and managed to find 350 Hanaoka survivors or their relatives.

The High Court appears to have actively pushed for compromise and acted as mediator, enlisting the support of the Chinese Red Cross Society as a conduit for distribution of the fund. Uchida argues that the Court's positive stance towards 'liquidating war damages' helped to restore the image of the Japanese judiciary. Referring to the statement produced by the court, Uchida explains that the judge had looked to the compensation offered by Germany to its former forced labourers 'instead of being constrained by conventional ways of compromise'.[22] He refers to the Hanaoka settlement as a 'milestone', comparing it favourably to the German 'Remembrance, Responsibility and the Future' fund set up in 2000 for former forced labourers or their families (2001b: 33).[23]

But not all assessments of the Hanaoka settlement were quite so positive, and a debate soon developed as to the true extent of the 'victory'. Opinion remains divided, particularly in China, where some view it as an important legal landmark and victory for the compensation movement, while others see it as a failure. For example, Chinese writer Li Min criticised the way the (Japanese) lawyers dealt with the plaintiffs on the matter of the agreement with Kajima, noting that the content of the final settlement was never discussed with, or agreed upon by, the survivors themselves. In fact, He Tianyi, who acted as adviser to the Huagang shounanzhe lianyihui, points out that from 2000 onwards the Chinese group and their supporters were rarely notified of meetings (2002: 10). In addition, the amount of compensation fell short of the original demands – of the ¥5 million demanded, the survivors were offered ¥500,000 each, of which they would actually only receive ¥250,000 because of the way the money was to be distributed (He 2002: 11). A number of Chinese writers point to the discrepancies between this award and the amounts provided to claimants in other, more successful, cases – for example the award of ¥20 million to Liu Lianren's family, or Li Xiuying's ¥1.5 million (Wu 2002: 1–2).[24] The Hanaoka settlement was also compared with the Mitsui case (see below) which included a financial settlement of ¥11 million for each plaintiff. Critics also referred to the money spent by the Japanese government on war pensions to its own nationals which amounts to over ¥40 trillion, in contrast to less than ¥1 trillion paid to Asian victims (Wang 2002: 9). Some described the money destined for the Hanaoka victims as 'incense money' (*xianghuo qian*), in other words, a trifling amount sufficient only to pay for the incense to offer prayers to one's ancestors, and a further insult to the victims (Li 2002).

Moreover, the spirit in which Kajima agreed to the compromise was highly criticised. In keeping with the company's reluctance to accept legal responsibility, Kajima's stance was that the trust fund did not constitute compensation in any way, but that it was being set up from the standpoint of friendship between China and Japan to be used for memorial ceremonies, 'self-help' and healthcare for the victims, and education for their grandchildren. Chinese academics were critical of the fund, describing it as relief money rather than compensation. The Chinese press was not so scathing, tending to use the word 'compensation', and emphasising the success of the case. The Japanese press struggled with the terminology, describing the money variously as a subsidy or grant, support money, compensation, relief money (Li 2002). The wording of the terms of settlement issued by Kajima's lawyers was couched in legal jargon and made no reference to plans for the construction of memorial halls as originally requested by the claimants. There was no further apology, but the settlement did reconfirm the previous statement of 1990.[25]

For such reasons, some of the plaintiffs (including Geng Zhun) announced that they would not accept the settlement, resigned from the Huagang shounanzhe lianyihui, and even talked about setting up a new group to push the company and government to accept legal responsibility.[26] Even for those who were willing to accept the settlement and proceeds of the fund, the process was still a long one. The company agreed to pay the funds, into an account to be managed by a steering committee, by the end of 2003. The first tranche of money for Henan survivors and their families was distributed in April 2003 (*People's Daily Online* (Chinese), 10 March 2003).

When considered in legal terms, the response of the company can be better understood, thought not necessarily condoned. Different forms of redress are available to a defendant. According to Brooks, reparations are 'responses that seek atonement for the commission of an injustice' whereas a settlement does not include an expression of atonement. Thus, in a settlement, the defendant can agree to pay a sum of money or agree to a non-monetary solution (e.g, education programmes, medical care). It 'does not concede any wrongdoing', but it allows both sides to compromise by providing the victim with some symbolic material compensation, while allowing the perpetrator 'a chance to end the dispute without a finding of liability'. If the solution is monetary, it can go directly to individuals (compensatory) or to a group (rehabilitative) (1999: 8–9). The Hanaoka *settlement* was just that – it included no expression of atonement, but provided a combination of monetary and non-monetary redress to the victims and their families, and the company absolved itself of further liability.

It seems, then, that the victory for the Huagang shounanzhe lianyihui was bittersweet. The views expressed by some Chinese about the Kajima fund are reminiscent of the criticisms of the Asian Women's Fund established by the Japanese government in response to the comfort women claims. Both funds seemed only to highlight the Japanese reluctance to accept legal responsibility while acknowledging moral responsibility.

FORCED LABOURERS VS. MITSUI MINING

Another example of a relatively successful claim was the case brought by former forced labourers aginst Mitsui Mining. During the war, of all Japan's mining companies, Mitsui Mining used the largest number of forced labourers. Nearly 6,500 labourers were 'employed' at various branches of Mitsui Mining, and just over 1,000 died during their time there.[27] Twelve former labourers who had been sent to Japan in 1943–44 and set to work in Mitsui-run coal mines in Fukuoka (Miike and Tagawa) brought their case against the company in 2000, with an additional three coming forward in 2001. The group of plaintiffs, led by former forced labourer Zhang Baoheng, was represented by a team of Chinese and Japanese lawyers. On the Japanese side, the main lawyer was Tachiki Toyoji. Suopei acted as the main support group. The demand was for compensation of ¥23 million for each plaintiff, in addition to a public apology from the company and the Japanese government. The verdict of this case was announced on 27 April 2002 by the Fukuoka District Court. The judge dismissed the demands for a public apology and compensation from the government, but did order Mitsui to pay ¥11 million each to the plaintiffs (in total ¥165 million or $1.39 million).[28] The judge, Kimura Motoaki, ruled that Mitsui should be held responsible for its wartime actions, and that the forced transportation of civilians for labour was an 'illegal act jointly conducted by the state and the companies' (*Japan Times Online*, 27 April 2002).[29] But he echoed other judges in his view that the Meiji constitution prevented the state from taking responsibility for payment of individual compensation. On the other hand, he did argue against the twenty-year statute of limitations, saying that 'it goes against the idea of justice', and against the bilateral treaties signed between China and Japan, arguing that these 'cannot be recognised as ending the plaintiffs' right to seek damages' (*Japan Times Online*, 27 April 2002; *Muzi.com*, 26 August 2002). The plaintiffs, however, later appealed against the ruling precisely because the state was not held accountable by the court, and the company also announced its intention to launch an appeal against the judgement.[30] Nonetheless, the relative success of the Mitsui case was welcomed by many in China and Japan and seen as an important step forward, providing important legal lessons for future cases. Guan suggests, for example, that the judge's criticism of the twenty-year statute of limitations, used so often in the past as a means of dismissing the cases, was one such important development, offering hope that other judges might dispense with this in future. That the court also upheld the right of individuals to claim compensation was also unprecedented. A further strength of the Mitsui case, in Guan's view, was the cooperation between Japanese and Chinese lawyers which prevented the sort of breakdown of communication experienced between the Huagang shounanzhe lianyihui and the Japanese lawyers who represented them (2002: 2–6).

The relative success of the Hanaoka and Mitsui cases must have acted as an impetus to other former forced labourers, since new cases were still being brought in late 2002. For example, in August 2002 a group of ten Chinese former forced labourers filed a suit seeking compensation of ¥20 million each against the Japanese government and four companies including Sumitomo Coal Mining and Mitsui Mining at the Sapporo District Court, and in February 2003, nineteen former forced labourers lodged a lawsuit in Fukuoka District Court against the Japanese government, Mitsui Mining and Mitsubishi Corporation (*Japantoday.com*, 26 August 2002; *China Daily*, 28 February 2003). This is not to suggest that such cases are any more successful – in July 2002, for example, the Hiroshima District Court rejected a suit filed by former forced labourers against Nishimatsu Construction. But there is a growing body of opinion, in both China and Japan, which feels that if groups wishing to seek compensation could work more closely, perhaps forming a more organised and coherent movement, then there would be a stronger chance that the Japanese courts would put more pressure on the

Japanese government and companies to make greater concessions. The mood among Japanese and Chinese academics and activists remains extremely upbeat about the prospects for a Japanese settlement for forced labourers similar to the German 'Remembrance' fund.

Former 'comfort women'

As described earlier, a great deal of literature now exists on the topic of the Japanese military's 'comfort women' system and, in particular, the attempts by Korean former comfort women to seek justice in the 1990s through an acknowledgement, official apology and compensation from the Japanese government. In the late 1990s the issues surrounding the comfort women system remained highly sensitive and controversial, attracting the attention of a growing transnational network. The attempts by revisionist groups in Japan to deny or downplay the role of the wartime government in the comfort women system have only served to strengthen the worldwide movement to gain recognition of, and justice for, the women who suffered. Until recently, however, the plight of *Chinese* women under this system was relatively unknown, and very few Chinese women spoke out in public.[31] By the late 1990s, however, new research into Chinese comfort women contributed to a fresh understanding of the extent of the system, and more Chinese comfort women began to talk more openly.

The total number of comfort women is generally accepted as approximately 200,000, but Chinese research now throws doubt on this figure. In the early 1990s a number of articles about Chinese and Korean comfort women began to appear in Chinese journals and newspapers, based on various local surveys and investigations. A teacher (Zhang Shuangbing) from Yu county in Shanxi carried out a survey in his area in 1992 and discovered 'several' former comfort women. A Shanghai journalist reported on a similar investigation later the same year.[32] An article written in 1992 by Su Shi in *KangRi zhanzheng yanjiu*,[33] outlines the sort of sexual abuse suffered by Chinese women at the hands of Japanese soldiers in North-east China. The article cites Chinese sources of the time which record the activities of the various clubs and coffee bars serving as 'comfort stations' throughout China, in addition to the numbers of Korean and Chinese girls and women held in such places (Su 1992: 10–19). Chinese research into the comfort women began in earnest in the late 1990s, with the creation in 1999 of the Research Centre on Chinese Comfort Women (Zhongguo weianfu wenti yanjiu zhongxin), attached to the Shanghai Normal University, History Department. The key scholars working on the issue are Su Zhiliang and Chen Lifei (Hayashi 2000: 2). Bu Ping of Heilongjiang Academy of Social Sciences has also published a number of articles on the issue. Japanese academics such as Yoshimi Yoshiaki, Hayashi Hirofumi and Kasahara Tokushi, to name but a few, have also contributed to our knowledge of Chinese comfort women. With the discovery of documentation in Tianjin, Shanghai and Nanjing in the late 1990s, the research carried out by Chinese and Japanese scholars has been important in understanding the scope of the comfort women system in China. For example a two-year project on the Nanjing Massacre was set up in 1998, part of which has looked at Japanese sexual violence in Nanjing and the regions.[34] There has been widespread coverage in China of the internationalisation of the issue, including the various UN reports, and in April 2000, an International Symposium on Chinese Comfort Women was held in Shanghai as a preparatory meeting for the Women's International War Crimes Tribunal on Japan's Military Sexual Slavery to be held in Tokyo in December 2000.[35]

This research has revealed more information about the scope of the comfort women system as a whole. Although many comfort stations in China were 'staffed' by Korean and Japanese women, a great many Chinese women and girls were forced into sexual slavery too or were subjected to sexual assaults (Hayashi 2000: 2). Comfort stations were established in twenty-one cities. In Shanghai alone there were an estimated seventy-seven stations (estimates vary; Hayashi mentions eighty-two; seventy-seven is Su Zhiliang's figure), in Wuhan between forty and fifty (ibid.: 3). The total number of stations is estimated to have been anything from several thousand up to ten thousand, some in operation for the entire duration of the war, some just for a number of months. According to Su Zhiliang and Chen Lifei, the total number of Chinese women forced into prostitution by the Japanese army could have exceeded 200,000, with the total number of comfort women of all nationalities reaching between 360,000 and 410,000 (Su and Chen 1998b; Su 2000: 19–23, 33).[36] Of that number, Su estimates that there are perhaps only 100 or so survivors, many of whom are now too elderly, infirm or simply unwilling, for obvious reasons, to face court hearings (ibid.). Although survivors from all over China have come forward to tell their stories (for example, from Shanxi, Anhui, Hunan, Hainan, Yunnan, Inner Mongolia, etc.), to date, only a small number of Chinese women have been willing to take their cases to the Japanese courts, and it was not until 1995 that the first lawsuit against the Japanese government was brought on behalf of Chinese comfort women. The next section considers four cases – three filed in Japan, one in the United States. None of them have met with success for the plaintiffs.

Japan-based cases

The first case brought on behalf of Chinese former comfort women was filed in August 1995 in the Tokyo District Court on behalf of four women (Li Xiumei, Liu Mianhuan, Chen Lintao and Zhou Xixiang) who were forced into sexual slavery in Shanxi. They sought an apology and ¥20 million each in compensation. The second suit, with the same demands, was brought on behalf of two more women from Shanxi (Wan Aihua, Gua Xicui) in February 1996. Both cases were brought about by the cooperative efforts of various Chinese, Japanese and international groups. Suopei, or rather its affiliated lawyers' group, undertook a series of study trips to China in the mid-1990s and managed to identify at least fifty women in Shanxi province who claimed to have been victims of the Japanese comfort women system. For example, in 1994 a delegation from the Japan Democratic Lawyers' Association (Nihon minshu hōritsuka kyōkai) under the leadership of Ōyama Hiroshi heard Li Xiumei's testimony and that of one other former comfort woman. In 1995 the group made a further four visits to China. Li Xiumei's case was brought about by cooperation between the Central Lawyers' Office in Beijing and Japanese lawyers (Matsuo 1998: 15–18). Bu Ping stresses the crucial role played by Japanese organisations (citizens groups and lawyers associations) without whom, he argues, the cases could not have been launched (2000b: 168).

But neither case has, thus far, been successful. The decision on the first case was announced in May 2001. One of the grounds for the case was that, under the Hague Convention (1907), an aggressor is liable to pay compensation for damage inflicted. The judge, however, ruled that the treaty did not allow for claims for individual compensation and dismissed the case. On 29 March 2002 the Tokyo District Court rejected the claims of the plaintiffs in the second case, but did acknowledge that Chinese women had suffered sexual violence at the hands of the Japanese military. Once again, though, the judge found that the grounds upon which the case had been brought (for example, the Hague Convention, Japanese civil law and Chinese civil law) did not apply. Both cases went to appeal and are still pending.

A third case was brought in 1998 by seven women from Shanxi, and the relatives of three others, who had been raped by Japanese soldiers during the war. They demanded an apology and compensation of ¥20 million each. Once again the verdict, announced on 24 April 2003, dismissed their claims, but the judge's ruling nonetheless offered some hope to those involved in the campaign. Judge Takizawa dismissed the claims on the grounds of the twenty-year statute of limitations, and the lack of a provision under international law that necessitates compensation from the Japanese government. But he acknowledged that 'the army and the government had not upheld their responsibility to prevent the assault[s]' and indicated that the government could seek a 'legal and administrative solution' (*Asahi Online*, 25 April 2003; *Mainichi Interactive*, 24 April 2003).

The plight of Chinese comfort women was further highlighted at the Women's International War Crimes Tribunal attended by eight former comfort women from China who were accompanied by a team of academics, lawyers and supporters.[37] The head of the Chinese investigating team, Zhou Hongdiao, Professor of International Law at Huadong Institute of Political Science and Law, opened his argument by stressing that China suffered the most from Japan's system of military sexual slavery, with stations set up throughout twenty-two provinces of China, and more than 200,000 Chinese women forced into sexual slavery. Three other members of the investigating team – Beijing lawyer Kang Jian, academic Chen Lifei (Huadong Normal

University) and head of the Nanjing Memorial Museum Zhu Chengshan –
then invited three Chinese women to give testimony (Wan Aihua, Zhong
Zhulin from Hubei, and Yang Mingzhen from Nanjing). The Chinese side
brought charges against the Japanese government, as well as individuals such
as Emperor Hirohito, Matsui Iwane, Okamura Yasuji and others.[38] Their
demands included an acknowledgement that war crimes had been committed, an official apology, compensation for each of the victims, and a memorial
for victims of sexual slavery (Su 2001b: 230).

Although various Japanese prime ministers have apologised to Korean and
Filipina comfort women, and compensation has been offered (albeit via the
rather controversial Asian Women's Fund), the same treatment has not yet
been afforded the Chinese comfort women (Jiang 1998: 13). This is in large
part due to the lack of information available on Chinese comfort women in
the early 1990s when the Koreans were first pushing for compensation. The
Japanese government's response to the claims of the early 1990s only
extended to those countries (and their governments) which had been
vigorously pushing for acknowledgement of the issue.[39]

As with the textbook issue, and the forced labourer compensation cases
described above, unless the Japanese government comes under direct pressure
from another government, it is unlikely that a political settlement will be
reached. The Chinese government stance has been passive, taking the view
that the Japanese government should deal with the issues 'sensibly' but
refraining from intervening directly. On the other hand, statements from
government-backed mass organisations such as the All China Lawyers'
Association seem to indicate tacit support for the cause (China 918net, 27
April 2002). For example, after the dismissal of the first case in May 2001, the
All China Lawyers' Association, the All-China Women's Federation and the
China Foundation for Human Rights Development issued a joint statement
in support of the appeal (CNN.com, 21 June 2001). For the time being, it
seems unlikely that the Japanese courts will order the state to pay compensation to Chinese comfort women outside the existing Asian Women's Fund
arrangement.[40]

US-based cases

Law firms in the United States have taken up the comfort women issue in
addition to that of forced labourers, but have had no more success than their
Japanese counterparts. In September 2000, for example, Michael Hausfeld of
Cohen Milstein filed a case with the Columbia District Court to seek com-
pensation from the Japanese government on behalf of fifteen named plain-
tiffs ('and all others similarly situated'), among them, four Chinese women,
Yuan Zhilin (Hankou), Li Xiuzhen, Guo Yaying and Zhu Qiaomei (all from
Shanghai, Congming county) (*Japan Times Online*, 20 September 2000).[41]
The lawsuit was brought on the basis of the Alien Tort Claims Act which
allows non-US citizens to bring claims against other non-US citizens (here

the Japanese state). By October 2001, however, the case had been dismissed by Judge Kennedy and had gone to appeal.[42] As with the forced labour cases, the court's decision was probably swayed by a statement of interest issued by the George W. Bush administration in May 2001 in support of the defendant's case (i.e., the Japanese government), arguing in favour of a dismissal. The main reason given in the statement of interest was that Japan is entitled to sovereign immunity under the Foreign Sovereign Immunities Act which disallows US courts from establishing jurisdiction over such lawsuits (Park 2002: 403–58). The actions taken by the Bush administration were criticised by US lawyers and academics as employing double standards, being self-serving and inconsistent on human rights and other reparations issues. Park argues, for example, that the United States 'ignored the human rights protection policy that it advocated in previous cases by urging the court not to hear the case' (ibid.: 456). 'Arbitrary self-interests' (i.e., the desire to maintain a stable relationship with Japan) were seen at the root of the US decision to file its statement of interest, and Park argues that given that the USA failed to take up the issue of sexual slavery in the immediate aftermath of the war, it has a 'moral responsibility to pursue reparations' now. Johnson (and others) see the US-based cases as a meaningful opportunity to raise awareness of the atrocities and thereby apply pressure on the Japanese government to act. But for this to happen, US government support is needed. With no such support forthcoming, the prospect for success in the US courts appears slight (Bazyler 2001; Johnson 2001; Park 2002).

Biological warfare and abandoned chemical weapons

During the Second World War, various Japanese facilities were involved in research into biological warfare (Unit 731 in Harbin, Unit 100 in Changchun, Unit 1644 in Nanjing, etc.). Unit 731 was engaged in research into and production of plague bacteria (cholera, typhoid, anthrax), along with bombs which could distribute such bacteria in sufficient quantities to contaminate huge areas of land and kill hundreds of people. The best-documented attacks took place in Ningbo and Quzhou in Zhejiang province, Changde in Hunan, on the Zhejiang/Jiangxi borders, and Yunnan. Japan's biological warfare programme took the lives of more than 100,000 Chinese (Nomura 1997). Japan's chemical warfare programme consisted of research centres (for example, Unit 516 Qiqihar) which developed and carried out experiments with poison gas. Regular army units throughout China also had officers trained in the use of chemical weapons. It is estimated that 2,000 chemical attacks (using, for example, mustard gas or tear gas), leading to over tens of thousands of deaths and many more casualties, took place during the war.[43]

Since the 1980s considerable research has been carried out by Western, Chinese and Japanese academics into Japan's chemical and biological warfare programme, boosted in recent years by the opening of US archives, in addition to the discovery of documents relating to Unit 731 in Chinese archives.[44] There are currently a number of cases pending in Japanese courts relating to chemical and biological warfare programmes carried out in China during the war. For the purposes of this chapter, one important legacy of the chemical warfare programme is the issue of abandoned chemical weapons and the injuries and illnesses they have caused since the end of the war. When Japan surrendered, orders were given to dispose of the vast amount of chemical weapons and agents. The rather crude disposal methods included burial, dumping in rivers, or simply mixing them in with the stockpiles of conventional weapons. Weapons were accidentally discovered by local Chinese people in the 1940s and became such a risk to citizens that in the early 1950s local governments destroyed some of the weapons, or collected and stored them. Injuries occurred during this process too, since those involved in their transportation neither knew what the weapons were, nor had the technical expertise to dispose of them safely. The bulk of the weapons (approximately 1.8 million by Chinese estimates) were moved to Dunhua and Meihekou (Jilin) where they were buried. Known locations of other weapons and chemical agents include Heilongjiang, Jiangsu, and Hebei (Zhao 2000: 187; Evans 1997: 42). Joint Chinese–Japanese investigations of these sites have been undertaken since the early 1990s. Driven by Chinese requests made during the 1992 Geneva Disarmament Conference that the Japanese acknowledge its disposal of chemical weapons, followed by the signing and later the ratification of the Chemical Weapons Convention (CWC),[45] China and Japan signed a Memorandum of Understanding in 1999, agreeing to cooperate on the destruction of abandoned chemical weapons, with Japan accepting responsibility to bear all costs of the exercise. Initially, the Japanese acknowledged that there were 700,000 chemical weapons to be disposed of, whereas the Chinese estimated 2 million (*Chūgoku nenkan* 1997: 113–18). The accidental discovery or explosion of poison gas weapons or agents has caused injury and illness to over 2,000 Chinese since 1945 (Evans 1997: 2). Weapons stores and abandoned chemical weapons were still being discovered by accident in North-east China in 2003. One such case occurred in August 2003 when approximately forty Chinese people fell ill (one of whom subsequently died) after a number of drums containing mustard gas were unearthed on a construction site in Qiqihar. The Chinese government issued a stern warning to the Japanese government to step up the disposal of such weapons, and the Japanese government, in response, expressed 'its heartfelt sympathy to the victims' and agreed to cooperate with China in dealing with the incident (MoFA, 12 August 2003).[46]

The lawsuits discussed below are similar to those of former forced labourers and comfort women in terms of the way they have brought together civil groups in China and Japan and raised awareness of the suffering of Chinese victims, but, as yet, have had limited success.[47] The section below considers two lawsuits and their progress through the courts.

Unit 731 germ warfare victims

The first lawsuit concerned the victims, or their relatives, of Unit 731's germ warfare programme and involved 180 plaintiffs. This represented one of the largest class actions, and the first relating to biological warfare.[48] The plaintiffs sought an apology and ¥10 million each for damages relating to illness and death from biological weapons produced at Unit 731 and deployed by the Japanese army in Zhejiang and Hunan provinces. The cases were brought about through the joint efforts of a group of Japanese lawyers headed by Ichinose Keiichirō and Tsuchiya Kōken, Chinese lawyers, and civil groups in Japan such as the Committee for the 731 Biological Warfare Lawsuit (731 saikinsen saiban kyanpēn iinkai). A number of individuals also became well known in China and Japan for their active involvement in the campaign, such as Wang Xuan (based in Japan), Chen Yufang (head of the Changde support group) and Wu Shigen (Quzhou village representative).

Although many people had heard about Unit 731's human experimentation, less was known in China about Japan's use of biological weapons. The various groups and individuals worked tirelessly to raise awareness about the case and the suffering of not only the 180 plaintiffs, but also the many thousands of other Chinese who were victims of Japan's germ warfare programme. A series of investigations was carried out in Zhejiang and Hunan provinces by a group of over 100 lawyers, academics and activists whose task it was to gather witnesses for the case and produce a list of names of Chinese who had been affected by biological warfare. They published booklets of their findings relating to particular villages or towns (for example, Chongshan and Quzhou) and reported their progress to symposia held in Shanghai, Beijing and Harbin.[49] Memorial ceremonies were also held in various Chinese towns, and memorial plaques or tablets erected. There was an educational side to the campaign too, with exhibitions arranged in schools in Chongshan, Lishui, Quzhou and Jingshan. The 731 saikinsen saiban kyanpēn iinkai mounted a poster exhibition in Japan which toured around the country, and made the poster panels available for loan to schools, cultural festivals and community centres. The lawyers involved in the case also took the exhibition to the United States in 1998 and made TV appearances to talk about their work. International awareness was further raised by such events as the International Citizens' Forum on War Crimes and Redress held in Tokyo in December 1999. One Chinese individual stood out in particular, and became a household name in China. Wang Xuan, living in Japan when she heard about the plans for a lawsuit, became actively involved in the process, returning to the village of Chongshan (to which she had been sent down during the 1960s) to persuade witnesses to testify in court. She held rallies, live 'webcasts' and radio phone-ins, attended international conferences, and became the focus of TV and radio documentaries both in China and abroad.[50] In 2002 she was awarded a China Central Television (CCTV) Touch China prize (*Gandong Zhongguo*) for her activities.

The funding for Chinese witnesses and their representatives to attend court proceedings in Tokyo was provided by support groups such as the Association for the Clarification of the Japanese Army's Biological Warfare (Nihongun ni yoru saikinsen no rekishi shijitsu o akiraka ni suru kai). In addition to the many Chinese witnesses and Japanese veterans, expert testimony was provided by some of the leading academics in the field, such as Sheldon Harris, Yoshimi Yoshiaki and Xin Peilin. The verdict was announced on 27 August 2002, and somewhat predictably dismissed all the plaintiffs' claims on the grounds that 'the defendant [Japan] has already disposed of its national responsibility according to international law' via the 1972 Japan–China Joint Statement. On the other hand, Judge Iwate did concede that 'the suffering caused by this case of germ warfare was truly immense and the former Japanese military's wartime actions were clearly inhumane', thereby acknowledging the facts of the case. In addition, he indicated that any compensation for the victims would be at the discretion of the Diet: 'If this nation were to consider some sort of compensation for the damages in this case of germ warfare, it is conceivable that it would be handled through domestic law or domestic measures.'[51] The verdict received a mixed response. Nanjing University professor Zhang Lianhong considered the court's acknowledgement of Unit 731 activities and their impact on the Chinese people as a victory for the plaintiffs, researchers, lawyers, and historians who had struggled so hard to provide evidence to the court. He emphasised the significance of the process as a whole, during which time former Japanese soldiers had provided new evidence about Unit 731 and apologised to victims' families, as a wonderful step forward. Quoting Wang Xuan, he said that the important thing was that the truth about the 'death factories', and the suffering of the Chinese people had been revealed to the world. On the other hand, a Nanjing lawyer described the verdict as lacking logic and violating the principles of justice and fairness (*People's Daily Online* (Chinese), 28 August 2002). This view was echoed by protestors in Changde (Hunan) who, having heard the verdict, called once again for an apology from the Japanese government and for 'respect for human rights and justice' (*People's Daily Online*, 28 August 2002). The response of the lawyers fighting the case was one of indignation and a determination to fight on. The comments they made when announcing their decision to appeal are no doubt echoed by the many other groups involved in the struggle for compensation: 'When the number of Japanese citizens who know the facts about germ warfare grows drastically and public opinion in favour of us surrounds the court and moves the conscience of judges, we believe that the right judgment will be given.'[52]

Abandoned chemical weapons

The second set of cases relates to abandoned chemical weapons. Two lawsuits were filed in 1996 and 1997. The first case was brought by thirteen plaintiffs seeking compensation (for financial and psychological damage) of nearly

¥200 million for illnesses caused by the accidental discovery of abandoned weapons. The second case involved five plaintiffs seeking a total of ¥80 million in compensation, for illnesses relating to the discovery of abandoned chemical weapons and one incident involving the explosion of a conventional shell. Both cases were supported by Suopei among others, and led by the Chūgokujin sensō higaisha baishō seikyū bengodan (in particular, Ōyama Hiroshi) in cooperation with Chinese lawyers (for example, Su Xiangxiang), academics and experts on chemical warfare from China and Japan (for example, Bu Ping and Xin Peilin both from Heilongjiang Academy of Social Sciences, Yoshimi Yoshiaki, Murakami Hatsuichi, and Matsuno Seichi.)[53] The lawsuits originated from a research trip undertaken by the lawyers' group in May 1996 when they met Chinese people suffering from the effects of toxic gases as a result of accidental discoveries of abandoned weapons. Since then, Chinese academics have carried out a series of investigations in Heilongjiang, researching the activities of Units 516 and 526 in and around Qiqihar, gathering primary evidence, and interviewing people who have reported chemical weapon-related injuries and illness.[54]

The first lawsuit dealt with three incidents, the first of which took place in October 1974 near Harbin. Four men on board a boat dredging the Songhua river discovered black liquid coming from the ship's pump causing the engine to stop. On closer examination they found that a shell had become lodged in the pump and had ruptured. The contents of the shell caused skin ulceration, nausea, shortage of breath and dizziness. The men suffered long-term illness, and one died in 1991 of a related illness. The second incident involved the discovery of a canister of what was later believed to be mustard gas during sewage repairs in Mudanjiang (Heilongjiang) in 1982. One of the workers, Zhong Jiang, suffered temporary loss of sight, followed by ongoing ailments such as blistering of the skin, headaches and chest pain. The third incident occurred in 1995, also in Heilongjiang, when three workmen were repairing a road and discovered a bomb which exploded, killing one of the men instantly. Another man died later of burns, and the third man sustained serious burns.[55]

The second lawsuit involved four separate incidents which occurred between 1950 and 1987 in various cities in Heilongjiang. The first case was that of a former school teacher who had examined a canister discovered during the building of a school dormitory in 1950. The canister contained mustard gas, and Mr Cui (along with seven other people who were not seeking compensation) sustained similar injuries to those mentioned above. The other incidents involved leaking shells discovered in a mine, a shell which exploded when unearthed in a garden, and mustard gas canisters found at a construction site and examined by Dr Li Guoqiang who worked in a local hospital.[56]

Prior to the verdicts, the lawyers bringing both lawsuits were upbeat about their chances, given that, unlike other lawsuits, these related (mostly) to more recent events which would not automatically run into the problem of the twenty-year statute of limitations. While this did not necessarily mean that they would win, they were determined that raising international awareness of the issue would at least help to inform public opinion within Japan, and change attitudes.[57] The case for the second lawsuit was completed before that of the first and the verdict was announced on 15 May 2003. Although the judges acknowledged the facts of the case, they dismissed all the plaintiffs' claims, supporting the case of the defence, which had argued that Japan had no jurisdiction in China and did not know the whereabouts of the weapons. The hypocrisy of the defence argument was not lost on the prosecuting lawyers who pointed out that, during both lawsuits, the lawyers for the defence failed to acknowledge the fact that the existence of abandoned chemical weapons was now widely acknowledged, and that the Japanese government had already entered into an agreement with China to locate and dispose of 700,000 abandoned weapons.[58] The verdict for the first lawsuit came a few months later in September 2003 when Judge Katayama ruled in favour of the plaintiffs, finding the Japanese government negligent in dealing with the abandoned chemical weapons, and ordering the government to pay ¥190 million (*China Daily Online*, 20 September 2003). This is clearly an important step forward in the compensation movement, and given the high profile of abandoned chemical weapons in the Chinese and Japanese press in recent years, it is likely that further cases will be brought against the Japanese government.

Conclusion

The cases described above represent just a sample of numerous lawsuits currently being fought in Japanese courts. The legal basis for their claims range from international law to Japanese and Chinese civil law, and lawyers for the prosecution charge that the Japanese government violated a series of treaties and conventions to which it was a party (either through ratification or by virtue of international customary law).[59] The Japanese courts have at times made concessions by acknowledging the facts of the case and that the plaintiffs have undergone tremendous suffering. This in itself represents a victory for those whose suffering has been ignored or denied by Japanese governments over the years. But in the majority of the cases, the reasons for dismissal are similar, with judges arguing, variously, that compensation claims were settled under international law via bilateral treaties, that under the Meiji constitution the Japanese state cannot be held liable, or that the twenty-year statute of limitations makes the claims invalid. This has drawn much criticism from Japanese academics and lawyers and, of course, the plaintiffs themselves. Tanaka Hiroshi points to the double standard of the Japanese government in paying substantial amounts in compensation and pensions to its own citizens and veterans, but little to non-Japanese victims (1995).[60] Matsuo is also critical of the Japanese government for trying to evade its responsibility, accusing it of having 'run away from the truth and merely quibbled over legalities' (1998: 44). It seems clear that the battles for compensation, both in Japan and the USA, are not having the desired effect of forcing the Japanese government to accept legal responsibility. In many ways, the court cases have exacerbated the problem, further highlighting the inability of the government to come to terms with the past and prolonging the hurt for ageing victims of Japanese aggression. Japanese companies, while accepting moral responsibility in some cases, have nonetheless been reluctant to settle the claims, both in and out of court.[61]

To return to Brooks' criteria for successful civil redress, the chapter has highlighted the flaws in the compensation movement in terms of their legislative weakness, and the lack of political pressure. Brooks suggests that claims must be in the hands of legislators, not the judiciary (1999: 7). While there have been attempts in Japan to implement legislation which would enable judges to deliver more favourable judgements to the plaintiffs, these have not been successful. In 1996, Social Democratic Party member Motooka Shōji, supported by twenty-five members of the Upper House, submitted a 'Bill for establishment of a fact-finding committee on the issue of victims of sexual coercion during the war' (Totsuka 1999). In 2000 Motooka submitted an 'Enhancement of Resolution for Issues concerning Victims of Wartime Sexual Slavery Act', calling for restoration of the women's honour (through an apology and monetary compensation) and the resolution of issues of sexual slavery.[62] A year later in March 2001 the Democratic Party submitted a similar bill to the Upper House to promote the resolution of the comfort women issue. None of the bills have been adopted, although Hayashi indicates that in the Lower House such bills have the support of at least 160 Dietmembers, including some members of the LDP. That said, the majority of Dietmembers 'still oppose or remain indifferent to such proposals' (Hayashi 2001: 576).

On the plus side, however, the compensation cases have fulfilled Brooks' criteria that claims must have merit, must be supported by as large a group as possible in order to apply political pressure on the legislators, and maintain internal solidarity (Brooks 1999: 7). Albeit with some exceptions, most of the judges in the lawsuits have acknowledged the practices of the Japanese military and government during the war, and the ongoing suffering of the plaintiffs. This demonstrates that the cases have provided sufficient evidence, in the form of documentary proof, witness statements, and expert testimony to convince the courts of their merit. The number of groups involved in the movement for compensation is also impressive. The range of activities and the level of public awareness that they have managed to attract in a relatively short space of time are certainly worthy of note. Wu and Zhu (2000: 158) argue that the groups are gradually gaining in strength and they stress the importance of the Japanese lawyers' and citizens' groups in helping to bring about an awareness among the Japanese people of the responsibility they must bear for their past. The interaction between Chinese and Japanese civil groups has been essential in raising awareness of many of the issues that Chinese, Japanese and US governments have suppressed over the years. It is this grass-roots interaction that could very well be the catalyst for more complete reconciliation in years to come. If the movement continues to grow, there is a chance that public opinion in Japan and China, along with domestic legislative efforts in Japan, and the international pressure brought to bear by transnational civil society could force the Japanese government to produce a compensation package and an apology sufficient to satisfy the plaintiffs and help to settle the past. But one of the weaknesses of the 'movement' is that it is not so much a fully-fledged 'movement' – that is, a group working for a shared cause – as a series of disparate attempts by independent groups to gain some acknowledgement and compensation in the courts. In addition, there have been instances (for example, the Hanaoka settlement) where internal solidarity has broken down, thereby weakening the case.

While not wishing to dismiss the achievements of the compensation movement, it is difficult not to conclude, as with the dispute over textbooks and the intepretation of history, that unless a political solution can be found – be it forced upon the Japanese government by the judiciary, US or Chinese governmental pressure, or international NGO activity – then subsequent compensation claims will continue to fail to reach their objectives. Even if some monetary compensation is awarded by individual companies, as has been the case, there is still a perceived need for the Japanese government to acknowledge legal responsibility and offer symbolic compensation in addition to a sincere apology. As this chapter has shown, the efforts of grass-roots groups are unstinting, and promise to continue unabated. If the compensation movement grows further in China, both governments may well be forced to come to some sort of agreement. If a financial settlement could be agreed upon, this would have an impact on the next stage of our ideal model of reconciliation, namely, attempts to settle the past. The next chapter discusses the difficulties the two countries currently face with regard to apologising for and commemorating the past.

5 Settling the past

Both the Chinese and Japanese governments made frequent reference in the 1990s to settling the past, indicating at least a willingness to move towards the final stage of our 'ideal' model of reconciliation in which apologies are made (and accepted), the past is commemorated, and attempts are made to move towards a communicative history. The Japanese government has adopted a number of approaches in this respect, from setting up funds, and offering official and personal apologies, to implementing educational programmes and exchanges. The response to these has been mixed. Yoneyama (1999: 8) argues that the region's shifting condition in the 1990s created an imperative for 'Japanese politicians and bureaucrats [to] carefully settle past wrongs against neighboring countries by laying to rest the memories about them' and points to Hosokawa's frank admission about Japan's war of invasion, the relaxation on history textbook authorisation by the Ministry of Education in the early 1990s, and the 1995 'Resolution to Renew the Determination for Peace on the Basis of Lessons Learned from History' as evidence of a willingness on the part of Japanese governments to remember and acknowledge the past. There are also numerous examples of Japanese individuals, war veterans and peace and reconciliation groups who have visited China to make their own peace. Others have a less positive view of Japanese efforts in the 1990s. Barkan argues that Japan is an exception to those governments, representative of a liberal society, who have been ready to 'admit to unjust and discriminatory past policies and to negotiate terms for restitution or reparation with their victims based more on moral considerations than on power politics', and his case study of Japan's handling of the comfort women issue concludes that the failure to reconcile was due to internal political pressures which prevented Japanese society from addressing its war guilt (Barkan 2000: 317). Japan's approach to reconciliation is often compared, in unfavourable terms, to Germany's record of overcoming the past, and the inability of 'the Japanese' to apologise or come to terms with the past represents a recurring theme in the international media and academic literature.

The success of Chinese and Japanese attempts to settle the past is, therefore, as mixed as the other aspects of reconciliation described in the previous chapters. This chapter considers three of the more intractable aspects of this

stage of the reconciliation process: (1) apologising for the past; (2) commemorating the past; and (3) remembering (or re-presenting) the past in
museums. It demonstrates how the same sort of domestic historical and political factors which influence disputes over textbooks and struggles for compensation also intrude into such issues as the wording of apologies, Yasukuni
Shrine visits, and the content of museum exhibits.

The apology issue

When Japan and China normalised relations in 1972, the question of an
apology was raised, and resolved. As described in Chapter 2, it was not
central to the negotiations in the run-up to the signing of the Joint Statement,
and the wording of the apology was deemed satisfactory by both parties at
the time. By the 1990s the domestic and international situation had changed,
and demands for apologies became the norm. As Table 5.1 shows, various
apologies or statements of remorse have been made by Japanese prime ministers and the Emperor to China, Korea and other Asian countries in the 1990s,
but it was the wording, timing, and style of Japan's apologies which became a
recurring issue between China and Japan.

The issues described in this chapter are to do with official apologies (an
apology from one collective to another). To remind ourselves of Tavuchis's
criteria a collective apology is one that is: (1) official, in the sense that the
prime minister of Japan (or whoever is acting on behalf of the state) acts
both 'as an authoritative member of the collectivity' and 'an unencumbered
individual'; and (2) on record, and therefore binding. Without such creden-
tials, an apology is worth nothing 'because it represents the unaccredited One
and not the mandate of the Many' (Tavuchis 1991: 101). An apology is also
often accompanied by an assurance that there will be no repetition of the
acts, although Tavuchis argues that such reassurances are superfluous if the
'offender is genuinely sorry'. If accepted by the recipient, an apology can
transform a relationship – Barkan states that

> by validating and showing respect for the victims' memory and identity,
> the very recognition of past injustices constitutes the core of restitution.
> It is a recognition that transforms the trauma of victimization into a
> process of mourning and allows for rebuilding.
>
> (Barkan 2000: 323)

It is this recognition that is seen to be lacking in the Japanese approach.

The main problem surrounding the apparent failure of the Japanese to
come to terms with the past is, from the Chinese point of view, the refusal of
successive Japanese governments to offer genuine, sincere apologies to the
Chinese government and people, *backed up by actions* to reinforce the apologies. This view is at odds with that held by a number of Japanese prime
ministers, politicians, the media, and, increasingly, the public who feel that

Table 5.1 Japan's apologies and statements of regret to Asian countries, 1952–2001

Date	Statement and apology

1952   Treaty with Taiwan: no reparations but 'regret' (*ikan*) for 'unfortunate events' (*fukōna jiken*).

1965   Treaty with South Korea: no apology in treaty and no reparations, but grants and 'good-will gestures' plus expression of true regret (*makoto ni ikan*), and deep reflection (*fukaku hansei suru*) on the unfortunate period (*fukōna kikan*).

1972   (Japan–China Joint Statement): no reparations, Japan 'keenly feels responsibility for' (*sekinin o tsūkan shite*) and deeply reflects upon the losses inflicted on the people of China during the war.

1984   Emperor Hirohito to President Chun Doohwan: 'I feel great regret that there was an unhappy phrase in relations between our two countries in a certain period of this century despite the close ties between us. I believe that such things should not be repeated.'
Prime Minister Nakasone: 'the fact cannot be denied that Japan caused great suffering to your country and your people during a certain period during this century. I would like to announce that the Japanese government and people express deep regret for the wrongs done to you and are determined to strictly caution themselves against repeating them in the future'.

1990   Emperor Akihito to President Roh Taewoo: 'When I think of the sufferings your people underwent during this unhappy phase, brought on by my country, I cannot help feeling the deepest regret.'

1991   Prime Minister Kaifu in Singapore: 'Once again I look back over the history of the early half of this century, and I solemnly express our sincere remorse for Japanese actions in the past which inflicted unbearable suffering and sorrow upon multitudes in the Asia Pacific region.'
Prime Minister Kaifu apologises to Roh Taewoo (using *owabi*).

1992   Emperor Akihito's visit to China: 'In the long history of the relationship between our two countries there was an unfortunate period in which my country inflicted great sufferings on the people of China. I deeply deplore this. When the war came to an end, the Japanese people, believing with a deep sense of remorse that such a war should never be repeated, firmly resolved to tread the path of peaceful nations and addressed themselves to national reconstruction.'

1993   Prime Minister Hosokawa acknowledges the war was a mistake and that it was a war of aggression. Also acknowledges suffering of Asians (at National Memorial Service for the War Dead): 'On this solemn occasion, I would like to offer my condolences again, across national borders, to all war victims and their families in neighbouring Asian countries, and all over the world.'
Prime Minister Hosokawa visits South Korea: 'During Japan's colonial rule over the Korean peninsula, the Korean people were forced to suffer unbearable pain and sorrow in various ways ... I hereby express genuine contrition and offer my deepest apologies for my country, the aggressor's acts'.

1995   Resolution to Renew the Determination for Peace on the Basis of Lessons Learned from History (see Appendix 3).
Prime Minister Murayama's 15 August statement apologising for the mistaken state policy in embarking upon the war (refers to aggression and colonial rule) (see Appendix 3).

1998   Prime Minister Obuchi Keizō to President Jiang Zemin (verbally): 'For a time in the past, there were unfortunate relations between Japan and China. The then prime minister's statement issued in 1995 expressed deep remorse for the acts of colonial rule and aggression by Japan for a time in the past, and registered most sincere apologies for them. The government of Japan takes

Table 5.1 continued

Date	Statement and apology
	this opportunity to again express such feeling of remorse and apologies to China.'
	Joint Declaration (text): 'The Japanese side is keenly conscious of the responsibility for the serious distress and damage that Japan caused to the Chinese people through its aggression against China during a certain period in the past and expressed deep remorse for them.'
2001	Prime Minister Koizumi visits Beijing: 'I express my heartfelt apology and condolences to the Chinese people who fell victim to aggression'.

Sources: Field (1995), Wakamiya (1998), Kitaoka (1995), Japanese Ministry of Foreign Affairs website.

apologies *have* been offered on a number of occasions, and that China uses the 'history card' when it is politically beneficial. The apology issue hit the headlines a number of times in the 1990s, but the most significant incidents for our purposes are the 1995 Resolution to Renew the Determination for Peace on the Basis of Lessons Learned from History (hereafter Diet resolution) and Prime Minister Murayama's statement, and the Jiang-Obuchi summit of 1998.

The 1995 Diet Resolution and Prime Minister Murayama's statement

Much has been written on the attempts made in the run-up to the 50th anniversary of the war to settle the past by producing a definitive, authoritative resolution in the Diet which would include an apology to Asian victims of the war, and an assurance that Japan would not tread the same path again (see Field 1995; Mukae 1996). Plans for the adoption of a resolution for the renunciation of war (*fusen ketsugi*) began in 1994, and the government (under Prime Minister Murayama Tomiichi of the SDP) set up a project team to realise this goal. The internal politics of the coalition government (SDP, LDP and Sakigake), in addition to opposition from Shinshintō meant that the final draft was a watered-down version of the original. Various groups, led by renowned hard-liners such as Okuno Seisuke and Nagano Shigeto (both of whom had angered the Chinese government in 1988 and 1994 respectively with their reckless remarks about the war), were set up within the LDP with the specific intention of 'torpedoing' the activities of the project team (Mukae 1996: 1015). When the resolution was voted upon in the Lower House in June, only 251 of the 502 Dietmembers cast a vote. Of those, the majority opposed the resolution (including JCP members who felt the resolution did not go far enough) and the rest abstained or were absent (Dower 1995). The wording of the resolution did not include the terms 'apology' or 'renunciation of war' as originally intended. The 'deep sense of remorse' expressed towards Asian people did not represent a major step forward and even though there was an acknowledgement that Japan had carried out 'acts of aggression' in the past, this was placed firmly within the context of 'colonial rule and acts of aggression in the modern history of the world', and the term 'war of aggression' was avoided (see Appendix 3 for the full wording).

The Chinese government had been following the progress of the planned resolution during the early part of 1995. During Prime Minister Murayama's visit to China in May he issued a statement of regret apparently in response to Chinese dissatisfaction over the open opposition of the LDP to the SDP's proposed wording (*Japan Times Weekly*, 8–14 May 1995: 1). Murayama redeemed the situation by issuing a personal statement on 15 August in which he referred to the mistaken state policy of the past and stated that: 'In the hope that no such mistake be made in the future, I regard, in a spirit of humility, these irrefutable facts of history, and express here once again my feelings of deep remorse and state my heartfelt apology' (Dower 1995). The Chinese government seems to have adopted Murayama's statement as a benchmark against which to evaluate subsequent official statements on the war, and often expresses its 'appreciation' of his apology. Although the statement was not representative of the Japanese government as a whole (as subsequent criticism from the LDP showed), Murayama nonetheless obtained a cabinet decision (*kakugi kettei*), a more binding procedure than a cabinet understanding (*kakugi ryōkai*). In so doing, 'he apparently wished his statement to be interpreted at home and abroad as the general will of the Japanese cabinet, which he hoped would politically bind future cabinets' (Mukae 1996: 1029). Surprisingly perhaps, subsequent Japanese prime ministers have indeed used Murayama's wording as a 'model' for their own statements and apologies. Prime Minister Hashimoto referred in 1996 to Japan's colonial rule and aggression during the Second World War, and said 'that his own interpretation of the war was in accordance with Murayama's 50th anniversary statement' (ibid.). Similarly, the wording of Prime Minister Koizumi's apology to the Chinese in 2001 (described below) was similar to that of Murayama's. But although Japanese prime ministers are no longer averse to issuing a verbal apology to the Chinese people and government (using the word *owabi*), the word has yet to appear in an official, diplomatic document. This became an issue in 1998.

The 1998 apology issue

Jiang Zemin's visit to Japan in November 1998 was marred by the inability of both leaders to fully agree on the wording of their joint declaration. The problem hinged on the inclusion of one word – apology (*owabi*). Jiang Zemin's visit was his first state visit to Japan as President of the People's Republic of China. Coming shortly after a successful visit by Kim Daejung the previous month – when the South Korean president agreed to settle the past (*kako no seisan*) in exchange for a written apology from the Japanese –

academics and journalists were hopeful that the same goal could be achieved during Jiang's visit. Indeed, prior to his arrival, President Jiang had himself emphasised the need for a solution to the long-running history problem, and as Satō (2001: 6) suggests, the conclusion of a joint declaration helping to resolve this aspect of the relationship would have been viewed as a political coup. Similarly, a successful summit would have helped Prime Minister Obuchi develop his 'future-oriented diplomacy' with China (*mirai shikō gaikō*).

Both the Chinese and Japanese bureaucracies had been considering the wording of a joint declaration for some months. The Chinese side, for example, had begun working on the first draft approximately six months before the visit, originally planned to take place in September, but postponed until November because of the Yangtze floods. On 9 August, Jiang had outlined his principle on the matter of history to Foreign Minister Kōmura Masahiko who was visiting China. Jiang stated that 'Japan's invasion of China brought great suffering to the Chinese people. We need to develop friendly relations based on both good and bad experiences' (*Asahi shinbun*, 24 November 1998: 5). During the previous night's meeting between representatives of both foreign ministries, the Chinese side had indicated that it would be satisfied with Japan's re-confirmation of the importance of Prime Minister Murayama's 1995 statement (*Asahi shinbun*, 29 November 1998: 3). However, following Jiang's postponement of his visit and then Kim Daejung's state visit, by mid-October the Chinese side were requesting that 'in line with the Japan–Korea joint declaration, an apology for invasion be included in the China–Japan joint declaration'. One Ministry of Foreign Affairs (MoFA) official's worries that a reversal of the order of the visits of the two heads of state would affect the history issue proved to be well founded (*Asahi shinbun*, 29 November 1998: 3). Japan's response to the new request from the Chinese was that the word 'apology' would not be incorporated into the text of the declaration since the issue had been covered in the 1972 Joint Statement and during the Emperor's speech in 1992 also (see Table 5.1). At this point the Chinese Foreign Minister stated that 'if the two issues of history and Taiwan were not dealt with clearly, then the leaders would not accept it', thus giving a clear hint that this could become a major obstacle (*Asahi shinbun*, 12 November 1998: 2).

There was a strong feeling within the MoFA that China was playing the 'history card' for domestic political reasons, and that Chinese demands should not be totally met. A second reason for Japan's reluctance to issue the apology was related to domestic public opinion in Japan. A number of newspapers had reflected upon the fact that there was a growing sense of resentment among the Japanese public of China's calls for apologies (*Asahi shinbun*, 27 November 1998: 1). Furthermore, if Prime Minister Obuchi were to 'give in' to all of China's demands, he would certainly be regarded as weak at a time when he could little afford to appear so (Satō 2001: 10). Although he had gained some popularity for his handling of the Kim Daejung visit, the government's handling of the North Korean missile 'crisis' in previous months (when missiles, later alleged by the North Koreans to be satellites, were launched in the direction of Japan), had not instilled any confidence in the public's opinion of their new prime minister.

While the MoFA stated that the Japanese government was willing to apologise for actions that warranted an apology, it suggested to the Chinese side that reaching a common view of history was too complicated and that they should agree to disagree. Jiang responded by acknowledging the difficulty of agreeing upon a common view but he was adamant that a 'correct attitude' should be shown by the Japanese side before the history matter could be resolved (*Asahi shinbun*, 27 November 1998: 1). The Japanese side confirmed that the history issue would certainly be dealt with in some form in the joint declaration (although there was no mention of an apology), but requested that the issue not be taken up during the summit meeting. By the middle of November the Japanese Ministry of Foreign Affairs was struggling to find a way of responding to the Chinese demands, while at the same time keeping elements within the LDP happy. There had been strong protest within the party over the Japan–Korea declaration, and Obuchi was facing the same opposition on the China declaration (*Asahi shinbun*, 12 November 1998: 2). A week before Jiang's arrival, although some in the LDP were in fact encouraging Obuchi to concede on the two most controversial points in the joint declaration (the second one being confirmation that Taiwan did not fall into the 'areas surrounding Japan'),[1] the prime minister stressed that an apology would not be included.

The final round of discussions between officials from both foreign ministries was held in Hakone on 22 and 23 November, during which it was agreed that, with regard to the Taiwan issue, Japan would reaffirm its 'understanding of China's position' (as first announced in the 1972 Joint Statement) and that emphasis would be placed upon the fact that relations between Japan and Taiwan are strictly non-governmental. Both sides agreed that, to further Sino-Japanese relations, government leaders would conduct annual visits and a 'hotline' would be established between Tokyo and Beijing. However, no agreement was reached on 'historical awareness' about the Sino-Japanese war, and the matter was left until the 24 November when Foreign Minister Kōmura was due to meet his counterpart Tang Jiaxuan (*Asahi shinbun*, 24 November 1998: 1). On that day, discussions focused on the inclusion of two words: 'aggression' and 'apology'. By the end of the hour-long meeting it was agreed that, while the word 'aggression' would be incorporated into the joint declaration, 'apology' would not. Satō suggests that Obuchi had offered, secretly, to include a written apology in the document on the condition that the Chinese government would provide an assurance that it would not raise the history problem in the future, as Kim Daejung had done. Beijing refused to agree to this, so the resulting compromise was that Prime Minister Obuchi would issue a verbal apology (using *owabi*) during his talks with President Jiang on the 26th (2001: 10).

It soon became clear to the Japanese side, however, that this solution was not satisfactory to Jiang Zemin, who made his position clear at the outset of the summit meeting. Reportedly speaking for 25 minutes on the issues of history and Taiwan, Jiang stated that he was opposed to the general feeling that the history issue had been discussed exhaustively, and he referred to Japan's militarist past and the suffering inflicted on the Chinese people (*Asahi shinbun*, 28 November 1998: 2). Jiang reiterated his position in his speeches at banquets hosted by the Emperor on the 26th and Prime Minister Obuchi on the 27th. While neither the Emperor nor Obuchi made any reference to the past in their welcoming speech, Jiang Zemin made it the focus of both his speeches. This attitude, according to the *Asahi shinbun*, took the Japanese side, which had tried to create a mood of friendship, by surprise (27 November 1998: 1). Some Japanese analysts argue that Jiang's reasons for dwelling so much on history problem had much more to do with an attempt to score points at home than a genuine desire to resolve the history problem. Nakamura argues, for example, that Jiang's relative lack of authority in China drove him to take a hard line on Japan as a means of drumming up support from the military or conservative factions in Beijing (*Asahi shinbun*, 24 November 1998: 2).

The final wording of the 'Joint Declaration on Building a Partnership of Friendship and Cooperation for Peace and Development' was as follows:

> Both sides believe that squarely facing the past and correctly understanding history are the important foundation for further developing relations between Japan and China. The Japanese side observes the 1972 Joint Communiqué of the Government of Japan and the Government of the People's Republic of China and the 15 August 1995 statement by former Prime Minister Tomiichi Murayama. *The Japanese side is keenly conscious of the responsibility for the serious distress and damage that Japan caused to the Chinese people through its aggression against China during a certain period in the past and expressed deep remorse for this.*
>
> (italics added)[2]

The inclusion of the word 'aggression' in the joint declaration was significant in as much as this was the first time the word had been used in an official diplomatic document. However, the Chinese side had failed to secure inclusion of the word *owabi*, which, by contrast, *had* appeared in the Korea–Japan declaration.[3] The otherwise positive results of Jiang's visit (for example, an agreement on the fourth yen loan package, and a 33-point action plan for co-operation and exchange between China and Japan for the twenty-first century)[4] were completely overshadowed as the media in Japan devoted most of its attention to Obuchi's choice of wording relating to history and Jiang's response.

Interestingly, the mainstream Chinese media glossed over what was being described elsewhere as a public relations disaster (Dreyer 2002: 379).[5] On the day of Jiang's arrival in Tokyo, the *Renmin Ribao* heralded it as a visit of utmost significance for the development of future friendly cooperation between the two sides (*Renmin Ribao*, 26 November 1998: 1). The following day, the front page of the newspaper carried a summary of the joint declaration and lengthy article detailing Prime Minister Obuchi's apology and Jiang Zemin's position on the history problem. The article did not indicate any dissatisfaction with the lack of a written apology (*Renmin Ribao*, 27 November 1998: 1). Subsequent press coverage in the *Renmin Ribao* included reports on Jiang's speech delivered at Waseda University, and a press conference, and in both cases the tone of the articles was upbeat. In the latter report, however, in response to a question about the failure of both sides to sign the joint declaration, Jiang was reported to have stressed the fact that the declaration represented a solemn pledge regardless of whether the document had been signed or not. When asked whether he thought Japan was in danger of reviving militarism, Jiang responded that the existence of a few people who continued to beautify history was evidence that Japan had not yet dealt squarely with its past, and he stressed the need for the younger generation to be provided with a correct view of history in the interests of Sino-Japanese friendship (*Renmin Ribao*, 29 November 1998: 1). Despite the furore, the issue did not appear to have a lasting adverse effect on the relationship as far as the official word from China is concerned. Reference to the visit is made on the Chinese Ministry of Foreign Affairs webpage in the section on the issue of history, and its tone is fairly positive:

> During his state visit to Japan in 1998, President Jiang gave a comprehensive, thorough and systematic elaboration of China's principles. The *Japanese side recognized its aggression against China for the first time and expressed its profound introspection and apology to the Chinese people.* The two sides mutually confirmed that it was an important basis for developing Sino-Japanese relations to recognize history correctly.
>
> (italics added)[6]

It should be noted that the apology issue does not always stall talks between Chinese and Japanese leaders, adding some weight to the view that Jiang Zemin was, on this occasion, playing the apology card. In stark contrast, the meeting between Chinese Premier Zhu Rongji and Prime Minister Obuchi in Beijing in July 1999 was characterised by an avoidance of history-related matters, with the exception of an acknowledgement by Zhu Rongji that the history problem 'was a sensitive political issue, and that important mutual understanding had been achieved at the time of President Jiang's visit to Japan'. Indeed, Zhu accepted that 'the majority of Japanese citizens had a correct perception of the past, understanding and supporting the friendship between Japan and China'.[7] One year later, in October 2000, Zhu stated in a television programme during a visit to Tokyo that 'China will not keep demanding apologies from Japan' but that the Japanese people should consider the fact that 'Japan has never officially apologized to the Chinese people in any of the official documents' (*Japan Times Online*, 15 October 2000). It is clear that, for the Chinese government, a written apology has become the benchmark against which to measure the sincerity of Japanese remorse.

Ironically, even if the Chinese government 'will not keep demanding apologies', it seems that Japanese prime ministers are willing to offer them anyway, particularly if relations have been shaken by such issues as textbooks or visits to the Yasukuni Shrine. Thus, in the wake of his August 2001 Yasukuni Shrine visit (described below), Prime Minister Koizumi's trips to China and South Korea in October were notable for his apologies for Japan's wartime aggression. In Beijing, Koizumi visited the Marco Polo Bridge, before visiting the Memorial Museum of the Chinese People's War of Resistance to Japan where he laid a wreath and expressed his 'heartfelt apology and condolences (*kokoro kara owabi to aitō*) to the Chinese people who fell victim to aggression'.[8] The Chinese response to Koizumi's apology was favourable. Media coverage noted that Koizumi was the first LDP prime minister to visit the Memorial Hall while in office (*People's Daily Online*, 9 October 2001, and Jiang Zemin commented that 'the phase of tension between Japan and China was relaxed as a result of today's talks' (Ministry of Foreign Affairs of Japan 2002: 58).

Nonetheless, there remains a huge divide between China and Japan (and, needless to say, within Japan) on the apology issue. Popular opinion in Japan, as we saw with President Jiang's 1998 visit, is suffering from 'apology fatigue'. Interestingly, there are signs in China that some people also think that Japan has apologised enough. An article written by a well-known *Renmin Ribao* editor, Ma Licheng, asserted that 'the Japanese apology issue has been resolved, and there is no need to be inflexible on the form [of the apology]' (*riben daoqian wenti yijing jiejue, bubi juni kebanxinghsi*, Ma 2002). His comments were not well received in the popular press or on Internet discussion boards, where he was branded a traitor, but his opinion may be gaining ground in China.[9] As we have seen, however, those Chinese who are fighting for compensation and a legal apology in the courts remain frustrated and angry. For them, the apologies offered by prime ministers like Koizumi are worthless, partly because of the actual wording – *owabi* is considered less weighty than *shazai* – but also because they are seen to lack sincerity, since, in Koizumi's case, they are usually preceded or followed by a visit to the Yasukuni Shrine or some other incident which only serves to undo any progress. Here we are reminded of Jiang Zemin's salutary words during his visit to Japan in 1998: 'No matter how beautifully the words are written, if they are not put into effect then they mean nothing' (*Asahi shinbun*, 24 November 1998: 5).

Commemorating the past: anniversaries, war memorials and museums

If controversies over the wording of apologies seem to have abated since the late 1990s, the same cannot be said about controversies surrounding Japan's commemoration of the past and its war dead, which, by contrast have come to the forefront of the Sino-Japanese diplomatic agenda in recent years. The 'memory boom' of the 1990s led to a proliferation of special events in many countries to mark anniversary years (1995 in particular), including the renovation or creation of new museums, and a renewed emphasis on memorial ceremonies. In China and Japan, anniversary dates and years have long been used as occasions for national remembering and mourning, but memorial ceremonies seem to have increased in importance in both countries in recent years.

In China, commemorations of war-related anniversaries take the form of various activities that reinforce memories of the country's suffering during the war, thereby strengthening a collective awareness of China's past. These events are particularly poignant, and enjoy greater press coverage, if China and Japan happen to be locked into a history-related controversy at the time. On key dates (7 July, 15 August, 3 September, 18 September), newspapers carry reports of the many commemorative events (some of which, it should be noted, are attended by Japanese veterans) taking place throughout the country, and editorials remind readers of the need to use history as a guide to the future. To cite just two examples, on 18 September 2001, the *People's Daily* reported on a number of official and non-official activities which took place all over China to commemorate the outbreak of the war, including symposia, unveiling of statues, and visits to memorials and museums. In Shenyang, Harbin and Changchun, a three-minute air raid siren was sounded and traffic on the road stopped to sound horns (*People's Daily*, 19 September 2001). On 15 August 2002, Chinese veterans gathered in Shenyang for a commemorative meeting, and in Nanjing testimonies of over 100 Japanese veterans, collected by a group of Japanese school teachers, were put on display and later published (Xinhua, 16 August 2002).

In Japan, key dates are those associated with the dropping of the atomic bombs (6 and 9 August) and Japan's surrender (15 August). The latter is most commonly associated with controversial visits of government leaders to the Yasukuni Shrine (discussed below), but 15 August is also marked by the National Memorial Service for the War Dead, an official ceremony which takes place at the Nippon Budōkan, attended by the Prime Minister, the Emperor and Empress, and between 5,000 and 6,000 war veterans and bereaved families. The pressure to implement an official, annual ceremony came from the Izokukai which wanted 'to publicly recognize their dead relatives' wartime service to the state' (Orr 2001: 138). Greeted with suspicion when it first took place in 1963, especially among the progressives and sections of the media, the ceremony tends to be overshadowed by the visits of government members to the Yasukuni Shrine. But the statements made by prime ministers at these ceremonies are a measure of their (personal) position on war responsibility, and are worth noting. Koizumi's speech in 2002, for example, was notable because it included his resolve to 'firmly maintain the nation's anti-war pledge' – the first reference to this since Prime Minister Murayama's 1995 speech. While Koizumi did not offer an apology to Asian victims of the war (as had Hosokawa and Murayama), he did follow Hashimoto's formula of expressing 'profound remorse' and 'sincere mourning'.[10] It should also be noted that the prime minister of the day usually precedes the National Memorial Service with a visit to the Chidorigafuji National Cemetery. This cemetery was established by the Japanese government after the war to entomb the souls of unknown soldiers who died in the war in China, and it has come to be the preferred venue for JSP and other opposition politicians to express their condolences to those who died in the war.

Remembering the dead: Yasukuni Shrine visits

For the Chinese government, however, the most problematic issue relating to commemoration of the war is that of Japanese prime ministerial visits to the Yasukuni Shrine. The problem first emerged in the 1980s when Nakasone Yasuhiro paid a visit, in his official capacity, on 15 August 1985. Hashimoto Ryūtarō's visits in 1994, 1995 and 1996 were also controversial, but it was not until Koizumi became prime minister that the issue developed into a diplomatic problem once again. As with the textbook issue, the Yasukuni Shrine has been the object of a long-running domestic struggle in Japan between liberals (who seek religious freedom and the strict separation of state and religion) and conservatives (who 'dream of reinvigorating the myths and symbols of emperor worship and the prewar status of State Shinto' (O'Brien 1996: 31)). Until a domestic consensus emerges on the Yasukuni Shrine problem, it is unlikely that the problem will be fully resolved between Japan and China. Before discussing the Chinese response to the Yasukuni Shrine issue, some background explanation is necessary.

The Yasukuni Shrine, where the souls of over 2.5 million war dead are enshrined, originated from the wishes of the new Meiji leaders to perform rituals for those who had died to create the new nation. Originally called the Shōkonsha (the place to which divine spirits are invited), the shrine was built in 1869 (Nelson 2003: 447). A decade later the shrine was elevated to 'Imperial Shrine of Special Status' and renamed Yasukuni (peaceful country) as part of a national programme to create a new state ideology with Shinto at its core. After 1879, Totman explains, Yasukuni's role was reinforced as the shrine at which those who had sacrificed their lives for the Meiji triumph received worship and imperial gratitude. As Japan's empire expanded, and more soldiers gave their lives to the nation, it became customary for the Emperors Meiji, Taishō and Shōwa to visit the shrine to honour the war dead and their 'heroic spirits' (Totman 2000: 294).[11]

After the Second World War, one of the priorities of the Occupation forces was to sever the link between state and religion, which Yasukuni and its branch memorial shrines embodied. After ordering the Emperor to stop visiting or sending envoys to the Yasukuni Shrine in April 1946, the Supreme Commander of the Allied Powers then went about disbanding the government offices in charge of shrine administration and all shrines were made legal corporations (Bix 2000: 622). The separation has remained intact despite attempts in the 1960s and 1970s by interest groups and politicians to 'reaffirm the special linkage between Shinto and government' by attempting to introduce legislation which would place the shrine under state protection (Totman 2000: 490).[12] There is no consensus in Japan on the Yasukuni Shrine issue. In addition to the long-running debate about the status of the shrine, other controversial aspects include the enshrinement of war criminals, and official ministerial visits to honour the war dead. On the one hand, groups like the Izokukai, the National Association of Shinto Shrines (Jinja Honchō), the Society to Honour the Glorious War Dead (Eirei ni kotaeru kai) and many LDP Dietmembers are in favour of official visits, while on the other, opposition parties, Christian and Buddhist groups protest at the visits, arguing that they represent a violation of Article 20 of the Constitution, which guarantees freedom of religion and the separation of religion and state.

Japanese (LDP) prime ministers and cabinet ministers made regular visits to the Yasukuni Shrine from 1951 onwards, during the shrine's spring and autumn festivals. Yoshida Shigeru made his first post-war visit in October 1951 (and made a further six visits up to 1954), and visits by other Dietmembers and civil servants followed. With the exception of pro-China Prime Ministers Hatoyama Ichirō and Ishibashi Tanzan, all prime ministers up to 1974 made visits to the shrine on a regular basis (see Tanaka 2002: 113). Emperor Hirohito also resumed worshipping at the Yasukuni Shrine on 16 October 1952, and made eight visits between then and 1975 (Bix 2000: 653). But the issue became particularly controversial in Japan in 1975 when Prime Minister Miki chose 15 August for his visit. After attending the National Memorial Service for the War Dead, the prime minister went to the Yasukuni Shrine as a private individual (*itsu shijin*). Tanaka describes what later became the 'four criteria' by which a visit was deemed to be a private visit: Miki was unaccompanied by any other (government) official; he travelled in the LDP presidential car (not the prime ministerial one); he signed the visitors' book without mention of his official title, and he paid for the *tamagushi* (an offering of a sprig of a sacred tree) with his own money (2002: 142). There was increased attendance at the shrine that day by members of the general public, and the perception, as reported in the press, was that the visit was undertaken by the Prime Minister of Japan, not Miki Takeo the private individual. Nonetheless, the government later insisted that the visit could not be classed as official and did not violate the constitution. Tanaka argues that Miki's visit, although undertaken as a 'private person', was an example of a new strategy, adopted by those groups in the LDP and beyond who had been foiled in their attempts to pass the Yasukuni Shrine bill, 'designed to accomplish *de facto* state protection by accumulating official obeisance visits' (2000). Similarly, Harootunian describes this development in terms of an 'expansive program aimed at restoring the unified body of state Shinto through constitutional revision'. By the early 1980s this had grown into a movement to establish Yasukuni as a central site for national ceremonies (1999: 157–8). The issue of official visits was taken up by a Diet study group which concluded in 1980 that 'formal visits by government officials to Yasukuni would run into direct conflict with Article 20 of the Constitution' (O'Brien 1996: 166), but this did not put a stop to such visits, and the 'four criteria' were often ignored. The style of prayer also became a focus of attention, and the press noted whether or not officials chose to follow the Shinto ritual (bowing twice, clapping twice, bowing once).

One of the most controversial aspects of the Yasukuni Shrine issue, as far as the Chinese are concerned, is the enshrinement there of the souls of Japanese war criminals. The souls of Class B and C war criminals were enshrined in 1959, but it was after the enshrinement of souls of the fourteen Class A war criminals in late 1978 that problems emerged. When Prime Minister Ōhira visited the shrine in the spring of 1979, and Prime Minister Suzuki in 1982, there was increased criticism in the Japanese press (Kobori 1998: 178). But the controversy between China and Japan began in earnest in the mid-1980s, when Nakasone Yasuhiro, a strong advocate of the failed Yasukuni bill, became prime minister. Nakasone set up a study group on the topic of official visits to the shrine, which, in contrast to the 1980 report, concluded (though not unanimously) that official visits 'might be constitutional'. Despite the lack of consensus in the final report, the government clearly 'wanted to use it as justification for permitting cabinet members to make formal tribute at the shrine' in August 1985 (Harootunian 1999: 158). Nakasone, and most of his cabinet, thus paid an *official* visit to the Yasukuni Shrine on 15 August – the fortieth anniversary of Japan's surrender in the Second World War, drawing criticism within Japan and from Asian governments.

Chinese response to the Yasukuni Shrine issue

The issue of Yasukuni Shrine visits by Japanese prime ministers has tended to flare up between China and Japan when the incumbent has been more closely associated with right-wing groups or views, or when Japan's defence or national policies have shifted to the right (for example, with increases in defence expenditure, or revision of SDF-related laws). Thus, the Chinese took a keen interest in Prime Ministers Nakasone, Hashimoto and Koizumi.

Prior to the 1980s, the Chinese showed little interest in the Yasukuni Shrine. There was no specific reference to Prime Minister Miki's visit to the shrine in 1975, although a *Renmin Ribao* editorial published on 3 September referred to 'a small group of people who dream of reviving militarism'.[13]

Prime Minister Suzuki's visit in 1982 was noted in an article in the *Zhongguo Qingnian bao* (China Youth Daily), which questioned who the prime minister was mourning (Whiting 1989: 53). In response to Nakasone's visit, however, the Chinese press carried a number of articles stressing that 'official visits to the Yasukuni Shrine hurt the feelings of the Japanese people and those Asian neighbours who suffered at the hands of Japanese militarism during the war of aggression' (*Renmin Ribao*, 15 August 1985). A Xinhua editorial (21 August 1985) also referred to the visit, reiterating the tone of the *Renmin Ribao* article and noting that the shrine housed the spirits of war criminals such as Tōjō Hideki. According to Whiting, the Chinese side made no official protest on the day of the visit for fear of unleashing strong public reaction in China (1989: 54), but their dissatisfaction was made clear in subsequent meetings (Nakajima 1986: 28).[14] The Chinese Ministry of Foreign Affairs had asked the Japanese government to 'handle the matter with prudence' in advance of the visit, and it continued to urge caution in early 1986. During Wu Xueqian's visit to Japan in April, in an oblique reference to Yasukuni, he talked about the emergence of problems that required careful consideration. Prime Minister Nakasone assured him that, in developing Sino-Japanese relations, it was important not to hurt each other's feelings (Whiting 1989: 61; Tian 1997: 583–6). Although Nakasone had refrained from visiting the shrine in the autumn and spring festivals, in the run-up to 15 August 1986, there was much debate as to whether or not an official visit would take place. Nakasone found himself under pressure from both sides – members of the LDP signed a resolution arguing that Japan would forfeit its right as a sovereign state if the visit did not go ahead, while the domestic and international press warned of the detrimental effects if it did. In the end, the negative international and domestic response to Nakasone's Yasukuni visit of 1985 put a stop to his official visits thereafter, but it did not signal the end of the Yasukuni problem.[15] It continued in the 1990s with non-governmental groups on each side of the divide organising conferences and rallies, and mustering support for their respective causes. LDP ministers continued to pay visits to the shrine, mainly in a private capacity, although some purposely obfuscated the type of visit by adding their ministerial title next to their name in the visitors book. Minister of International Trade and Industry Hashimoto Ryūtarō (also chairman of the Izokukai) caused a stir in 1994 by following Shinto ritual, rather than the previous practice of one bow. In July 1996, Hashimoto attended in his official capacity (now as prime minister) and elicited much criticism at home and abroad (Nelson 2003: 457).

In the late 1990s, senior LDP leaders continued to make the case for official visits (for example, Chief Cabinet Secretary Nonaka Hiromu and his successor Aoki Mikio in 1999 and 2000, respectively). With continued pressure on the LDP coming from the usual quarters, a new Yasukuni Shrine Problem Discussion Group was established in July 2000. The membership of ten included representatives of the Izokukai, the LDP, and the Dietmembers' Shinto Politics League (Tanaka 2000). In the meantime, Tokyo Governor Ishihara

Shintarō made an official visit to the shrine in August 2000, and in the following year newly installed Prime Minister Koizumi attended the shrine on 13 August. Chinese responses to Koizumi's visits since August 2001 appeared to be more low key than their reaction to Nakasone's 1985 visit, but, as described below, nonetheless disrupted high-level exchanges between the two governments and threatened to overshadow the 30th anniversary celebrations.

Prime Minister Koizumi and the Yasukuni Shrine problem

Koizumi had openly discussed the issue of visits to the Yasukuni Shrine during the LDP presidential campaign in April 2001, announcing that he would consider visiting the shrine on 15 August 'with the feeling that we should never go to war again, and to console the souls of those who died after having no choice but to go to war' (*Japan Times Online*, 6 August 2001). This gave the Chinese government and media something to watch over the next few months, and raised the usual suspicions that Japan was undergoing something of a revival of militarism. The Chinese response to Koizumi's various announcements came from Foreign Minister Tang Jiaxuan who stated in a meeting with the three secretaries general of the ruling coalition (LDP, New Komeitō and New Conservative Party) on 10 July that 'We cannot accept having the leader of Japan visit the Yasukuni Shrine, where a number of Class A war criminals are enshrined' (*Asahi Online*, 11 July 2001). Jiang Zemin further warned the three politicians that the 'issue could ignite serious trouble' (*Daily Yomiuri Online*, 11 July 2001). In the run-up to August, Chinese officials tried to urge the prime minister not to visit the shrine. When it became clear that a visit would go ahead, the Chinese asked if he could at least go on a day other than 15 August (Hardacre, H-Japan posting, 13 August 2001). Koizumi 'compromised' by going on 13 August, issuing a statement explaining his decision to change the date of the visit:

> As the anniversary of the end of the war came closer, vocal debates have started at home and abroad as to whether I should visit Yasukuni Shrine. In the course of these debates, opinions requesting the cancellation of my visit to Yasukuni Shrine were voiced not only within Japan but also from other countries . . . Taking seriously such situations both in and outside of Japan, I have made my own decision not to visit Yasukuni Shrine on that day, and I would like to choose another day for a visit.
>
> (Koizumi 2001)

The visit nonetheless provoked a critical response from the Chinese, and even more so from the Koreans. Although the Japanese government showed some concern about the potential backlash from its neighbours, there seemed to be a sense that they could gain their understanding. Deputy Chief Cabinet Secretary Abe Shinzō explained, for example, that 'as for deteriorated relations (with China and South Korea), we have to dispel misunderstanding and earnestly make explanations to them' (*Japan Times Online*, 6 August 2001).

While the South Koreans took a hard stance on the issue (by immediately cancelling a number of exchanges and refusing to meet Japanese delegations), the Chinese took a slightly softer, but nonetheless firm, line. In Beijing, Vice Foreign Minister Wang Yi summoned Japanese Ambassador Anami Koreshige on the afternoon of 13 August to make a 'solemn representation' in which Wang pointed to the damage inflicted on the China–Japan relationship as a result of Koizumi's visit. Wang acknowledged that 'Koizumi gave up his original plan to visit the Shrine on the sensitive day of 15 August and made remarks on historic issues, in which he admitted Japanese aggression and expressed introspection, *but his actual practice contradicts and runs against what he said*' (italics added). Furthermore, Wang warned that the visit 'would inevitably affect the healthy development of future bilateral ties between China and Japan', adding that Asian countries would wait and see if Koizumi carried out his pledge to 'strengthen international coordination and develop friendly relations with neighboring countries'.[16]

Koizumi's one-day visit to China in October was partly aimed at developing friendly relations and smoothing over the Yasukuni issue, and appeared to be successful in this regard.[17] As noted above, the Chinese response was favourable and seemed to put the relationship back on an even keel. The prime minister's trouble-free visit may well be explained by an agreement reached prior to his arrival whereby the Chinese side requested that he visit the Marco Polo Bridge, show an understanding of history, indicate his intentions about future Yasukuni Shrine visits, and use the words 'apology', 'regret' and 'remorse'. In return, the Chinese side would avoid reference to the Yasukuni Shrine and textbook issues (Przystup 2001a).[18] But the problem re-emerged in spring 2002 when Koizumi once again visited the shrine. Koizumi explained that his reasons for visiting the shrine that day were to mourn for all those who had given up their lives for Japan since the Meiji Restoration and who had sacrificed themselves for the prosperity and peace of today's Japan.[19] Described as a surprise visit in the Chinese press, it once again drew an official protest in which Vice-Foreign Minister Li Zhaoxing made the same sort of comments to Ambassador Anami as his predecessor had done a few months previously. Li said that for Koizumi to re-visit the shrine 'in defiance of the strong opposition from the people of Japan's neighbouring countries' was 'detrimental to Sino-Japanese relations' (*People's Daily Online*, 21 April 2002). Demonstrations were held in China by survivors of the Nanjing Massacre who gathered at the Nanjing Memorial Hall, and written protests were sent from Chinese groups to the Japanese prime minister (*People's Daily Online*, 23 April 2002). The issue spilled over into other aspects of Sino-Japanese relations, with China postponing a visit of Director General Nakatani Gen of the Japan Defence Agency planned for May (CNN.com, 24 April 2002).

In Japan, the visits drew much criticism too. Koizumi's insistence on visiting the shrine was no doubt intended to please the relevant constituents and, therefore, keep his ratings high. But the fact that the first visit took place on the 13th rather than the 15th, and that it was carried out in a private capacity, did not, in fact, curry favour with his conservative supporters, who considered Chinese and Korean protests as nothing but interference in Japan's domestic affairs and objected to Japan's grovelling foreign policy. Opposition to the visit also came from the media, the general public, religious groups and opposition parties, though for different reasons to those expressed by the right-wing groups. Some Japanese groups sent letters of protest to the prime minister, and messages of support to the Chinese.[20] Similar to his predecessors, Koizumi did not have the full support of his party. Foreign Minister Tanaka Makiko felt that Koizumi should not have visited the shrine at all, and other senior members of the LDP such as Yamasaki Taku, Fukuda Takeo and Nonaka Hiromu expressed similar views.

Koizumi seemed to placate his critics by stating that he did not intend to pay a visit to the shrine in August 2002, but he did visit the shrine again the following year in January. Koizumi appeared to be trying to steer a path between foreign and domestic opponents, on the one hand (by not attending the shrine on sensitive dates, issuing apologies and renewing his vows for peace), and the pro-Yasukuni groups, on the other (by visiting the shrine and mourning those who sacrificed their lives in war). But the Chinese (and Koreans) remain extremely wary of such visits as long as the souls of Class A war criminals are enshrined there. The Chinese government makes no distinction between official or private visits, pays little attention to whether the prime minister makes one bow or two, or how he signs his name in the visitors' book, and makes no reference to the constitutionality of such acts. For the Chinese, the Yasukuni Shrine is quite simply a symbol of Japan's military past, and a prime ministerial visit represents an attempt to justify the war and glorify war criminals.

The Chinese government's response to Koizumi's January 2003 visit to the shrine came in the form of another solemn representation (*yanzhong jiaoshe*) in which Vice-Foreign Minister Yang Wenchang expressed strong dissatisfaction and indignation.[21] Since Koizumi first indicated, in April 2001, his intention to visit the shrine, the wording of the Chinese statements of warning and protest had grown stronger, and the Chinese dissatisfaction with Koizumi became increasingly evident. As a result, the Japanese prime minister did not attend the 30th anniversary celebrations in China in September 2002, although he did meet Jiang Zemin later in the year at the APEC Leaders' Meeting in Mexico where Jiang raised the Yasukuni Shrine issue a number of times. Attempts to re-schedule a visit to China for the prime minister failed to come to fruition in late 2002, and were scuppered in early 2003 in the wake of his January visit to the Yasukuni Shrine. By April, however, it seemed that the (new) Chinese leadership was more open to the idea of a resumption of high-level contact. Foreign Minister Kawaguchi's trip to China in early April was marked by a relative lack of discussion of the Yasukuni Shrine issue, although Prime Minister Wen Jiabao and Foreign Minister Li Zhaoxing stressed the importance of 'using history as a mirror for the future'. Other meetings which took place in April between the top Chinese leadership and leaders of Japanese opposition and ruling parties served to underscore this message, but also provided the opportunity for Koizumi and the Chinese side to work the problem out through informal channels. By May, a meeting between Prime Minister Koizumi and President Hu Jintao in St Petersburg marked the (probably temporary) end of cool relations, and arrangements were later made for Foreign Minister Li to visit Japan in August (Przystup 2003c).

It is difficult to see how the Yasukuni Shrine issue can be resolved between Japan and its Asian neighbours, given the complexity of the problem within Japanese domestic politics. In September 2002, Zeng Qinghong, senior official in the Communist Party of China and 'Japan-hand', suggested that if Prime Minister Koizumi wanted to continue paying homage at the Yasukuni Shrine, then the spirits of the war criminals must be removed. Some Japanese would agree with this suggestion, or would at least concur that there is a need for an alternative site of commemoration free of the symbolism of Yasukuni Shrine. As in previous decades, the Koizumi government set up a study group (Advisory Group to Consider a Memorial Facility for Remembering the Dead and Praying for Peace) to debate this very issue. The group concluded in December 2002 that there is a need for a 'national, nonreligious, and permanent facility where the nation as a whole can remember the dead and pray for peace'. It envisaged that the new facility would complement the existing facilities (the Yasukuni Shrine and Chidorigafuji cemetery), but would fulfil an 'independent purpose'. Those to be remembered at the new facility would include all those who died either during Japan's post-Meiji wars or since (i.e., soldiers, civilians and non-Japanese), and the facility could be a park or open space suitable for large gatherings and ceremonies (though not government-sponsored events). The new memorial would represent:

> a place to pray for the peace of Japan and the world on the basis of remembrance of the dead and reflection on the horrors of war, not a place to comfort the souls and honor the names of specific individuals.
>
> (Advisory Group 2002)

Needless to say, the report was greeted with some criticism within Japan from those who see no need for a new memorial site and argue that Japanese prime ministers would still be free to visit the Yasukuni Shrine.[22] On the other hand, such a facility might at least placate the Chinese who recognise the need for Japanese to mourn their war dead, but object to the militaristic connotations of the Yasukuni Shrine.[23] As of early 2004, China's objections to Prime Minister Koizumi's now regular attendance at the Yasukuni Shrine in spring and autumn were becoming more emphatic, and threatened once again to disrupt bilateral relations.

War (and peace) museums in China and Japan

A further element of this stage of the reconciliation process relates to a different type of commemoration in the form of museums and exhibitions, and underscores, as with textbooks, the yawning gap between Chinese and Japanese national narratives on the war. The number of museums increased worldwide in the 1990s. They diversified in both form and content, becoming more interactive and 'life-like' (using dioramas or interactive computer software, for example), offering exhibitions online, and dealing with more controversial, sensitive topics which in turn gave rise to domestic and international controversy (Macdonald 1996: 1). The potential for controversy in museum exhibitions originates from the role of the museum as a site where a nation's heritage, qualities, and history are recorded and viewed and 'whose displays create and reinforce a vision of the past that constitutes a part of the collective memory' (Zolberg 1996: 70). In line with global trends, the number of museums in China and Japan increased in the 1980s and 1990s. These were largely government-funded in the case of history or war museums, but in Japan private funding helped in the creation of new peace museums and peace projects. While the content of war museums in Japan and China has yet to become the subject of a diplomatic upset between the two countries, this may well arise in the future since the tone and content of exhibits at, for example, the museum attached to the Yasukuni Shrine (Yūshūkan) or at the Shōwa Hall (Shōwa kan) in Japan, and the Memorial Museum of the Chinese People's War of Resistance to Japan in Beijing or Harbin's Martyrs' Museum reflect the diametrically opposed narratives of each nation's history.

In China, museums and memorials dealing with the War of Resistance against Japan proliferated after the mid-1980s, often to coincide with important anniversary years and in line with the official re-assessment of the role of Nationalist forces during the war. At the same time, however, the new narrative involved 'much stronger rhetoric against Japan' (Mitter 2000: 280), and formed part of the intermittent patriotic education campaigns. A number of new sites of memory and mourning were created, or refurbished, to reflect this view. The Memorial Hall for Victims of the Nanjing Massacre opened in 1985, the 40th anniversary of the end of the war, which was also marked by a host of other events, exhibitions, television documentaries and publication of major works on the subject. The Memorial Museum of the Chinese People's War of Resistance to Japan (hereafter War of Resistance museum) was opened in Wanping, Beijing in 1987 (the 50th anniversary of the start of the war), with a new section in 1997. Fushun Prison, which housed Japanese war criminals (and the 'Last Emperor' Henry Pu-yi) in the 1950s, was transformed into a base for patriotic education in the 1980s, and was refurbished in the late 1990s. The Crime Evidence Exhibition Hall of Japanese Imperial Army Unit 731, opened in 1985, was extended in 1995 (with some funding from a Sino-Japanese friendship group) and again in 2001. The Shenyang September 18th History Exhibition Hall was opened in 1991. In December 2002, the 65th anniversary of the massacre, the Memorial Hall for Victims of the Nanjing Massacre opened a new installation – a bronze road imprinted with the footprints and signatures of over two hundred survivors of the massacre (Xinhua, 13 December 2002).[24]

As Mitter points out, these museums are more than just venues for domestic consumption of the latest line in political education and propaganda, since they say something about China's relationship with Japan, the Japanese and the rest of the world. 'The War of Resistance Museum has a role in educating the international community; like the Museum of the Nanjing Massacre, it also aims to educate Japanese visitors' (Mitter 2000: 285). The numbers of Japanese visitors to this and other museums increased in the 1990s, and Japanese visitors to Unit 731, for example, far outstrip those of any other nationality. Mitter also notes that the War of Resistance museum adheres to the long-held official line that a small handful of Japanese militarists was responsible for Japanese actions during the war, thereby enabling Japanese officials to attend these sites without too much domestic backlash. He notes, for example, that Prime Minister Murayama attended the opening of a new section of the museum in 1995 (ibid.: 285). In addition, the exhibitions usually end with a section on Sino-Japanese friendship, with examples of Japanese veterans or ordinary citizens who have shown deep remorse for Japan's invasion of China and helped the two sides to deepen the bonds of friendship. This, once again, reflects the official line that the Japanese people as a whole are pacifists and supportive of a lasting friendship between the two countries. Other Japanese prime ministers and leading politicians have since made visits to various memorial sites in China. In 1997, Hashimoto became the first prime minister to visit China's North-east (formerly Manchuria) where he attended the memorial to the September 18th Incident in Shenyang. LDP Secretary General Nonaka Hiromu visited Nanjing in 1998, and Prime Minister Koizumi visited Beijing's War of Resistance museum in 2001 (Yang 2002).

Japan also witnessed a museum boom in the 1990s. The Yūshūkan at the Yasukuni Shrine was extended and refurbished in the late 1990s, and in 1999 the Shōwa Hall (Shōwa kan) was opened. The concessions to Sino-Japanese friendship found in Chinese museums are lacking in Japan's war museums. While the Yūshūkan focuses on the military sacrifices and the heroes who fought and died in Japan's wars, the Shōwa kan tells the story of life in Japan during the Second World War, focusing on the daily hardship of mothers and children. Both museums studiously avoid descriptions of Japanese military behaviour in China or explanations of why the country found itself in such economic distress in the 1930s and 1940s. The emphasis is on the Japanese as victims, thereby reinforcing the conservative view of history.

The battle between progressives and conservatives described in the discussion of Japan's domestic textbook issues extends to these sites of memory. The Shōwa kan was the result of many years of lobbying by the Izokukai to have a national memorial to Japan's war dead. Originally planned for 1995 to mark the 50th anniversary of the end of the war, building work was delayed because of the domestic debate about the nature of the museum. The conflict pitted the Ministry of Health and Welfare (under whose remit the project fell), some in the LDP, and the Izokukai against progressive historians, politicians, residents local to the planned location of the museum (Kudan), and the National Council of Bereaved Families for Peace (Heiwa Izokukai). The main criticisms of the plans for the new museum were that the content lacked reference to Asian victims of the wartime Shōwa period and, therefore, historical objectivity (Hammond 1995).[25]

Peace museums in Japan have tried to redress the lack of objectivity in war museums. The Hiroshima Peace Memorial Museum, which had for many years failed to explain the reasons for the dropping of the bomb, was reorganised in the early 1990s to take this into account. Similarly, the Nagasaki Atomic Bomb Museum was re-worked in 1996 to provide more explanation of Japan's wartime policies, in addition to the human costs of the nuclear age. New museums, such as Osaka Peace (opened in 1991 and funded by the Osaka municipal government) and Kyoto's Museum of World Peace (opened in 1992, attached to Ritsumeikan University), both focus on the suffering of the victims of Japan's aggression and the fifteen-year war. Many other smaller, often privately run, peace museums throughout Japan tackle the subject in a similar way. One example is Grass Roots House, a privately run peace centre in Kōchi founded in 1989 and devoted to disseminating information about the war and promoting peace education. In addition to hosting a permanent exhibition, it also organised 'peace trips' to China in the early 1990s, with the aim of bringing Chinese and Japanese together to talk about the war.[26] Peace museums regularly come under attack from right-wing groups. Coinciding with the beginning of the textbook offensive in the mid-1990s, groups such as Nihon yoron no kai, Nihon kaigi and the right-wing press stepped up their condemnation of peace museums for promoting what they called a 'biased and masochistic' view of the war. In July 1997 some photographs in the Osaka Peace exhibition had to be removed in response to protests from the Nihon yoron no kai which alleged that the photographs were fakes (Nakakita 2000: 232–3), and in an ironic twist of fate, the Nihon kaigi managed to secure Osaka Peace (on the grounds that it is a public building) as the venue for its January 2000 conference on 'The biggest lie of the 20th century: a thorough investigation of the Nanjing Massacre'. This event was heavily criticised within Japan and, needless to say, drew comment from the Chinese (ibid.).

Conclusion

The difficulties faced by both the Chinese and Japanese in reaching some sort of accommodation on a settlement of the past are, of course, inextricably linked with the many problems experienced in the other stages of reconciliation discussed in this book. The ongoing debate in Japan about how to mourn the war dead in a way that appeases those Japanese who lost family members during the war, while respecting those whose families were the victims of Japan's military behaviour in Asia, may be moving closer to a solution, but progress will be slow. As the previous chapters highlighted, there remain huge gaps and contradictions between the different types of memory and remembrance, and different interpretations of history. These, often diametrically opposed, approaches to the past – official and private, Chinese and Japanese, left-wing and right-wing, Maoist and post-Maoist – all converge on the issues of apology, commemoration and remembrance. As we have seen, without some level agreement on one (or more) versions of history, on who were the victims, and who the victimisers, then little progress can be made towards acknowledgement of moral responsibility. Without such acknowledgement, there can be no apology, forgiveness or agreement on how to remember and mourn the dead. Clearly, progress has been made over the years at different levels, and it is still underway, but, as this chapter has shown, the process is marked by a 'one step forward, two steps back' formation. The enthusiasm with which Chinese and Japanese leaders embrace the notion of a future-oriented relationship, supposedly based on a common understanding of the past, clashes with domestic needs in both countries to legitimise very different understandings of that past. This stage of the reconciliation process is, therefore, perhaps the most difficult to achieve since it is rife with fundamental differences based on the politics of commemoration, and a continued emphasis at state level on a form of remembering which recalls the glories and heroes of past wars and which, in turn, forms the basis of each nation's identity.

6 Conclusion

Towards a future-oriented relationship?

> At the core of any reconciliation process is the preparedness of people to anticipate a shared future. For this to occur they are required not to forget but to forgive the past, and thus be in a position to move forward together.
>
> (Rigby 2000: 12)

The aim of this book was to explore the progress made in the 1990s between Chinese and Japanese people, at both elite and sub-elite level, towards reconciliation. There are various means by which reconciliation can take place, such as war crimes trials, reparations, apologies, collective amnesia and truth commissions. As the book has shown, the Chinese and Japanese have attempted a number of these approaches at various points in the past fifty years. The celebratory events arranged for the 30th anniversary of diplomatic normalisation showed that tremendous progress has been made. But as we have seen, one of the biggest obstacles to a smooth relationship has been the frequent recurrence of problems left over from the past. Although Chinese and Japanese leaders frequently talked about the need to settle the past and come to a mutual understanding about history in the 1990s, a series of diplomatic incidents revealed their inability to deal with the past. Disputes over prime ministerial visits to the Yasukuni Shrine and the content of history textbooks, continued to disrupt the relationship in much the same way as they had in the 1980s. But new issues emerged too – compensation cases and disagreements over the wording of apologies only served to highlight how far both sides still had to go to achieve a more complete reconciliation.

As Chapter 2 explained, a number of factors impeded reconciliation during the Cold War period. Although the Tokyo war crimes trials and trials held in China brought some individuals to justice, it is widely felt that the war crimes trials failed to deal fully with Japan's transgressions in China. In particular, the architects and the perpetrators of biological and chemical warfare and sexual slavery were not tried. Within the context of the Cold War, Japan and China were soon divided by the hostile political environment and there was very little interaction until the 1970s and 1980s. The issue of reparations was discussed during negotiations for normalisation between

Japan and China in the 1970s but, adopting a 'magnanimous policy', the PRC renounced its claims. Compensation for individuals was not considered in the 1970s and only emerged in the 1990s as part of the developing trends in both the international and domestic environments.

The political systems and accompanying ideologies that developed in China and Japan in the early post-war (and for China in the early post-civil war period) had the effect of suppressing any dialogue between the two sides about the war, thus impeding progress towards reconciliation. In China, the lack of legal or political rights meant that victims of Japanese wartime abuses, even had they been willing to speak about their experiences, were not necessarily allowed to do so unless the authorities so wished it (for example, only in 1985 were Nanjing survivors officially encouraged to tell their stories). This is not to say that historical research was not underway or that the war was not discussed at all. On the contrary, the Communist Party's 'grand narrative' in which the Communists were victorious in the War of Resistance against Japan became the mainstay of the party's legitimacy, forming the core of the country's collective memory and therefore its collective identity. The grand narrative would (and could) not be questioned until the 1980s, when the academic environment was relaxed and more independent research could be undertaken. During this time, China's younger generation, which had no direct experience of the war came to be taught only about the 'bad Japanese' in their textbooks and media. When the Chinese leadership attempted to move away from this view, for example, in an attempt to improve relations with Japan and cast Japan in a better light,[1] they faced a huge challenge in the form of deeply held antipathy towards the Japanese which the party had encouraged for so long, and which, of course, had been reinforced by the wartime experiences related by parents and grandparents.

The Japanese 'grand narrative' also presented problems for the prospects of reconciliation, both domestically and bilaterally. Early attempts by scholars, teachers, some war veterans and politicians to discuss the facts of Japan's aggression during the fifteen-year war were overshadowed by the more dominant view that the 1930s and 1940s represented a 'dark valley' for Japan and the Japanese, an aberration for which the instigators had been punished, reparations made, and justice done. Intermittent struggles between the progressives and conservatives helped to keep history in the present, through high profile court cases such as Ienaga Saburō's textbook lawsuits and domestic debates over the content of school history textbooks. That there had been little domestic reconciliation between these two contending views of history prior to the internationalisation of textbook problem from the 1980s onwards, made reconciliation between China and Japan on the same issue somewhat problematic.

Sino-Japanese reconciliation: measuring success

In his explanation of strategies for achieving reconciliation, Kriesberg notes that reconciliation is not a process conducted by a single actor, but is the result of the efforts of different groups and individuals employing various strategies, sequentially as well as simultaneously. One important set of actors in the reconciliation process are those who work at grass roots to advance such causes as compensation claims or new legislation, and whose 'struggles are an essential component in advancing reconciliation' (1999: 121–2). As we have seen, grass-roots organisations and individuals in China and Japan have fought tirelessly throughout the 1990s to promote reconciliation. They have combined their efforts with international organisations that have helped to broaden the awareness of their experiences and apply pressure on Japanese companies and the government to respond. This response has been chequered and, as this book has shown, the struggles for truth, justice and settlement of the past are still ongoing.

As Chapter 3 showed, the battle over textbooks between China and Japan will no doubt continue as along as the domestic divisions in Japan exist. While the Chinese government and academics acknowledge that 'a handful of rightists' are responsible for perpetuating the Greater East Asia War view of the past, they are also aware of a general shift to the right in Japan since the mid-1990s which affects not just education policy but other policy areas too, and this is a cause for concern. For some Japanese, the neo-nationalist, anti-Japanese tendencies which emerged in China in the 1990s are also a concern and impact upon the prospects for mutual understanding. On the other hand, the attempts by Chinese and Japanese academics to move towards a common history of the war, as evidenced in the many conferences, joint publications and the 'common history textbook' project, have helped to counteract the revisionist trends in Japan and suggest that China and Japan are a step closer to producing an agreed version of history. The transnationalisation of the textbook issue, and the widespread criticism of the output of groups like the Tsukuru kai are also notable, and the results of the future rounds of textbook screening will be interesting to monitor.

Chapter 4 discussed the Chinese movement for compensation and the pursuit of justice for individual Chinese. There seems to be a consensus that the court cases, events such as the Women's International War Crimes Tribunal, and out-of-court settlements (such as the Hanaoka settlement) have helped, if only partially, to meet the victims' need for justice and recognition. The process of recording one's testimony, having that testimony heard in court or in a people's tribunal, and receiving acceptance by others of one's suffering does seem, for some at least, to offer some relief or help restore honour and dignity.[2] In many cases, the legal battles for compensation are not necessarily, or perhaps not even, about monetary gain. The plaintiffs have indeed demanded financial redress, but they have also insisted upon official apologies, memorial plaques or monuments, the inclusion of their histories in textbooks, and so on. They are seeking validation and a broader, international, understanding of how they have suffered during and since the war, and reparations need not be measured by their monetary value. But, as we have seen, there have been problems with some of these activities and their outcomes. For some people 'the issue cannot be finally settled until the Japanese government accepts full legal responsibility and acts accordingly' (Hayashi 2001: 580). While a number of judges have acknowledged Japan's moral responsibility, they have not been able (or willing) to push for legal responsibility, since to do so would require new legislation and a change in the relationship between the judiciary and government.

Some people assert that there is a limit to how far the compensation movement can grow in China, given that the majority of those seeking justice are approaching old age. As we have seen, a number of plaintiffs have died since bringing their cases to court. But the family members and support groups continue the battle. As Winter and Sivan point out, 'younger people, uninitiated into the actual experience, carry emotion-laden stories very effectively. For some, carrying a survivor's narrative can approximate survivorship itself' (1999: 18). In addition, the efforts of Chinese academics and lawyers in bringing to light the experiences of former forced labourers and sex slaves, as described in Chapters 3 and 4, show no sign of slowing down. Indeed, research into these topics only began in earnest in the early 1990s and there is much more to do. There is a firm conviction among the Chinese involved in these efforts that the movement for redress will only grow stronger in future years.

Activities associated with settling the past – apologies and commemoration – remain problematic too, as described in Chapter 5, and there appears to be a growing divide between what is acceptable to the two governments and peoples. The Chinese government under Zhu Rongji announced that it would stop demanding apologies from the Japanese government, but Prime Minister Koizumi seems happy to continue to offer them. By contrast, many Chinese people feel that the Japanese government has not apologised sincerely, while many Japanese feel that no further apologies are necessary. Commemorating the war on key anniversaries remains a central event in both countries. For the Chinese government, official visits of Japanese prime ministers and ministers to the Yasukuni Shrine are simply unacceptable, and many Japanese citizens concur with this point of view. On the other hand, the Chinese readily acknowledge that the Japanese have a right to mourn their own war dead and in this regard, a politically 'neutral' war memorial with no links to Shinto, and no reference to Japan's war criminals, may well placate the Chinese and defuse this particularly sensitive issue.

Domestic support for resolution of the past in both countries is now considerable, but could be strengthened if each of the individual campaigns and groups could unite to create a stronger, more institutionalised set of organisations.[3] This would be easier to achieve in Japan than in China where, under the current political circumstances, the support groups are not able to register as formal social organisations. The political climate in China still places considerable constraints on the activities of such groups. When activists defend their patriotic rights as victims of Japan's war of aggression, they are implicitly criticising the Chinese government for failing to represent their interests by waiving reparations in 1972. Just as the Korean comfort women movement was partly about a confrontation with the patriarchal forces which had kept the events of the war concealed for fifty years (Piper 2001: 143), so too is the Chinese compensation movement potentially about anti-government action.[4] At the same time, the movement serves as a useful reminder (and one that hails not from the CCP, but from the people themselves) of the horrors inflicted during the war, thereby helping to reinforce Chinese unity at a time when the Chinese government is seeking to bolster its legitimacy through patriotic education campaigns.

A more cohesive movement might produce the political pressure needed to achieve greater success. There is a growing consensus that if sufficient pressure is put on the Japanese government by Japanese, Asian and international organisations, and if more victims (or their relatives or representatives) come forward to claim compensation and demand official apologies, then the Japanese government would have little choice but to respond in a more favourable way, perhaps along German lines.[5] Part of this pressure would have to come from the Chinese government itself. While a number of Chinese academics note the current passive stance of the Chinese government, they do acknowledge that if the compensation movement gets bigger, then the Chinese government would have to respond, perhaps by seeking a political resolution with the Japanese government.[6] Yet both the Chinese and Japanese governments seem keen to maintain a status quo on the issue of reparations and apologies, and this is usually attributed to an unwillingness to disrupt the economic relationship. As the economic relationship strengthens over the next few decades, some argue that the issue of history will have less and less influence. A number of academics stress the growing interdependence of the Japanese, Chinese, and indeed the Asian economies. It seems that for the decision-makers in each country, the history problem is moving further and further down the agenda. Although history will continue to cause friction, this is considered to be a relatively minor issue, and, moreover, one that is better left alone, precisely because it is considered so intractable.[7]

Both the Chinese and Japanese governments often reiterate their respective views that issues such as statements of regret, compensation, and the problem of abandoned chemical weapons have been dealt with in the various agreements and declarations signed by the two sides since 1972. By the late 1990s, it seemed that the two governments were willing to put the past in the past, and move towards a 'vision of a shared future'. The reasons for this approach had less to do with a mutually agreed resolution of the past, and more to do with political and economic exigencies. By contrast, many Chinese and Japanese who had been directly or indirectly touched by the experiences of the war were still struggling to get their stories into the open, and to seek justice through official acknowledgements, apologies and individual compensation. At the beginning of the twenty-first century, the attempts of the two governments in seeking to pursue their future-oriented foreign policies are at odds with those at grass roots who see their own struggles as incomplete. Ironically civil groups need the support and cooperation of their governments if they are to succeed. Reconciliation between the two countries is undoubtedly making progress, but there is still a long way to go.

Appendix 1 Chronology of textbook controversies and trials

1955 First 'textbook offensive' campaign. Criticisms of 'biased' history textbooks and tightening of textbook authorisation by MoE.

1965 Ienaga Saburō brings first case against the government. 1974 Tokyo District Court partial victory; Ienaga appeals to High Court, 1986 Tokyo High Court (Suzuki) overturns district court ruling, Ienaga appeals to Supreme Court. 1993 Supreme Court dismisses case.

1967 Ienaga Saburō brings second case against the government. 1970 partial victory in Tokyo District Court (Sugimoto), MoE appeals to Tokyo High Court; 1975 HC dismisses MoE claim, MoE appeals to Supreme Court; Supreme Court refers back to High Court. 1989 Tokyo High Court dismisses case.

1982 Second 'textbook offensive'. June: Japanese press (erroneously) warns of pre-war tone in textbooks. July–August: China and Korea protest and demand changes. August: Chief Cabinet Secretary Miyazawa agrees to amend textbook guidelines, but no amendments made to textbooks.

1984 January: Ienaga files third lawsuit. 1989 Tokyo District Court (Katō) awards partial victory; Ienaga and MoE appeal to higher court, 1993 High Court makes further ruling in Ienaga's favour (on Nanjing), Ienaga appeals to Supreme Court on other points. 1997 Supreme Court (Ono) rules in favour of Ienaga (on Unit 731).

1986 June: Chinese (official) and Korean (unofficial) protests over *Shinpen Nihonshi* (A New History of Japan, written by Nihon o mamoru kokumin kaigi). Prime Minister Nakasone orders revisions.

1989 February: MoE inserts ruling in Course of Study that national anthem should be sung and flag hoisted on graduation days. June: Ienaga's second lawsuit reverses first verdict.

1993 March: Supreme Court Verdict on Ienaga's first lawsuit in favour of MoE. August: Chief Cabinet Secretary Kono Yōhei acknowledges and apologises for 'comfort women' system. October: Tokyo High Court Ienaga third lawsuit verdict, finds that authorisation was unconstitutional in three places.

1994 April: Fujioka Nobukatsu *et al.* embark on movement to 'reform modern history teaching'.

1996 Third 'textbook offensive'. June: reports on results of textbook screening of middle-school history textbooks show that all seven books contain reference to 'military comfort women' (*jūgun ianfu*). June: LDP members form Akarui Nihon group. December: Atarashi Rekishi Kyōkasho o Tsukuru Kai formed to protest against 'masochistic history' and to call for reform of history curriculum.

1997 January: Tsukuru kai asks Education Minister to delete descriptions of comfort women from textbooks. July: Nihon Kaigi asks PM Hashimoto to delete descriptions of comfort women from textbooks. August: successful verdict for Ienaga's third lawsuit.

1998 July: Education Minister Machimura criticises negative elements of descriptions of modern history in textbooks.

1999 January: MoE 'informally' asks textbook publishers for more balance in textbooks. November: textbook examiner resigns after criticising the 'neighbouring countries' clause.

2000 September: Press reports about the regression in middle-school history textbooks for use from 2002 – only one textbook refers to comfort women.

2001 February: Public protest against Tsukuru kai history textbook (*Atarashii rekishi kyōkasho*) by Japanese historians; Korean Foreign Ministry expresses concern about the new history textbook. March: China asks that Fusōsha make changes to *Atarashii rekishi kyōkasho*. April: MoE announces authorisation results (*Atarashii rekishi kyōkasho* passes). May: Chinese and Korean governments protest. July: Japanese government announces that the textbook contains no factual errors; Korea takes retaliatory measures by stopping Japanese cultural imports.

Source: Arai (2001: 178–87)

Appendix 2 Selected list of NGOs and other organisations involved in history-related issues (Chinese, Japanese and North American)

Name/type of group	Chinese/Japanese name	URL
Groups supporting compensation cases		
Society to Support the Demands of the Chinese War Victims (Suopei)	中国人戦争被害者の要求を支える会	http://suopei.org/index-j.html
Committee on Chinese Forced Labour (Hanaoka incident)	中国人強制連行を考える会	http://www.jca.apc.org/hanaokajiken/
Committee to Support Chinese 'Comfort Women' Court Cases	中国人「慰安婦」裁判を支援する会	Not available
Lawsuit for Compensation for Unit 731 Biological Warfare	731部隊細菌戦国家賠償請求訴訟	http://www.anti731saikinsen.net
Campaign Committee for 731 Biological Warfare Court Case	731 細菌戦裁判キャンペーン委員会	http://homepage2.nifty.com/731saikinsen
Association for the Clarification of the Japanese Army's Biological Warfare	日本軍による細菌戦を明らかにする会	http://www1.ocn.ne.jp/~sinryaku/akirakakai.htm
Hanaoka Victims' Group	花岡受難者联谊会	Not available
Research Centre on Chinese Comfort Women (Shanghai Teaching University)	中国慰安妇问题研究中心（上海师范大学）	Not available
General, pro-reconciliation groups		
JCA-NET (Japan Computer Access Network) – hosts many of the women's, pro-reconciliation and peace-related Japanese NGOs		http://www.jca.apc.org

Name/type of group	Chinese/Japanese name	URL
Asia-Japan Women's Resource Center		http://www.aworc.org/org/ajwrc/ajwrc.html
Violence against Women in War-Network, Japan (VAWW-NET, Japan)	VAWW-NET ジャパン	http://www1.jca.apc.org/vaww-net-japan/
All-Japan Association of Bereaved Families for Peace	平和遺族会	Not available
Chinese Returnees Association (Chūkiren)	中国帰還者連絡会(中帰連)	http://www.ne.jp/asahi/tyuukiren/web-site/top_16.htm
Centre for Research and Documentation on Japan's War Responsibility	日本の戦争責任資料センター	http://www.jca.apc.org/JWRC/index-j.html
Textbook/history-related groups		
Japanese Society for History Textbook Reform	新しい教科書を作る会	http://www.tsukurukai.com/
Association for the Advancement of a Liberalist View of History	自由主義史観研究会	http://www.jiyuu-shikan.org/
Children and Textbooks Japan Network 21	子供と教科書全国ネット 21	http://www.ne.jp/asahi/kyokasho/net21/top-f.htm
Tawara Yoshifumi (homepage)		http://www.linkclub.or.jp/~teppei-y/tawara%20HP/index.html
Asian Network for History Education, Japan	歴史教育アジアネットワーク	http://www.jca.apc.org/asia-net/index.shtml
War and Peace Museums		
Peace Osaka	ピースおおさか	http://www.mydome.or.jp/peace/
Kyoto Museum for World Peace	国際平和ミュージアム	http://www.ritsumei.ac.jp/mng/er/wp-museum/e/eng.html
Grass Roots House	平和資料館　草の家	http://ha1.seikyou.ne.jp/home/Shigeo.Nishimori/grh.htm
Yūshūkan (Yasukuni Shrine)	遊就館	http://www.yasukuni.or.jp/
Shōwa Hall	昭和館	http://www.showakan.go.jp/
Fushun War Criminal Exhibition Hall	抚顺战犯管理所	http://www.leifeng.com/Travel/war/in_1.asp
Shenyang 9/18 History Museum	九一八歴史博物館	http://www.918museum.org.cn/

Name/type of group	*Chinese/Japanese name*	*URL*
The National Museum of Chinese History (Beijing)		http://www.nmch.gov.cn/gb/index.asp
Memorial Hall for the Victims of the Nanjing Massacre	南京大屠杀遇难同胞纪念馆	http://njdts.china1840–1949.net.cn/
Chinese websites devoted to war-related issues		
Chinese WWII forced labourers	中国二战劳工人网	http://www.warslave.net
China September 18th Patriotic Website	中国918·国网	http://www.china918.net
North American organisations		
Nikkei for Civil Rights and Redress (NCRR)		http://www.ncrr-la.org
Global Alliance for Preserving the History of WWII in Asia		http://www.gainfo.org/index.html
Alliance for Preserving the Truth of the Sino-Japanese War		http://www.sjwar.org/
Canada Association for Learning and Preserving the History of World War II in Asia (Canada Alpha)		http://www.vcn.bc.ca/alpha/frontpage.htm

Appendix 3 Important statements, treaties, declarations and apologies

The following seven texts are given here:

1   1972 Joint Communiqué of the Government of Japan and the Government of the People's Republic of China.
2   Statement by Chief Cabinet Secretary Miyazawa Kiichi on history textbooks, August 1982.
3   Statement by Chief Cabinet Secretary KonoYōhei on the 'comfort women' issue, 4 August 1993.
4   Personal letter of apology to comfort women from Prime Minister Koizumi Junichirō.
5   Resolution to Renew the Determination for Peace on the Basis of Lessons Learned from History, June 1995.
6   Prime Minister Murayama Tomiichi's statement, 15 August 1995.
7   Japan-PRC Joint Declaration on Building a Partnership of Friendship and Cooperation for Peace and Development, 26 November 1998.

1. Joint Communiqué of the Government of Japan and the Government of the People's Republic of China, 29 September 1972 (excerpt)

The Japanese side is keenly conscious of the responsibility for the serious damage that Japan caused in the past to the Chinese people through war, and deeply reproaches itself.

(5) The Government of the People's Republic of China declares that in the interest of friendship between the Chinese and the Japanese peoples, it renounces its demand for war reparation from Japan.

Source: http://www.mofa.go.jp/region/asia-paci/china/joint72.html
(accessed 6 March 2004)

2. Statement by Chief Cabinet Secretary Miyazawa Kiichi on history textbooks, 26 August 1982 (excerpt)

(1) The Japanese Government and the Japanese people are deeply aware of the fact that acts by our country in the past caused tremendous

suffering and damage to the peoples of Asian countries, including the Republic of Korea (RoK) and China, and have followed the path of a pacifist state with remorse and determination that such acts must never be repeated. Japan has recognized, in the Japan-RoK Joint Communiqué of 1965, that the 'past relations are regrettable, and Japan feels deep remorse,' and in the Japan-China Joint Communiqué, that Japan is 'keenly conscious of the responsibility for the serious damage that Japan caused in the past to the Chinese people through war and deeply reproaches itself.' These statements confirm Japan's remorse and determination which I have stated above and this recognition has not changed at all to this day.

(2) The spirit in the Japan-RoK Communiqué and the Japan-China Joint Communiqué naturally should be respected in Japan's school education and textbook authorization. Recently, however, the Republic of Korea, China, and others have been criticizing some descriptions in Japanese textbooks. From the perspective of building friendship and good will with neighboring countries, Japan will pay due attention to these criticisms and make corrections at the Government's responsibility.

(3) To this end, in relation to future authorization of textbooks, the Government will revise the Guideline for Textbook Authorization after discussions in the Textbook Authorization and Research Council and give due consideration to the effect mentioned above.

Source: http://www.mofa.go.jp/policy/postwar/state8208.html
(accessed 9 February 2004).

3. Statement by Chief Cabinet Secretary Kōno Yōhei on the issue of 'comfort women', 4 August 1993

Undeniably this was an act with the involvement of the military authorities of the day that severely injured the honour and dignity of many women. The government of Japan would like to take this opportunity once again to extend its sincere apologies and remorse to all those, irrespective of place of origin, who suffered immeasurable pain and incurable physical and psychological wounds as comfort women . . . We hereby reiterate our firm determination never to repeat the same mistake by forever engraving such issues in our memories through the study and teaching of history . . . The Korean Peninsula was under Japanese rule in those days, and their recruitment, transfer, management, and so forth were conducted generally against their will through such means as coaxing and coercion.

Source: *Japan Echo*, August 1997.

4. Personal letter of apology to comfort women from Prime Minister Koizumi Junichirō (issued only upon acceptance of payment from Asian Women's Fund) (excerpt)

As the Prime Minister of Japan, I thus extend my most sincere apologies and remorse to all the women who underwent immeasurable and painful experiences and suffered incurable physical and psychological wounds as comfort women.

We must not evade the weight of the past, nor should we evade our responsibilities for the future.

I believe that our country, painfully aware of its moral responsibilities, with feelings of apology and remorse, should face up squarely to its past history, and accurately convey it to future generations.

Source: http://www.mofa.go.jp/policy/women/fund/pmletter.html
(accessed 10 July 2003).

5. Resolution to Renew the Determination for Peace on the Basis of Lessons Learned from History, June 1995 (complete)

On the occasion of the 50th anniversary of the end of World War II, this House offers its sincere condolences to those who fell in action and victims of wars and similar actions all over the world.

Solemnly reflecting upon many instances of colonial rule and acts of aggression in the modern history of the world, and recognising that Japan carried out those acts in the past, inflicting pain and suffering upon the peoples of other countries, especially in Asia, the Members of this House express a sense of deep remorse.

We must transcend the differences over historical views of the past war and learn humbly the lessons of history so as to build a peaceful international society.

This House expresses its resolve, under the banner of eternal peace enshrined in the Constitution of Japan, to join hands with other nations of the world and to pave the way for a future that allows all human beings to love together.

Source: Dower (1995)

6. Statement by Prime Minister Murayama Tomiichi, issued on 15 August 1995 (excerpt)

During a certain period in the not too distant past, Japan, following a mistaken national policy, advanced along the road to war, only to ensnare the Japanese people in a fateful crisis, and through its colonial rule and aggression, caused tremendous damage and suffering to the people of many countries, particularly to those of Asian nations.

In the hope that no such mistake be made in the future, I regard, in a spirit of humility, these irrefutable facts of history, and express here once again my feelings of deep remorse and state my heartfelt apology.

Source: *Japan Times Weekly*, 21–27 August 1995: 6.

7. Japan-PRC Joint Declaration on Building a Partnership of Friendship and Cooperation for Peace and Development, 26 November 1998 (excerpt)

Both sides believe that squarely facing the past and correctly understanding history are the important foundation for further developing relations between Japan and China. The Japanese side observes the 1972 Joint Communiqué of the Government of Japan and the Government of the People's Republic of China and the 15 August 1995 Statement by former Prime Minister Tomiichi Murayama. The Japanese side is keenly conscious of the responsibility for the serious distress and damage that Japan caused to the Chinese people through its aggression against China during a certain period in the past and expressed deep remorse for this. The Chinese side hopes that the Japanese side will learn lessons from the [*sic*] history and adhere to the path of peace and development.

Source: http://www.mofa.go.jp/region/asia-paci/china/visit98/joint.html (accessed 6 March 2004).

Notes

Introduction

1 Both messages were sent on the occasion of the 30th anniversary of the normalisation of China–Japan relations on 29 September 2002. For the full text, see the Japanese Ministry of Foreign Affairs website, available at http://www.mofa.go.jp

2 The Yasukuni Shrine in Tokyo is where the souls of Japanese war criminals are enshrined. Japanese prime ministerial and ministerial visits there on important anniversaries such as 15 August (the date of Japan's defeat in the Second World War) have become a regular bone of contention between the Chinese and Japanese governments. The Yasukuni Shrine issue is described in more detail in Chapter 5.

3 The Shenyang incident refers to the forcible removal by Chinese police of five North Koreans who had attempted to enter the Japanese consulate in Shenyang in May 2002. The behaviour of the Chinese police was considered by some to be an infringement of Japanese sovereignty. *Japan Times Online*, 10 August 2002.

4 In December 2001 the Japanese coastguard fired upon a ship, suspected to be North Korean, which had entered Japan's waters. The ship sank in the Chinese exclusive economic zone (EEZ) and a diplomatic quarrel broke out over raising the ship. For more details on these and other events in Sino-Japanese relations refer to the quarterly summaries in *Comparative Connections*, http://www.csis.org/pacfor/ccejournal.html

5 The website refers to seven sensitive issues in Sino-Japanese relations. In addition to the three categories relating to the war, these are Taiwan, the Diaoyu (Senkaku) islands, Japanese–American Security Cooperation, and the Guanghua dormitory issue. For more details see http://www.fmprc.gov.cn/eng/29726.html. Some Chinese referred to the most contentious issues of the late 1990s as the 'two Ts and the two Hs', that is, Taiwan, the USA–Japan (security) treaty, the history problem, and human rights (Rozman 1999: 393). By early 2003, those I spoke to in China talked about the '5 Ts': Taiwan, territory (Diaoyu/Senkaku islands), textbooks, the USA–Japan treaty, and trade.

6 The use of the euphemistic term 'comfort women' is hotly debated and widely regarded as an inaccurate and insulting description of a system of military sexual slavery implemented by the Japanese army during the war. While the author concurs with this view, the term is nonetheless used throughout this book since it most often used in the Chinese and Japanese literature and by groups involved in compensation claims.

7 This text is taken from the Chinese Ministry of Foreign Affairs webpage available at http://www.fmprc.gov.cn

8 The page can be found at http://www.mofa.go.jp

9 Examples include the filing of a class-action lawsuit in the United States against the Japanese government in August 2000 by fifteen former comfort women (four

of whom were Chinese) who sought compensation and an apology. This was the first case of former sex slaves filing a lawsuit in the USA, and the first time that the Japanese government was named as defendant. Previous compensation cases were filed against Japanese companies. Such lawsuits were filed under the eighteenth-century 'Alien Torts Claims Act' which enables foreign citizens to sue other foreign citizens and entities for abuses of international law. The claim here in this case was that the comfort women system violated *jus cogens* norms of international law and was not covered by sovereign immunity (see *Japan Times Online*, 20 September 2000).

10 The economic relationship is not without its problems. In the past, Japanese investors have been reluctant to become involved in what they regard as a relatively unstable investment environment in China. The Chinese government has worked hard to rectify such problems, encouraging further economic co-operation by pledging to improve the investment environment in China. In 2000–1 a number of problems emerged on the trade front which caused some concern, such as Japanese accusations of Chinese dumping. Trade friction will no doubt become a perennial issue as Chinese products begin to compete with locally produced goods on the Japanese domestic market. See *Comparative Connections* for updates on various instalments of disputes over trade.

11 See, for example, Drysdale and Zhang (2000), Hilpert and Haak (2002) and Söderberg (2001).

12 The security dilemma states that

> in an uncertain or anarchic international system, mistrust between two or more potential adversaries can lead each side to take precautionary and defensively motivated measures that are perceived as offensive threats. This can lead to countermeasures in kind thus ratcheting up regional tensions, reducing security, and creating self-fulfilling prophecies about the danger of one's security environment.
>
> (Christensen 1999: 49–50)

13 Midford goes on to argue that only by showing good behaviour does Japan stand a chance of reassuring its neighbours that it no longer harbours militaristic intentions and of convincing its former victims of its peaceful intentions. In this respect Japan's strategy of engagement since the early 1990s has begun to pay off gradually and achieved a certain amount of success in terms of confidence building. For a discussion of the positive and negative dynamics of Japan's engagement policy, see Drifte (2003).

14 Public opinion polls are time-sensitive – the Shenyang incident may have had much to do with this response.

15 See Yang (2002) for a succinct discussion of the use of the history card in Sino-Japanese relations.

1 Reconciliation and Sino-Japanese relations

1 Up to the Second World War the word reparations was generally used to describe monetary compensation paid by one state to another state, or in Barkan's words 'some form of material recompense for that which cannot be returned, such as human life, a flourishing culture and economy, and identity' (2000: xix). The word has since come to describe other forms of redress as well.

2 This event was organised by Japanese and Asian NGOs. It had no legal power, but the aim was to establish that Japanese military sexual slavery during the war constituted a crime against women and a crime against humanity. The tribunal caused a great deal of controversy. See Hayashi (2001).

3 For an overview of interpretations of Japan's evolving foreign policy see Hook *et al.* (2001), Chapters 1 and 2.
4 The All China Lawyers' Association (ACLA) belongs to this category of new social organisations, and is relevant here due to its support for the pursuit of compensation by former slave labourers and comfort women in Japanese courts. White *et al.* count it as a semi-official body, since it receives funding and staffing from the government. It lacks the voluntary nature of other groups, since all lawyers must join the organisation, but it plays an important role in coordinating and regulating this 'revitalised' profession (1996: 107).
5 For information on these, and other, groups, see Wanandi (2000).
6 Examples are the Global Forum of Japan, the Japan Centre for International Exchange and its sister organisation Global Thinknet, and the China Association for International Friendly Contact.
7 For discussions of how Track Two and other forms of communication between China and Japan have improved, see Wada (2000) and Asano (1998).

2 Sino-Japanese reconciliation during the Cold War

1 This in itself is problematic since it assumes that individuals rather than collectives (i.e., societies as a whole) are responsible for, or complicit in, the war crimes.
2 See Minear (2001, Chapter 5) for a full discussion of the problems of attempting to use a trial to create an authentic historical record of events.
3 For summaries and examples of these points of view see Dower (1999: 442–84), Minear (2001), Hosoya *et al.* (1986), and Maga (2001).
4 Specifically, they were found guilty on Count 55 'Disregard of duty to secure observance of and prevent breaches of Laws of War' (Minear 2001: 203).
5 For information on the suppression of evidence about biological and chemical experimentation, see Harris (1994).
6 Trials held by the Soviet Union are believed to have resulted in the execution of 3,000 Japanese, but some of those associated with Unit 731 were given lenient sentences. For example, twelve Japanese were tried at the Khabarovsk trial of December 1949 on charges of plotting to use biological weapons. All confessed and were repatriated to Japan by 1956 (Dower 1999: 449; Harris 1994: 229–30). In 1950 the Chinese Communists called for all Japan's top war criminals, including Emperor Hirohito, to stand trial for bacteriological warfare at an 'International War Crimes Tribunal' (Piccigallo 1979: 173).
7 The only trials to deal with comfort women were the Dutch trials held in Jakarta in 1948. They dealt only with Dutch comfort women. See Hicks (1995: 128–9).
8 Piccigallo's figures, based on Japanese Ministry of Justice data, are: 883 men on trial, 504 convicted, 149 death sentences, 83 life sentences (1979: 173). The Nanjing trial found four men guilty of participating in the Nanjing massacre (Tani Hisao, Mukai Toshiaki, Noda Tsuyoshi and Tanaka Gunkichi). For an account of the Nanjing trial see Yamamoto (2000: 190–233).
9 For an account of life in Fushun Prison, see the journal produced by the veterans' association *Chūkiren* Nos 1 and 2 (1997/6 and 1997/9) in which former internees write about the 'Fushun miracle' – the process by which they came to acknowledge, and repent for, the crimes they had committed in China.
10 For an excellent overview of this debate, see Wakabayashi (2000).
11 For more details on the nature of the Nanjing debate of the 1990s, see Fogel (2000), Yang (1999) and Yamamoto (2000).
12 The example refers to the criticism in the Chinese press in 1952 of Americans in the Nanjing Safety Zone who, according to the article, failed to protect Chinese citizens as the Japanese invaded in 1937.
13 For example, the Allied UN Declaration of January 1942, the Yalta Agreement,

the Cairo and Potsdam declarations and the Basic Post-Surrender Policy of the Far East Commission.

14 This was the 'Outline of China's claims for reparations from Japan' (*Zhanhou duiRi jianghe tiaojian gangyao*). Further statements emerged in 1947. See Yamagiwa (1991).

15 These figures have changed over time. The 1991 Human Rights White Paper published by the State Council of the PRC in November gave the following figures for damage suffered during the eight-year war against Japan: 21 million killed or wounded, 10 million massacred, 2 million labourers who died in North-east China, direct economic losses worth $62 billion, and indirect economic losses worth $500 billion (State Council of the PRC 1991). In 1995 Sun Pinghua, Chairman of the China–Japan Friendship Association, stated on the occasion of the 50th anniversary of the end of the war that the number of dead and injured totalled 35 million, and financial losses amounted to more than $100 billion (he was probably referring to direct financial loss). In 1998, President Jiang Zemin referred to a total of $600 billion in economic damage (Ryū 1999: 60).

16 The economic aid packages arranged between Chinese and Japanese governments since 1979 are generally regarded as reparations by proxy, but these packages were not discussed as part of the negotiations for normalisation in 1972 and cannot be regarded as official reparations.

17 Articles 14 (a) and (b) of the San Francisco Peace Treaty read as follows:

> 14 (a)
> It is recognized that Japan should pay reparations to the Allied Powers for the damage and suffering caused by it during the war. Nevertheless it is also recognized that the resources of Japan are not presently sufficient, if it is to maintain a viable economy, to make complete reparation for all such damage and suffering and at the same time meet its other obligations.
> Therefore
> 1. Japan will promptly enter into negotiations with Allied Powers so desiring, whose present territories were occupied by Japanese forces and damaged by Japan, with a view to assisting to compensate those countries for the cost of repairing the damage done, by making available the services of the Japanese people in production, salvaging and other work for the Allied Powers in question
> 2. (I) Subject to the provisions of subparagraph (II) below, each of the Allied Powers shall have the right to seize, retain, liquidate or otherwise dispose of all property, rights and interests of (a) Japan and Japanese nationals, (b) persons acting for or on behalf of Japan or Japanese nationals, and (c) entities owned or controlled by Japan or Japanese nationals (abridged).
> (b) Except as otherwise provided in the present Treaty, the Allied Powers waive all reparations claims of the Allied Powers, other claims of the Allied Powers and their nationals arising out of actions taken by Japan and its nationals in the course of the prosecution of the war, and claims of the Allied Powers for the direct military costs of the occupation.

18 Article 26 states:

> Japan will be prepared to conclude with any State which signed or adhered to the United Nations Declaration of 1 January 1942, and which is at war with Japan, or with any State which previously formed a part of the territory stated in Article 23, which is not a signatory of the present Treaty, a bilateral Treaty of Peace on the same or substantially the same terms as are provided for in the present Treaty, but this obligation on the part of Japan will expire

three years after the first coming into force of the present Treaty. Should Japan make a peace settlement or war claims settlement with any State granting that State greater advantages than those provided by the present Treaty, those same advantages shall be extended to the parties to the present Treaty.

19 For details on the negotiations see Yin (1996: 255–317).
20 The phrase 'The Republic of China voluntarily waives demands for compensation in services' was suggested by the Taiwanese on 19 March 1952 but the Japanese side wanted the phrase to read 'waives *all* demands for compensation'. The final version of the treaty read as follows: 'As a sign of magnanimity and good will towards the Japanese people, the Republic of China voluntarily waives the benefit of the services to be made available by Japan pursuant to Article 14(a) of the San Francisco Treaty.' Note that this phrase was not included in the treaty proper but appeared in section 1(b) of the Protocol attached to the treaty. Article 12, into which Taiwan wanted to insert the phrase about reparations instead read as follows in line with Japanese wishes: 'Any dispute that may arise out of the interpretation or application of the present Treaty shall be settled by negotiation or other pacific means.' Article 3 of the treaty allowed, ostensibly, for an agreement on the issue of claims against Japan to be negotiated separately. Such an agreement was never concluded between the two parties.
21 The background to China–Japan normalisation has been dealt with in some detail by a number of scholars. See, for example, Ogata (1988), Ijiri (1987), Fukui (1977) and Zhao (1993).
22 See for example Shimizu (1994). Himeda (1994: 150–5) also argues that the changes in the political situation in East Asia between 1945 and 1950 were such that the compensation issue was dropped without Japan having to deal with its war responsibility.
23 Note that this one-off payment was not considered a sufficient or satisfactory compensation by former British PoWs themselves (among others) who started their campaigns in the Japanese courts for an apology and compensation from the Japanese government in the late 1980s, resulting only in an *ex gratia* payment from the *British* government in 2000. For an interesting case study of the British former PoWs' struggle for compensation, see Preece (2001).
24 Tawara (1998) further points out the imbalance of Japan's reparations when compared with the government's payments to Japan's own veterans and bereaved families and also with Germany's record. In total, the amount of reparations made by the Japanese government to Asian countries was over ¥500 billion. Adding in renounced overseas industry, it would come to less than ¥1 trillion. Pensions for war veterans and consolation payments to their widows amounted to approximately ¥45 trillion between 1952 and 1997, and is currently about ¥2 trillion per annum. By 1994 Germany had paid over ¥7 trillion, and is not due to complete payments of ¥8.5 trillion until 2030 (ibid.: 127).

3 Uncovering the truth

1 The book included chapters written by Nishio Kanji and Takahashi Shirō, members of the Tsukuru kai.
2 Criticisms of Peace Osaka (Osaka International Peace Centre) – which was built in the 1990s with the aim of conveying to the younger generation the tragedies of war and a respect for peace – were launched in 1996 at the height of the textbook offensive (Nakakita 2000: 232–3).
3 For a more detailed account of the struggle for history education, see Nozaki and Inokuchi (1998).
4 The textbook screening process is as follows: a publisher submits a manuscript

('white-cover text') to the MoE textbook division. One ministry inspector and three external inspectors produce a report which is passed on to the Textbook Authorisation Research Council (TARC). The TARC reviews the report and makes a recommendation (pass/fail/recommendations for revision). If changes are required, the authors must revise the text and re-submit it.

5 Professor Ienaga sued the Japanese government three times to protest against the revisions made to his textbooks. These cases are listed in Appendix 1, and Nozaki and Inokuchi provide a detailed account of the lawsuits and their outcomes (1998).

6 In fact, the claim that the textbooks authorised in 1982 contained the word 'advance' in relation to Japan's actions in China was an error on the part of the Japanese press which first reported the results of the screening process, and which formed the basis of the Chinese government's protest. See Johnson (1986), Rose (1998), Kim (1983), Dirlik (1996), and Hirano (2000) for detailed accounts of the 1982 textbook issue.

7 Note that the Japanese media took a different view of the state of textbooks in 1984, arguing that screening in 1984 was seen to be as tight as ever, even though the term 'invasion' or 'aggression' had remained untouched by textbook examiners in line with the 1982 pledge. The *Daily Yomiuri* reported that textbook writers felt that screening had in fact become even stricter, despite the Chinese and South Korean protests of 1982 (2 July 1984, 'War History Textbooks Again Purged Heavily'). The number of victims of the Rape of Nanjing remained an area of concern to Ministry of Education examiners also, and textbook writers were asked to provide sources and/or indicate that there is no consensus on the number of victims. The *Japan Times* reported on the Ministry of Education's continuing trend towards the sanitisation of war atrocities in high-school textbooks, noting that the textbooks for use in 1985 had 'deleted all reference to the notorious Ishii Regiment and its biological experiments in China, on the grounds that "historians are still in the process of gathering historical data".' In addition, passages referring to the 'abuse' of women during the Rape of Nanjing were questioned by the textbook examiners who argued that 'such things were common practice in war' (2 July 1984, p. 2). The Chinese response to the 1984 screening consisted of some critical press coverage. For example, Xinhua criticised the Ministry of Education's rejection of authors' explanations of the start of the hostilities in 1937 in terms of Japanese troops attacking Chinese troops, preferring instead to keep the original version (in the 1982 textbooks): 'the Sino-Japanese war was triggered by conflicts between Japanese and Chinese troops stationed near Peking'. On the other hand, Xinhua approved of the use of 'aggression' rather than 'advance' (into Manchuria), and noted that the phrase referring to the Nanjing Massacre being 'triggered by resistance by the Chinese military and civilians' had been dropped (*Daily Yomiuri*, 2 July 1984 'Chinese blast "inaccurate" new textbooks' and *Japan Times*, 3 July 1984, 'China raps history accounts in new high school textbooks').

8 But this softening of the Ministry of Education's stance did not necessarily signal a complete change of policy. Tawara and Ishiyama argue that after 1982 neither the Ministry of Education nor the government made *fundamental* improvements to the textbook system as a whole, and there was never any acknowledgement that the system had been flawed or errors made. Also, textbook authorisation continued to 'beautify the emperor system', and middle-school social science and civics textbooks were used to push for support of the creation of a 'country that can go to war' (1995: 68).

9 The New Frontier Party was formed by Hata Tsutomu and Ozawa Ichirō in 1993 as a breakaway party from the LDP, and was therefore largely conservative in its political leanings.

10 For a discussion of the revision of the defence guidelines and its implications, see

Hook *et al.* (2001: 140–2). In May 2000 Prime Minister Mori commented that 'Japan is truly a divine country (*kami no kuni*) centred on the Emperor' (*Asahi shinbun*, 16 May 2000, evening edition). For a discussion of the significance of the national flag and anthem issue in Japan, see Aspinall and Cave (2001). For examples of the Chinese view of the Japanese 'turn to the right' in the 1990s, see Bu (2000b: 177), and also Bu (2000a: 175–7). Wang Xinsheng, Liu Shilong and Jin Xide made similar comments to me in interviews.

11 A strategy used by the Japanese military in China and South-east Asia – kill all, burn all, loot all.

12 For critical analyses of the Tsukuru kai's activities and the new textbook, see Tawara (2000), Nelson (2002), Beal *et al.* (2001), Morris-Suzuki (2000), Kersten (2003) and Takahashi (2003).

13 The 2002 *Kyōkasho Repōto* gives an adoption figure of 0.039 per cent, compared with, say, Tokyo Shoseki's *Atarashi shakai: Rekishi* (New society: history) which was adopted by the majority (51.3 per cent) of schools (Shuppan Rōren 2002: 66).

14 This group originated from The National League for Support of the School Textbook Screening Suit (Kyōkasho kentei soshō o shi'en suru zengoku renrakukai), the support group behind Ienaga Saburō's various court cases, which was disbanded in 1998 after Ienaga's partial victory.

15 For further information on these groups, visit the home page of Children and Textbooks Japan Network 21 and the Asian Network for History Education, Japan (Rekishi kyōiki Ajia nettowāku). Please refer to Appendix 2 for URLs.

16 December 2000 Appeal by Japanese Historians and History Educators, available at http://www.ne.jp/asahi/kyokasho/net21/e-yukou-seimei2001205.html (accessed 4 October 2001).

17 'Deeply concerned about the regressive history textbooks, we urge the Japanese government to take appropriate action' available at http://www.iwanami.co.jp/jpworld/text/statement01.html (accessed 23 July 2001) .

18 An English translation of the conference declaration can be found at http://www.angelfire.com/ny2/village/textbook-conf.html (accessed 6 August 2003).

19 The Chinese had previously lodged their concern in September 2000 in response to the news about plans for the new textbook (Su 2001a: 131).

20 The *Renmin Ribao* continues to be the official mouthpiece of the CCP, and its content remains under tight control from central government. It therefore serves as a useful indicator of the official line on an issue such as Japanese history textbooks. A rough count of articles printed in the *Renmin Ribao* (and its online version *Renminwang*) revealed that between 3 April 2001 and 14 July 2001 approximately 65–70 articles appeared which related in some way to the textbook issue. These came under the headings: 'the distortion of history issue', 'China's attitude', 'other countries' responses', 'related articles', and 'Japanese right-wing ravings (*kuangyan*)'. They ranged from short press release-type articles simply noting the diplomatic exchanges of the day to longer, more critical, articles and editorials explaining the Japanese textbook system and the attempts of right-wing groups to distort history.

21 It would seem that in responding to China's demands, the Japanese government, (and in this case, the publisher Fusōsha), paid greater attention to the South Korean protests than to the Chinese – as was the case with the 1982 textbook problem. Su Zhiliang suggests that the different treatment offered to Korea (for example, on the apology issue as well as the textbook problem) is a deliberate policy to weaken the Korea–China relationship, and isolate China (Su 2001a: 139). A more likely explanation is that the South Korean campaign was more sustained and organised (as it had been in 1982 also), and was helped by the cooperation with Japanese NGOs who joined forces with their Korean counterparts to demonstrate and put pressure on the Japanese government and the textbook

company. On the Korean side, the Korean Civilian Movement for Correcting Japan-distorted Textbooks (http://www.japantext.net) – a coalition of 80 civic groups formed in 2001 – joined forces with 10 Japanese groups (including the Kyōkasho netto 21) to campaign against the textbook and the activities of the Tsukuru kai groups (*Korea Herald*, 31 January 2002).

22 For reports on conferences held in China on history-related problems, see various issues of *KangRi zhanzheng yanjiu*. One workshop held at the Institute of History at Beijing University in January 2001 brought together Chinese scholars to discuss the problem of textbook revisionism; another in April 2001 was hosted by the Chinese Academy of Social Sciences (CASS) and involved thirty leading historians (see special issue of *KangRi zhanzheng yanjiu*, 2000, issue 2).

23 For a summary of the outcome of the Japan–South Korea Joint Study Group on History Textbooks, see Kimijima (2000). In 2001, Prime Minister Koizumi and President Kim Daejung agreed on the establishment of another Joint Historical Research Organisation.

24 On the Chinese side, the project includes Rong Weimu, Su Zhiliang, Bu Ping, Wang Xiliang and others, and, on the Japanese side, Tawara Yoshifumi, Arai Shin'ichi and others. Those I spoke to were hopeful that once the middle-school text was completed, they would be able to produce a high-school version too. For reports on the Nanjing and Tokyo conferences, see the Asian Network for History Education, Japan available at http://www.jca.apc.org/asia-net

25 See, for example, the description of activities undertaken between 1993 and 1997 for the History Association, Sino-Japanese History Education Exchange and Cooperation Visits (Rekishikyō nitchū rekishi kyōiku kōryū no tabi) in Rekishi kyōikusha kyōgikai (1997: 303).

26 See http://www.mofa.go.jp/policy/postwar/outline.html (accessed 10 July 2003).

27 For details on this and other youth exchanges on the war issue, see Shōwa kōkō chiri rekishi kenkyūbu (1998).

28 The content of some of these websites can be distinctly anti-Japanese and dubious in terms of factual accuracy, attesting to the democratic nature of the Internet. Chinese websites and discussion boards can be virulently anti-Japanese, and the government has closed down some sites. Similarly, the websites run by Japanese nationalist groups contain highly inflammatory content.

4 The search for justice

1 For discussion of this movement for compensation, see Ts'ai (2001). For a list of all compensation cases brought in Japanese courts from 1972 to 2000, see Tawara Yoshifumi's home page http://www.linkclub.or.jp/~teppei-y/tawara%20HP/index.html

2 This is also the view of the Chinese scholars I interviewed. Bu Ping refers to the end of the Cold War as the end of the San Francisco system which meant that 'the US could no longer cover up Japan's war responsibility, forcing the issue of Japan's war responsibility (which had not been acknowledged) into the open, and opening the route to compensation'. The 'incompleteness' of the post-war tribunals and the US protection of Japan are at fault. The second reason for the proliferation of cases is the growth of civil society in Japan since the end of the war, and Japan's economic growth. Third is the interaction of Japanese NGOs in international matters and the power of these groups to put pressure on domestic policy makers (Bu 2000a: 170–1).

3 Much has been written on comfort women and the struggle for recognition. For a selection written in English see Yoshimi (2000), Barkan (2000), Soh (1996) and Tanaka (2001).

4 For details on how the fund was to be run see Brooks (1999: 128–31) and Soh (2001).

5 For a list of 23 NGOs involved in the comfort women movement see *Bulletin of Concerned Asian Scholars*, 1994 26 (4) http://csf.Colorado.edu/bcas (accessed 5 July 2003).

6 A number of Japanese NGOs actively supported the recommendations of the UN Commission on Human Rights. See '23 Japanese NGOs Issue Joint Appeal in Support of McDougall', http://ww.korea-np.co.jp (accessed 2 May 2002).

7 Information on the details and dates of the various proposals are inconsistent. It seems that a number of proposals were submitted to the NPC in 1991 and to the joint conference of the NPC and the CPPCC in 1992. See Asahi Shinbunsha, *Sengohoshō mondai shūzaiban* (1994), and the special issue of *Falü yu shenghuo* (*Law and Life*), July 1992. See also Okuda and Kawashima (2000: 227) for Tong Zeng's activities and the Chinese governmental response. *Chūgoku Kenkyū* 1991 (vol. 21) contains the full text of Tong Zeng's proposal.

8 Jiang (1998: 11) provides the same figures, explaining that the estimated amount of compensation due to China because of the Japanese invasion of 1931–45 amounted to $30 billion (presumably using the estimate produced by the GMD in 1946 rather than the CCP's figure produced in 1951), of which $18 billion was due as compensation. See also Okuda and Kawashima (2000: 227) for Tong Zeng's activities and the Chinese response.

9 Tong Zeng's activities were curbed in the mid-1990s when he was sent to Qinghai to work for the China Geriatric Society.

10 This is the short title for the group, which takes its name from the Chinese word for compensation.

11 See Tawara's homepage for a more complete list. Appendix 2 has the URLs of this and other websites relating to compensation cases.

12 For details on where the forced labourers were sent and the Japanese companies involved, see Sensō giseisha (ed.) (1995). Statistics vary. Some Chinese media reports have set the figure at 50,000; Murayama gives 47,000 for Chinese, 1m for Koreans (1999: 140); *Shūkan Kinyōbi* gives 40,000 (1994: 16). According to the Japanese Ministry of Foreign Affairs, the numbers are 38,395 forcibly moved to Japan, of whom 6,830 did not survive.

13 For information on how the material was discovered, see NHK (1994).

14 An example of joint cooperation between Chinese, Japanese and American law firms or Bar Federations is described in the November 2000 edition of the quarterly newsletter of The Chinese Holocaust (produced by the Temporary Chinese Holocaust Museum of the United States). Professor Zhang Yibo (Liaoning Provincial Party School) and lawyer Yang Li (born in Shenyang but practising in New York) were active in making contact with approximately 1,000 former forced labourers. In cooperation with other lawyers, Yang brought a suit against Mitsui and Mitsubishi in May 2000 on behalf of two American-based Chinese, Wen Jenhan and Wang Songlin, plus 8,200 others. The lawyers involved in the case were Xing Anxhen, Liu Huanxin (China), Onodera Toshitaka and Takahashi Akira (Japan) and Yang Li (US). Chinese Holocaust Museum Newsletter, 4 November 2000. http://www.chineseholocaust.org/chmq4.html (accessed 9 January 2002).

15 'Lawsuits to seek compensation from Japanese corporations that used slave laborers during WWII', http://www.milberg.com (accessed 12 June 2002).

16 Chinese Holocaust Museum Newsletter, November 2000; *New York Times*, 23 August 2000, 'China Hopes for Labor Compensation'.

17 Statements of interest represent the US government view and have tended to preclude claims against the Japanese government or companies under the 1951 San Francisco Peace Treaty (Bazyler 2001: 75).

18 See 'Plaintiffs' Response to United States' Statement of Interest', in Hwang Geum

Joo versus Japan, case number 00CV02233 submitted by Cohen, Milstein, Hausfeld and Toll. Available at http://www.cmht.com (accessed 3 July 2002).

19 This refers to a riot at the camp in June 1945 by the internees, which was quickly put down by the camp guards and led to the torture and killing of 100 Chinese slave labourers (Macintyre 1996).

20 For the exact wording of the settlement, see *Wakai jōkō* (Settlement terms) http://www.jca.apc.org/~hanaoka/wakaisho.html (accessed 28 May 2003). See also CNN.com 29, November 2000. According to this report, the first ever successful claim against a Japanese company had been settled in July 2000 with Nachi-Fujikoshi Corp Machine Tools agreeing to pay ¥30 to 40 million to three Korean claimants.

21 Kathy Masaoka and Ayako Hagihara (undated) 'NCRR joins Tokyo group to report on landmark settlement' http://www.ncrr-la.org (accessed 24 June 2002).

22 For more details of the court case, see Niimi (1998), Uchida (2001a, 2001b).

23 The similarities between the Hanaoka fund and the German fund *are* striking, but in a less positive sense than Uchida implies. The German fund was to amount to 10 billion marks, paid half by the German government and half by companies who had benefited from the toil of 10–15 million forced labourers during the war. Niven explains, however, that the 1.5 million people still alive in 2000 would receive a 'pittance' of 5,000 to 15,000 marks, and only if the German companies actually paid the money to the fund. As of early March 2001, 'only 3.6 billion marks' had been paid in, and 'even this money had not always been willingly provided' (Niven 2002: 234).

24 Li Xiuying survived a vicious attack by Japanese soldiers during the occupation of Nanjing and was one of the plaintiffs involved in a lawsuit brought against the Japanese government in 1995 (for more information on this ongoing case, see Suopei home page, referring to the lawsuit 'Nanjing/Unit 731/Indiscriminate bombing'). In the meantime, she and her lawyers brought an anti-defamation lawsuit in 1999 against Japanese writer Matsumura Toshio who had accused her of being a 'false witness' in a book on the Nanjing Massacre published in 1998. The Tokyo Supreme Court ruled in her favour in April 2003, fining Matsumura, but not demanding a public apology (*People's Daily Online*, 11 April 2003).

25 For the full wording of the 1990 Statement, the 2000 settlement and other Hanaoka-related documents and articles, see http://www.jca.apc.org/~hanaoka

26 A damning criticism of the treatment by the Japanese lawyers of the Huagang shounanzhe lianyihui was sent in the form of an open letter to the lawyers by one of the plaintiffs, Sun Li. See http://www.jca.apc.org/~hanaoka (accessed 28 May 2003).

27 The statistics according to Sensō higaisha o kokoro ni kizamu Nanjing shūkaihen (1995) are: eleven Mitsui branches, using 6,476 labourers, of whom 1,072 died.

28 Transcripts of the judgements (in Japanese) can be found at: http://courtdomino2.courts.go.jp by searching for the case numbers (1550, 1690, and 3862).

29 Suopei list the case on their *Saiban nittei* page (http://suopei.org/event/saiban-j.html). See also www.20.u-page.so-net.ne.jp/yc4/ikenaga/topic.htm

30 As of May 2003, the appeals were still pending in the Fukuoka High Court. For updates on the progress of this and other cases go to: http://www.suopei.org/event/saiban-j.html

31 One exception was Wan Aihua who spoke harrowingly at the International Public Hearing on Post-war Compensation by Japan held in Tokyo, December 1992, describing how she had been disowned by her family and never married because of her experiences (Hicks 1995: 217; Su 2000b: 168).

32 Su and Chen (1998a) provide an overview of research into Chinese comfort women. See also Jiang (1998) and Tanaka (2001).

33 Produced by the Chinese Academy of Social Sciences, Modern History Research Centre since 1991.

34 See *Sensō Sekinin Kenkyū*, 2000, vol. 27, which contains a series of reports on research into comfort stations in Shanghai and Nanjing undertaken by Chinese and Japanese academics and researchers.

35 See for example, Bu (2000b) and Su (2001b). There have been a number of joint China–Japan and international conferences on the comfort women and other issues. Reports on these conferences can be found in journals such as *Riben xuekan* and *KangRi zhanzheng yanjiu*.

36 The mathematical calculation by which this figure is reached is somewhat complex, and can only be an estimate. For an abridged English translation of the article by Su and Chen see 'A Brief Discussion of the Institution of "Comfort Women" among Japanese Invading Armies in China', in *Social Sciences in China* vol. 21, no. 1, 2000, pp. 125–46. For a Japanese viewpoint which agrees with some of Su and Chen's estimates, see the special issue of *Sensō Sekinin Kenkyū*, no. 27, 2000, pp. 2–34 ('Chūgoku Shanhai, Nankin no Nihongun ianfu tokoro').

37 For details of the names of those who attended the tribunal, see Su (2001b: 225–33).

38 Okamura confessed in his memoirs to his role in establishing a comfort station in Shanghai in 1932 (see Hicks 1995: 19). Considered 'Number One Japanese war criminal in China' in the mid-1940s, he was nonetheless acquitted in Shanghai in 1949 (Piccigallo 1979: 167).

39 Originally the AWF was concerned with activities in the Philippines, Korea and Taiwan. In 1997 and 1998, the trustees of the AWF signed memoranda of understanding with the governments of the Netherlands and Indonesia respectively, and various projects have since been implemented in these countries. The wording of the MoFA's 'Recent Policy of the Government of Japan on the Issue known as "Wartime Comfort Women"' (as of January 2003) states that the Japanese government will 'continue its effort to seek the understanding from the Governments and authorities and other parties of the countries and regions concerned with regard to the activities of the AWF', thus offering a means by which Chinese comfort women could be offered support. Given the controversy surrounding the AWF in Korea, Taiwan and the Netherlands, however, such a move (which would have to be undertaken by the Chinese government) would probably exacerbate the problem. See http://www.mofa.go.jp/policy/women/fund/policy.html (accessed 10 July 2003).

40 The Shimonoseki branch of the Yamaguchi Prefectural Court has thus far been the only court to rule in favour of (Korean) comfort women. In 1998 it ordered the Japanese government to pay ¥300,000, but that ruling was overturned in 2001. See Nearey (2001).

41 The full text of the 'Comfort women complaint', brought by Cohen, Milstein, Hausfeld and Toll is available at http://www.cmht.com (accessed 3 July 2002).

42 For the Memorandum Opinion on Comfort Women Case, see http://www.cmht.com (accessed 3 July 2002).

43 Bu Ping 'A research report on Japanese use of chemical weapons during WWII' (unpublished manuscript). Estimates vary widely, for example, Ji Xueren gives 80,000 injured and 10,000 deaths (cited in Deng and Evans 1997: 102).

44 See for example Sheldon Harris (1994), Powell (1981), Williams and Wallace (1989), Guo (1997), Zenkokukyō (1997).

45 This is the 'Convention on the Prohibition of the Development, Production, Stockpiling and Use of Chemical Weapons and on their Destruction', a multilateral treaty which entered into force in 1997 and which China and Japan both ratified. Under the CWC any state which has abandoned chemical weapons in the territory of another state is obliged to declare information about the chemical

weapons and must provide financial, technical, expert and other help to retrieve, store and destroy them (Evans 1997).

46 See 'Statement by Press Secretary', available at http://www.mofa.go.jp announce/announce/203/8/0812.html (accessed 6 March 2004).

47 It should be noted that Japanese citizens were also victims of biological warfare. See Tamanoi (2000).

48 In fact, the lawsuit was made up of two cases – the first case was filed in August 1997 (108 claimants, case number 16684), the second in December 1999 (72 claimants, case number 27579) – but they were treated as one.

49 For more details on the investigative process and the trial itself, see http://homepage2.nifty.com/73/saikinsen (accessed 22 July 2002) and the webpages of the Association for the Clarification of the Japanese Army's Biological Warfare (see Appendix 2 for URLs).

50 The BBC aired a documentary (*Unit 731*) in February 2002 which focused on Wang Xuan's campaign.

51 http://www.anti731saikinsen.net/en/bassui-en.html (accessed 7 July 2003).

52 http://www.anti731saikinsen.net/en/seimei-en.html (accessed 7 July 2003).

53 For further background on this case, see http://suopei.org/saiban/dokugasu/gasnews_j.html (accessed 3 July 2002).

54 The Support Group for Victims of Japan's Abandoned Chemical Weapons (Nihon ga nokoshita doku gasu higaisha o sasaerukai) has produced a series of pamphlets about this case, and produces regular newsletters. It organises symposia and fund-raising events in conjunction with Suopei, and other groups such as ABC kigyō iinkai, Nihon Chūgoku yūkō kyōkai, and Nihon no sensō sekinin shiryō sentā. See, for example, *Doku gasu shiryō* (Materials on Poison Gas), vols 1–3.

55 http://suopei.org/saiban/dokugasu/jiken.html (accessed 3 July 2002).

56 http://suopei.org/saiban/dokugasu/jiken.html (accessed 3 July 2002).

57 http://suopei.org/saiban/dokugasu/jiken.html (accessed 3 July 2002).

58 The verdict can be found at http://courtdomino2.courts.go.jp by searching for case number 22021.

59 These include the Hague Convention 1907 (signed by Japan); the Treaty of Versailles 1919 (not signed by Japan; but Japanese were on the panel of fifteen who created the document); the International Convention for the Suppression of the Traffic in Women and Children 1921–22 (ratified by Japan in 1925); the Geneva Convention 1949; the Slavery Convention, 1815 (not signed by Japan but international customary law by the twentieth century); International Labour Organization Concerning Forced or Compulsory Labour (ratified by Japan 1932). See Nearey (2001).

60 This is not so cut and dried. Government assistance to Japan's *hibakusha*, for example, was very slow and inadequate. See Orr (2001), Chapter 6.

61 By 2000, a number of cases involving Japanese companies, in addition to the Kajima/Hanaoka case, had been settled. Examples are NKK, Nippon Steel and Mitsubishi Heavy Industries (Fisher 2000: 36). The latter refused to pay out in accordance with the court's suggestion (*The Economist*, 8 July 2000).

62 For a transcript of the proposal, see http://www.vcn.bc.ca/alpha/learn/SexualAct.htm (accessed 4 October 2001).

5 Settling the past

1 This refers to the wording of one section of the revised US-Japan Defence Guidelines which contained an ambiguous reference to the nature of Japan's response should an emergency arise in 'areas surrounding Japan'.

2 The full text of the declaration can be found at http://www.mofa.go.jp/region/ asiapaci/china/visit98/joint.html (accessed 18 January 1999).

3 It is perhaps worth noting that while the Japan–China declaration included the word aggression, the Japan–Korea declaration did not. This was despite attempts by the Korean negotiators to have it included (*Asahi shinbun*, 20 October 1998: 7). The wording of the relevant section of the Japan–Korea joint declaration, which echoes former Prime Minister Murayama's statement of 15 August 1995, is as follows:

> Looking back on the relations between Japan and the Republic of Korea during this century, Prime Minister Obuchi regarded in a spirit of humility the fact of history that Japan caused, during a certain period in the past, tremendous damage and suffering to the people of the Republic of Korea through its colonial rule, and expressed his deep remorse and heartfelt apology for this fact.

The English translation of the full text can be found at http://www.mofa.go.jp (accessed 21 February 2004).

4 After their first meeting on the 26th, for example, Jiang and Obuchi were able to announce plans for the latter two years of the fourth yen loan package. A total amount of ¥390 billion was settled on for fiscal years 1998–2000 for a total number of twenty-eight projects. This was an increase on the total of ¥580 billion for fiscal years 1996–98 and centred on environmental projects, development of rural areas, and, in the wake of the Yangtze floods, dam construction. On the cultural side, both sides agreed to set up a youth exchange programme, starting from 1999, with the aim of sending a total of 15,000 young people on reciprocal visits in fields such as sport, education, culture and science. For the full list of activities outlined in the action plan, see Satō (2001).

5 For some of the British coverage see *The Economist*, November 1998, *Electronic Telegraph*, 25 November 1998 and 27 November 1998.

6 http://www.fmprc.gov.cn (accessed 3 August 2002).

7 http://www.mofa.go.jp (accessed 9 August 1999).

8 For the full text in Japanese, see http://www.mofa.go.jp (accessed 21 February 2004).

9 This view was confirmed in various interviews in Beijing, March 2003.

10 The wording of the various prime ministerial addresses can be found at http:// www.kantei.go.jp. Koizumi's 2002 address can be found at http:// www.kantei.go.jp/foreign/koizumispeech/2002/08/15sikiji_e.html.

11 The shrine's role was reaffirmed in 1939 with another reorganisation of Shinto shrines and an increase in the number of memorial shrines (Totman 2000: 435). A national network of shrines was created with Yasukuni at the top, over 100 regional shrines acting as local branches of Yasukuni (*gokoku jinja* – country-protecting shrines), and thousands of local war memorials (*chūkonhi* – monument for loyal souls) (O'Brien 1996: 2).

12 Between 1969 and 1974 five attempts were made to put the 'Yasukuni Shrine Protection Bill' through the Diet, but it was defeated by the opposition parties on each occasion (Tanaka 2000).

13 *Renmin Ribao*, 3 September 1975 'Jinian kangRi zhanzheng xingli 30 zhounian' (Commemorating the 30th anniversary of victory in the anti-Japanese war), reproduced in Tian (1997: 190).

14 Anti-Japanese student demonstrations in China in September and October targeted Nakasone in particular, protesting against an apparent rise in Japanese militarism and Japan's second (economic) invasion of China. While the protests were also a product of dissatisfaction with the Chinese government, they nonethe-

less demonstrated the way anti-Japanese sentiment in China could easily be ignited.

15 In the wake of Nakasone's official visit, religious and opposition groups filed lawsuits claiming that official obeisance visits violated the Constitution. The results of two of these cases offered hope to those who wanted to maintain a strict separation between the state and religion, since both (Iwate and Ehime) ruled that official visits by the prime minister were unconstitutional (Tanaka 2000). But other cases produced contradictory judgments, highlighting the domestic confusion over the issue. See O'Brien (1996) for a discussion of these lawsuits. Koizumi's August 2001 visit to the Yasukuni Shrine also prompted a lawsuit, brought by over 1,200 plaintiffs (see Tanaka 2002: 210).

16 'Vice Foreign Minister Wang Yi urgently summons Japanese Ambassador Koreshige Anami to make solemn representations' http://www.fmprc.gov.cn/eng/16855.html (accessed January 16 2002).

17 The visit was also an important opportunity to explain Japan's response to the September 11 attacks on the World Trade Center and gather support for President Bush's anti-terrorist strategies.

18 By contrast, Koizumi's visit to Korea, where he laid a wreath at the National Cemetery, was marked by anti-Japanese rallies in major Korean cities where civil groups protested about textbooks, the lack of action to back up an apology and other Japan–Korea disputes. See *Korea Times Online*, 15 October 2001, 'Anti-Koizumi protests engulfs Korea', http://www.imadr.org/attention/japan.yasukuni.html (accessed 26 July 2003).

19 Yasukuni jinja sanpai ni kansuru shokan http://kantei.go.jp/jp/koizumispeech/2002/04/21shokan.html

20 For an example of the sort of protests being sent to Prime Minister Koizumi see 'Koizumi shushō Yasukuni jinja sanpai iken ajia soshō dan "kōgi seimei"' http://www3.justnet.ne.jp/~hal9000/yasukuni/kougi0421.htm

21 Chinese Foreign Ministry, 14 January 2003, Waijiaobu fubuzhang Yang Wenchang jiu Riben shouxiang canbai Jingguo shenshe xiang Rifan tichu yanzheng jiaoshe (Vice Foreign Minister Yang Wenchang makes solemn representation to Japan in response to prime minister's visit to Yasukuni Shrine), http://www.fmprc.gov.cn (accessed 27 July 2003).

22 For a sample of the counter-argument to a new facility, see *Japan Echo*, June 2003 and the Yasukuni Shrine website (http://www.yasukuni.jp).

23 Tang Jiaxuan to LDP/New Komeitō/New Conservative Party delegation to China in July 2001. See *Asahi shinbun Online*, 11 July 2002.

24 For more details about the origins of these various museum and memorials see Li (1992), Duan (1992), and Tanaka (2002). The exhibition relating to the anti-Japanese war at Beijing's Museum of History and Museum of the Revolution was undergoing refurbishment at the time of writing.

25 For the counter-plan produced by the Heiwa Izokukai, see Arai (1994).

26 I am grateful to Carol Rank for bringing this organisation to my attention. See Appendix 2 for URL.

6 Conclusion

1 Whiting (1989) discusses the attempts of the Chinese media in the 1980s to develop a more positive image of Japan.

2 Dudden comments on the importance of restoring dignity to the surviving women at the Women's Tribunal:

It is vital that Japanese society accord dignity to these women in order for their stories to be believed and take hold as a social concern. Acceptance of a narrator's credibility rests on the respect of the listeners who claim to share the same history.

(2001: 593–4)

3 For example, Wang Xiliang sees this as a necessity if the movement is to have any success in future.
4 Eykholt points out that 'criticism of government concessions to Japan had appeared clandestinely' in the early 1980s (2000: 37). Individual victims also refer to the government's magnanimous policy (i.e., the decision to waive reparations in 1972), but insist that the debts of blood must still be repaid by the Japanese government (see letter to Hashimoto from Ma Yingzi, quoted in Su 1999: 372).
5 Interview with Rong Weimu, Institute of Modern History, CASS, March 2003.
6 Interviews with Jin Xide of the Institute of Japanese Studies, CASS, and Wang Xinsheng, Beijing University, History Department, March 2003.
7 Interviews with Wang Xinsheng and Jin Xide, March 2003.

Bibliography

Online newspapers and news services

Asahi Online 11 July 2001 'Beijing stands firm on Yasukuni' http://www.asahi.com (accessed 23 July 2001).
—— 19 March 2003 'China's new leadership line-up eyes firmer Japan ties' http://www.asahi.com (accessed 14 June 2003).
—— 25 April 2003 'Court rejects suit over wartime rapes' http://www.asahi.com (accessed 9 July 2003).
BBC News Online 8 October 2001 'Koizumi apologises to China' http://news.bbc.co.uk (accessed 11 July 2002).
China 918.net April 27 2002 'Dongjing fayuan queren rijun ceng dui zhongguo funu shishi xingbaoli' (Tokyo court acknowledges Japanese military practised sexual violence against Chinese women) http://www.china918.net (accessed 11 July 2002).
China Daily Online 29 January 2002 'Good Sino-Japanese ties beneficial' http://www1.chinadaily.com.cn.
CNN.com 29 November 2000 'Japan builder to compensate Chinese WWII workers, report says' http://www.cnn.com (accessed 10 April 2001).
—— 21 June 2001 '"Sex slaves" win support against Japan' http://cnn.worldnews (accessed 21 June 2001).
—— 31 December 2001 'Downward spiral for Japan-Sino ties' http://cnn.worldnews (accessed 26 August 2002).
—— 24 April 2002 'China delays Japan trip after shrine visit' http://cnn.worldnews (accessed 26 August 2002).
Daily Yomiuri Online 22 April 2001 'Beijing grumbles over Lee visa, history text' http://www.yomiuri.co.jp (accessed 22 April 2001).
Daily Yomiuri Online 11 July 2001 'Jiang criticizes Koizumi over visit to Yasukuni' http://www.yomiuri.co.jp (accessed 13 July 2001).
Electronic Telegraph 25 November 1998 'Jiang hopes to end the saga of war apologies' http://www.telegraph.co.uk (accessed 16 April 1999).
—— 27 November 1998 'Jiang attacked over war apology failure' http://www.telegraph.co.uk (accessed 16 April 1999).
Japan Times Online 20 September 2000 'Ex-sex slaves file suit in U.S.' http://www.japantimes.co.jp (accessed 23 October 2000).
—— 14 October 2000 'Mori, Zhu vow to build a better future' http://www.japantimes.co.jp (accessed 23 October 2000).
—— 15 October 2000 'Japan "has never apologized": Zhu' http://www.japantimes.co.jp (accessed 23 October 2000).

—— 13 July 2001 'Family wins 20 million yen for laborer's time on the run' http://www.japantimes.co.jp (accessed 13 July 2001).

—— 6 August 2001 'Yasukuni visit "will certainly be made", says Yamasaki' http://www.japantimes.co.jp (accessed 8 July 2001).

—— 27 April 2002 'Forced laborers win suit' http://www.japantimes.co.jp (accessed 2 July 2002).

—— 10 August 2002 'Koizumi indicates trip to China is off the itinerary' http://www.japantimes.co.jp (accessed 26 August 2002).

Korea Herald 31 January 2002 'South Korean, Japanese civic groups form joint body on textbooks' http://www.koreaherald.co.kr (accessed 10 February 2002).

Kyodo News 18 October 2000 'US lawyer sees huge awards for Chinese war crime victims' http://www.findarticles.com (accessed 21 June 2001).

Mainichi Interactive 24 April 2003 'Sex slaves denied damages for wartime abuse' http://mdn.mainichi.co.jp (accessed 9 July 2003).

Muzi.com 26 August 2002 'Chinese men sue Japanese government' http://dailynews.muzi.com (accessed 26 August 2002).

—— 20 September 2002 'China wants war criminals removed from Yasukuni Shrine' http://latelinenews.com (accessed 26 September 2002).

People's Daily Online (English) 3 April 2001 'China slams Japan over history textbook' http://english.peopledaily.com.cn (accessed 3 August 2002).

—— 9 July 2001 'Japan's decision on textbook unacceptable' http://english.peopledaily.com.cn (accessed 3 August 2002).

—— 19 September 2001 'Nation commemorates September 18' http://www.china.org.cn (accessed 13 July 2003).

—— 9 October 2001 'Japanese PM Koizumi apologizes to the Chinese people' http://fpeng.peopledaily.com.cn (accessed 14 June 2003).

—— 15 January 2002 'Experts advise Chinese WWII laborers to file class action' http://english.peopledaily.com.cn (accessed 12 June 2002).

—— 21 April 2002 'Chinese Vice-FM summons Japanese Ambassador over Japanese PM's shrine visit' http://english.peopledaily.com.cn (accessed 13 August 2002).

—— 23 April 2002 'Massacre victims protest Japanese PM's shrine visit' http://english.peopledaily.com.cn (accessed 13 August 2002).

—— 28 August 2002 'Victims of germ warfare protest over Japanese court ruling' http://english/peopledaily.com.cn (accessed 28 August 2002).

—— 11 April 2003 'Chinese war survivor wins anti-defamation lawsuit in Tokyo' http://english.peopledaily.com.cn (accessed 9 July 2003).

People's Daily Online (Chinese) 12 April 2001 'Wo zhuRi dashi yaoqiu Ri yansu duidai lishi jiaokeshu wenti' (Chinese Ambassador demands that Japan deals ser iously with the textbook problem) http://www.people.com.cn (accessed 16 May 2001).

—— 13 April 2001 'Wo daibiao zai lianheguo renquanhuishang qianze riben jiaokeshu waiqu lishi' (China condemns Japan's distorted history in UN Human Rights Committee) http://www.people.com.cn (accessed 16 May 2001).

—— 7 May 2001 'Tang Jiaxuan waizhang yu Riben waixiang Tianzhong Zenjizi tong dianhua' (FM Tang Jiaxuan and Japan's FM Tanaka Makiko talk on the phone) http://www.people.com.cn (accessed 16 May 2001).

—— 8 May 2001 'Lishi burong waiqu; zhengyi bisheng xie'e' (History is not easily distorted; justice must prevail over evil) http://www.people.com.cn (accessed 9 May 2001).

—— 10 May 2001 'Waijiaobu fayanren zaitan "jiaokeshu"' (Foreign Ministry spokesperson talks about 'the textbook' once more) http://www.people.com.cn (accessed 16 May 2001).

—— 28 August 2002 'Xijunzhan susong yiyi hezai' (What is the significance of the germ warfare case?) http://www.people.com.cn (accessed 28 August 2003).

—— 10 March 2003 'Zhanhou duiRi susong di yi an shengsu Zhongguo laogong huode peichang' (Chinese forced labourers receive compensation in first post-war compensation victory) http://www.people.com.cn (accessed 10 March 2003).

Xinhua 16 April 2001 'Chinese leader Wen Jiabao discusses history textbook with Japanese guests' BBC Monitoring Asia Pacific http://web.lexis-nexis.com.

—— 16 August 2002 'Memory of Japan's wartime crimes still clear' http://www.china.org.cn (accessed 13 July 2003).

—— 13 December 2002 'Nanjing marks 65th anniversary of Japanese massacre' htpp://www.china.org.cn (accessed 20 July 2003).

Newspapers

Asahi shinbun 12 November 1998: 2 'Rekishi, Taiwan shinchō na hyōgen' (Cautious expression over history and Taiwan).

—— 24 November 1998: 5 'Mirai o hiraku nitchū kankei ni' (Opening up a future for Sino-Japanese relations).

—— 24 November 1998: 6 'Nitchū, unmei kyōdotai no jidai' (China and Japan – an era of destined community).

—— 27 November 1998: 1 'Rekishi ninshiki, Kō shuseki wa kibishii shisei' (President Jiang takes a hard line on historical consciousness).

—— 27 November 1998: 2 'Rekishi shuyaku, Nihon ni kugi' (Japan is warned that history plays a major role).

—— 28 November 1998: 2 'Shūshō wa mirai, shuseki wa kako' (Prime Minister talks about the future, President about the past).

—— 29 November 1998: 3 'Kō shuseki "rekishi ninshiki" no kodowari' (President Jiang's problem with 'historical consciousness').

China Daily 19 September 2000: 3 'Japanese prisoners of war rue misdeeds.'.

Japan Times Weekly 8–14 May 1995: 1 'Murayama to offer war regrets in China.'.

South China Morning Post 29 December 2001 'Little cause to Celebrate as Beijing-Tokyo ties falter'.

—— 22 March 2003 'Writing new history'.

Books, journals and reports

Advisory Group (Advisory Group to Consider a Memorial Facility for Remembering the Dead and Praying for Peace) (2002) Report, 24 December. Available HTTP: <http://www.kantei.go.jp/foreign/policy/2002/1224houkoku_e.pdf> (accessed 2 March 2004).

Arai S. (1994) *Sensō hakubutsukan* (War museums), Tokyo: Iwanami Shoten.

—— (2001) 'Rekishi mondai kanren nenpyō' (Chronology of textbook problems), *Sekai*, 696: 178–87.

Asahi Shinbun Sengo Hoshō Mondai Shuzaiban (ed.) (1994) *Sengo hoshō to wa nani ka* (What is post-war compensation?), Tokyo: Asahi shinbunsha.

Asano R. (1998) 'China and Japan: improving direct communication', in M. Nishihara (ed.) *Old Issues, New Responses: Japan's Foreign and Security Policy Options*, Tokyo: Japan Centre for International Exchange.

Aspinall, R. and Cave, P. (2001) 'Lowering the flag: democracy, authority, and rights at Tokorozawa high school', *Social Science Japan Journal*, 4 (1): 77–93.

Austin, G. and Harris, S. (2001) *Japan and Greater China: Political Economy and Military Power in the Asian Century*, London: Hurst and Company.

Awaya K., Tanaka H., Hirowatari S. *et al.* (1994) *Sensō sekinin, sengo sekinin: Nihon to Doitsu wa dō chigau ka* (War responsibility, post-war responsibility: how do Japan and Germany differ?), Tokyo: Asahi Shinbunsha.

Barkan, E. (2000) *The Guilt of Nations: Restitution and Negotiating Historical Injustices*, Baltimore, MD: Johns Hopkins University Press.

—— (2001) 'Between restitution and international morality', *Fordham International Law Journal*, 25: 46–63.

Barmé, G. (1993) 'History for the masses', in J. Unger (ed.) *Using the Past to Serve the Present: Historiography and Politics in Contemporary China*, Armonk, NY and London: M.E. Sharpe.

—— (1996) 'To screw foreigners is patriotic: China's avant-garde nationalists', in J. Unger (ed.) *Chinese Nationalism*, New York and London: M.E. Sharpe.

Bazyler, M. J. (2001) 'Holocaust restitution in the United States and other claims for historical wrongs: an update', available HTTP: <http://www.aclu.org/library/iclr/2001/iclr2001_9.pdf> (accessed 2 July 2002).

Beal, T., Nozaki Y. and Yang J. (2001) 'Ghosts of the past: the Japanese history textbook controversy', *New Zealand Journal of Asian Studies*, 3 (3): 177–88.

Berry, M. (2003) 'Cinematic representations of the rape of Nanking', in P. Li (ed.) *Japanese War Crimes: The Search for Justice*, New Brunswick: Transaction.

Bian X. (2001) '"Xinlishi jiaokeshu" yu zhanhou Riben guojia de lishi renshi' (The 'New History Textbook' and post-war Japanese historical consciousness), *KangRi zhanzheng yanjiu*, 4: 184–207.

Bix, H. P. (2000) *Hirohito and the Making of Modern Japan*, New York: HarperCollins.

Borden, W. S. (1984) *The Pacific Alliance: United States Foreign Economic Policy and Japanese Trade Recovery, 1947–1955*, Wisconsin: University of Wisconsin Press.

Bradley, M. P. and Petro, P. (2002) *Truth Claims: Representation and Human Rights*, New Brunswick: Rutgers University Press.

Brook, T. and Frolic, B. M. (eds) (1997) *Civil Society in China*, Armonk, NY: M.E. Sharpe.

Brooks, R. L. (1999) *When Sorry isn't Enough: The Controversy over Apologies and Reparations for Human Injustice*, New York: New York University Press.

Bu P. (2000a) 'Guanyu Riben lishi jiaokeshu wenti' (On Japan's history textbook problem), *KangRi zhanzheng yanjiu*, 4: 154–79.

—— (2000b) 'Weianfu wenti yu Riben de zhanzheng zeren renshi' (The comfort women issue and Japan's war responsibility consciousness), *KangRi zhanzheng yanjiu*, 2: 161–81.

—— (2001) 'Riben jingguo shenshe wenti de lishi kaocha' (On the history of the problem of Japan's Yasukuni Shrine), *KangRi zhanzheng yanjiu*, 4: 163–83.

—— (undated) *Research Report on Japanese Use of Chemical Weapons during World War II*, Heilongjiang Academy of Social Sciences.

Cairns, A. (2003) 'Coming to terms with the past', in J. Torpey (ed.) *Politics and the Past: On Repairing Historical Injustices*, Lanham, MD: Rowman & Littlefield.

Chang, I. (1997) *The Rape of Nanking*, London: Penguin.

Chen J. (2000) 'Chinese workers in Japan during World War II', *Social Sciences in China*, 21 (1): 147–56.

Chinese Academy of Social Sciences (2002) 'Di yi ci ZhongRi yulun diaocha' (The first China-Japan public opinion poll), *Riben xuekan*, 6: 19–23.

Ching, F. (1996) 'Diaoyu dispute: complex issues', *Far Eastern Economic Review*, 3 October: 32.

—— (2002) 'Another crisis feeds distrust', *Japan Times*, 16 May.

Christensen, T. J. (1999) 'China, the US-Japan alliance and the security dilemma in East Asia', *International Security*, 23 (4): 49–80.

Chūgoku kenkyūjo (ed.) (1991) *Nitchū kankei to sensō sekinin – baishō mondai o megutte* (Sino-Japanese relations and war responsibility – the issue of compensation), Tokyo: Chūgoku kenkyūjo.

—— (1997) *Chūgoku nenkan* (China yearbook). Tokyo: Shinhyōron.

Coomaraswamy, R. (1996) *Report on the Mission to the Democratic People's Republic of Korea, the Republic of Korea and Japan on the Issue of Military Sexual Slavery in Wartime*, UN Commission on Human Rights (E/CN.4/1996/53/Add.1).

Deng H. and Evans, P. (1997) 'Social and environmental aspects of abandoned chemical weapons in China', *The Nonproliferation Review*, Spring–Summer: 102–8.

Dirlik, A. (1996) 'Past experience if not forgotten is a guide to the future', in M. Miyoshi and H. D. Harootunian (eds) *Japan in the World*, Durham, NC: Duke University Press.

Dower, J. W. (1995) 'Japan addresses its war responsibility', *ii: The Journal of the International Institute*, 3 (1): 8–11.

—— (1999) *Embracing Defeat: Japan in the Aftermath of World War II*, London: Penguin.

Downs, E. S. and Saunders, P. C. (1998) 'Legitimacy and the limits of nationalism: China and the Diaoyu islands', *International Security*, 23 (3): 114–46.

Dreyer, J. T. (2001) 'Sino-Japanese relations', *Journal of Contemporary China*, 10 (28): 373–85.

Drifte, R. (2003) *Japan's Security Relations with China since 1989: From Balancing to Bandwagoning?* London and New York: RoutledgeCurzon.

Drysdale, P. and Zhang D. (eds) (2000) *Japan and China: Rivalry or Cooperation in East Asia?* Canberra: Asia Pacific Press.

Duan Y. (1992) 'QinHua Rijun Nanjing datusha yunan tongbao jinianguan de zhan-lan huadong' (Exhibition activities at the Memorial Hall for the Victims of the Nanjing Massacre), *KangRi zhanzheng yanjiu*, 4: 175–89.

Dudden, A. (2001) ' "We came to tell the truth": reflections on the Tokyo Women's Tribunal', *Critical Asian Studies*, 33 (4): 591–602.

—— (2002) 'The politics of apology between Japan and Korea', in M. P. Bradley and P. Petro (eds) *Truth Claims: Representation and Human Rights*, New Brunswick: Rutgers University Press.

The Economist (2000) 'Japan's murky past catches up', 8 July: 61–2.

—— (2001) 'Japan starts picking on China', 10 February: 43.

Evans, P. O. (1997) 'Destruction of abandoned chemical weapons in China', Bonn International Center for Conversion, paper 13, available HTTP <http://www.bicc.de/publications/papers/paper13/paper13.pdf> (accessed 6 March 2004).

Eykholt, M. (2000) 'Aggression, victimization, and Chinese historiography of the

Nanjing massacre', in J. A. Fogel (ed.) *The Nanjing Massacre in History and Historiography*, Berkeley, CA: University of California Press.

Fewsmith, J. and Rosen, S. (2001) 'The domestic context of Chinese foreign policy: does "public opinion" matter?' in D. M. Lampton (ed.) *The Making of Chinese Foreign and Defence Policy in the Era of Reform, 1978–2000*, Stanford, CA: Stanford University Press.

Field, N. (1995) 'The stakes of apology', *Japan Quarterly*, 42 (4): 405–18.

Fisher, B. A. (2000) 'Japan's postwar compensation litigation', *Whittier Law Review*, 22 (1): 35–46.

Fisher, R. J. (1999) 'Socio-psychological processes in interactive conflict analysis and reconciliation', in H. W. Jeong (ed.) *Conflict Resolution: Dynamics, Process and Structure*, Aldershot: Ashgate.

Florini, A. M. (2000a) 'Transnational civil society networks', available HTTP: <http://www.ceip.org/programs/global/semflorini.htm> (accessed 19 March 2002).

—— (ed.) (2000b) *The Third Force: The Rise of Transnational Civil Society*, Tokyo: Japan Centre for International Exchange.

Fogel, J. A. (ed.) (2000) *The Nanjing Massacre in History and Historiography*, Berkeley, CA: University of California Press.

Fuji N. (1998) 'Nihonjin no hokori wa kaifuku sareta ka' (Has Japanese pride been restored?), *Seiron*, 8: 118–27.

Fujioka N. (1996) *Kyōkasho ga oshienai rekishi* (History the textbooks do not teach), Tokyo: Sankei shinbun.

Fukui H. (1977) 'Tanaka goes to Peking: a case study in foreign policymaking', in T. J. Pempel (ed.) *Policymaking in Contemporary Japan*, Ithaca, NY: Cornell University Press.

Gluck, C. (1992) 'The idea of Showa', in C. Gluck and S. R. Graubard (eds) *Showa: The Japan of Hirohito*, New York and London: W.W. Norton.

Goldhagen, D. J. (1997) *Hitler's Willing Executioners: Ordinary Germans and the Holocaust*, London: Abacus.

Gong, G. W. (ed.) (1996) *Remembering and Forgetting: The Legacy of War and Peace in East Asia*, Washington, DC: Center for Strategic and International Studies.

Guan J. (2002) 'Sanjing kuangshan laogong suopeian yu "huagang hejie" zhi bijiao' (Comparing the Mitsui Mine forced labour compensation plan and the 'Hanaoka settlement'), *Dongbei lunxianshi yanjiu*, 23 (2): 2–6.

Guo C. (1997) *Qinhua Rijun xijun zhanzheng jishi* (A record of Japan's biological warfare during the invasion of China), Beijing: Yanshan chubanshe.

Guo Y. (1998) 'Patriotic villains and patriotic heroes: Chinese literary nationalism in the 1990s', *Nationalism and Ethnic Politics*, 4 (1–2): 163–88.

Hammond, E. H. (1995) 'Politics of war and public history: Japan's own museum controversy', *Bulletin of Concerned Asian Scholars*, 27 (2): 56–9.

Hardacre, H. (2001) 'Prime Minister Koizumi and the Yasukuni Shrine', H-Japan online posting, available e-mail: H-Japan@h-net.msu.edu (13 August 2001).

Harootunian, H. (1999) 'Memory, mourning, and national morality: Yasukuni Shrine and the reunion of state and religion in postwar Japan', in P. van den Veer and H. Lehmann (eds) *Nation and Religion: Perspectives on Europe and Asia*, Princeton, NJ: Princeton University Press.

Harris, S. H. (1994) *Factories of Death: Japanese Biological Warfare, 1932–45, and the American Cover-up*, London and New York: Routledge.

Hayashi H. (2000) 'Chūgoku de no iansho genchi chōsa ni tsuite' (On the survey of comfort stations in China), *Senso sekinin kenkyū*, 27: 2–3.

——(2001) 'The Japanese movement to protest wartime sexual violence', *Critical Asian Studies*, 33 (4): 572–80.

He T. (1997) 'Riben qinhuazhansheng yiliu wenti gaishu (An overview of problems left over from Japan's war of invasion)', *KangRi zhanzheng yanjiu*, 4: 141–58.

——(2002) 'Shi peichang haishi jiujiqian?' (Is it compensation or relief money?), *Dongbei lunxianshi yanjiu*, 23 (2): 9–11.

Henson, M. R. (1999) *Comfort Woman: A Filipina's Story of Prostitution and Slavery under the Japanese Military*, Lanham, MD: Rowman and Littlefield.

Hicks, G. (1995) *The Comfort Women: Sex Slaves of the Japanese Imperial Forces*, London: Souvenir Press.

——(1997) *Japan's War Memories: Amnesia or Concealment?* Aldershot: Ashgate.

Hilpert, H. G. and Haak, R. (eds) (2002) *Japan and China: Cooperation, Competition and conflict*, Basingstoke: Palgrave.

Himeda K. (1994) 'Sengo hoshō no kokusai hikaku – Chūgoku ' (An international comparison of post-war compensation – China), *Sekai*, 591: 150–5.

Hirano M. (2000) 'Revisiting the 1980s textbook issue in Japan: reactions in China, South Korea and other Asian countries', *STICERD*, IS/00/403: 29–48.

Honda K. (1972) *Chūgoku no tabi (Travels in China)*, Tokyo: Asahi shinbunsha.

Hook, G.D., Gilson, J., Hughes, C.W. and Dobson, H. (2001) *Japan's International Relations: Politics, Economics and Security*, London: Routledge.

Hosoya C., Ando N., Onuma Y. and Minear, R. (eds) (1986) *The Tokyo War Crimes Trial: An International Symposium*, Tokyo: Kodansha.

Howard, K. (2003) *True Stories of the Korean Comfort Women*, London: Cassell.

Hsiao, G. T. (1974) 'The Sino-Japanese rapprochement', *China Quarterly*, 57: 101–23.

Hughes, C. (1997) 'Globalisation and nationalism: squaring the circle in Chinese international relations theory', *Millennium: Journal of International Studies*, 26 (1): 103–24.

Huyssen, A. (1995) *Twilight Memories: Marking Time in a Culture of Amnesia*, New York and London: Routledge.

Ienaga S. (1986) 'The historical significance of the Tokyo Trial', in C. Hosoya, N. Ando, Y. Onuma and R. Minear (eds) *The Tokyo War Crimes Trial: An International Symposium*, Tokyo: Kodansha.

Ijiri H. (1987) 'The politics of Japan's decision to normalize relations with China, 1969–72', unpublished thesis, University of California.

Inoguchi T., Hakamada S., Yamauchi, M. *et al.* (1999) '*Challenge 2001: Japan's foreign policy toward the 21st century*', available HTTP <http://www.mofa.go.jp/policy/other/challenge21.html> (accessed 15 July 2003).

Inokuchi H. and Nozaki Y. (2001) 'The latest report on the Japanese government screening of junior high social studies textbooks', H-Japan online posting. Available e-mail: H-Japan@h-net.msu.edu (23 January 2001).

Iokibe M. (1999) 'Japan's civil society: an historical overview' in T. Yamamoto (ed.) *Deciding the Public Good: Governance and Civil Society in Japan*, Tokyo: Japan Centre for International Exchange.

Irie Y. (1997) 'Rekishi kyōkasho daisensō' (The war over history textbooks), *Bungei Shunjū*, February: 306–15.

Iriye A. (1999) 'Nonstate actors as forces of globalization' in T. Yamamoto (ed.)

Deciding the Public Good: Governance and Civil Society in Japan, Tokyo: Japan Centre for International Exchange.

Ito A. (1991) 'Nitchū yūko undō to baishō mondai' (The Sino-Japanese friendship movement and the compensation issue), *Chūgoku kenkyū*, 21: 4–11.

Japanese Society for History Textbook Reform (1998) *The Restoration of a National History*, Tokyo: Japanese Society for History Textbook Reform.

Jenner, W. J. F. J. (1992) *The Tyranny of History: The Roots of China's Crisis*, London: Penguin.

Jeong H.W. (1999a) 'Research on conflict resolution', in H. W. Jeong (ed.) *Conflict Resolution: Dynamics, Process and Structure*, Aldershot: Ashgate.

—— (ed.) (1999b) *Conflict Resolution: Dynamics, Process and Structure*, Aldershot: Ashgate.

Jetro (2000) 'Japan-China trade', *China Newsletter*, 144: 21–4.

Jiang H. (1998) *Zhongguo weianfu* (China's comfort women), Xining, Qinghai: Renmin Chubanshe.

Jiang L. (2002) 'Zhongguo minzhong dui Riben hen shao you qinjingan' (Very few Chinese feel close to the Japanese), *Riben xuekan*, 6: 1–18.

Jin X. (2000) 'The background and trend of China-Japan partnership', available HTTP: <http://www.cass.net.cn/chinese/s30_rbs/ch-ccjrs/en-hbgxx.htm> (accessed 18 August 2002).

—— (2002a) '21 shijichu ZhongRi guanxi de tezheng yu keti' (Characteristics and issues in Sino-Japanese relations in the early twenty-first century), *Riben xuekan*, 4: 50–61.

—— (2002b) *ZhongRi guanxi: fujiao 30 zhounian de kaolu* (Sino-Japanese relations: thoughts on the 30th anniversary), Beijing: Shijie Zhishi.

Johnson, C. (1986) 'The patterns of Japanese relations with China, 1952–1982', *Pacific Affairs*, 59: 402–23.

Johnson, N. I. (2001) 'Justice for "Comfort Women": will the alien tort claims act bring them the remedies they seek?', *Penn State International Law Review*, 20 (1): 253–74.

Kersten, R. (2003) 'Revisionism, reaction and the "symbol emperor" in post-war Japan', *Japan Forum*, 15 (1): 15–31.

Kim H. N. (1979) 'The Fukuda government and the politics of the Sino-Japanese peace treaty', *Asian Survey*, 19 (3): 297–313.

Kim, I. M. (1976) *Tennō no guntai to Chōsenjin ianfu* (The Emperor's forces and Korean comfort women), Tokyo: San'ichi shobō.

Kim, Paul (1983) 'Japan's bureaucratic decision-making on the textbook', *Public Administration*, 61: 283–94.

Kim, Puja (2001) 'Global civil society remakes history: "The Women's International War Crimes Tribunal 2000"', *Positions*, 9 (3): 611–20.

Kim T. (1998) 'A reality check: the "rise of China" and its military capability toward 2010', *Journal of East Asian Affairs*, 12 (2): 321–63.

Kim Y. C. (2001) 'Japanese policy towards China: politics of the imperial visit to China in 1992', *Pacific Affairs*, Summer: 225–42.

Kimijima K. (2000) 'The continuing legacy of Japanese colonialism: the Japan-South Korea joint study group in history textbooks', in L. Hein and M. Selden (eds) *Censoring History: Citizenship and Memory in Japan, Germany and the United States*, Armonk, NY: M.E. Sharpe.

Kinoshita J. (1986) 'What the war trials made me think about', in C. Hosoya,

N. Ando, Y. Onuma and R. Minear (eds) *The Tokyo War Crimes Trial: An International Symposium*, Tokyo: Kodansha.

Kitaoka S. (1995) 'The folly of the fiftieth-anniversary resolution', *Japan Echo*, Autumn: 66–74.

Kleinman, A. S. (1996) 'An unassimilable past and the diplomacy of the future: international relations in East Asia fifty years on', in G. Gong (ed.) *Remembering and Forgetting: The Legacy of War and Peace in East Asia*, Washington, DC: Center for Strategic and International Studies.

Kobayashi Y. (1998) *Sensōron* (On war), Tokyo: Gentōsha.

Kobori K. (1998) *Yasukuni jinja to Nihonjin* (The Yasukuni Shrine and the Japanese), Tokyo: PHP.

Koizumi J. (13 August 2001) 'Statement by Prime Minister Junichiro Koizumi', available HTTP: <http://www.kantei.go.jp/foreign/koizumispeech/2001/0813danwa_e.html> (accessed 16 August 2002).

Komori Y. (1998) *Nashonaru hisutorii o kōete* (Transcending national history), Tokyo: Tokyo Daigaku.

Kriesberg, L. (1999) 'Paths to varieties of intercommunal reconciliation', in H. W. Jeong (ed.) *Conflict Resolution: Dynamics, Processes and Structure*, Aldershot: Ashgate.

Lampton, D. M. (ed.) (2001) *The Making of Chinese Foreign and Defence Policy in the Era of Reform, 1978–2000*, Stanford, CA: Stanford University Press.

Lee, I. (2003) 'Probing the issues of reconciliation more than fifty years after the Asia-Pacific war', in P. Li (ed.) *Japanese War Crimes: The Search for Justice*, New Brunswick and London: Transaction.

Li H. (1992) 'Shenyang jiu yi ba shibian chenlieguan jianjie (A brief introduction to the September 18th Incident Exhibition Hall), *KangRi zhanzheng yanjiu*, 4: 190–2.

Li M. (2002) 'Shifou peichangqian? You shui shuole suan?' (Is this compensation or not? Who should determine?), available HTTP: <http://www.china918.net/91808/newxp/ReadNews.asp?NewsID=263&BigClassName=gongsuo> (accessed 11 July 2002).

Li, P. (ed.) (2003) *Japanese War Crimes: The Search for Justice*, New Brunswick and London: Transaction.

Li Z. (1999) *Zhanzheng suopei* (War reparations), Beijing: Xinhua.

Liu D. (2002) 'Fazhan ZhongRi guanxi zhi wo jian' (My views on how to develop Sino-Japanese relations), *Riben xuekan*, 4: 1–11.

Louie, K. and Cheung, C. (1998) 'Three kingdoms: the Chinese cultural scene today', in J. Y. S. Cheng, (ed.) *China Review, 1998*, Hong Kong: Chinese University Press.

Ma L. (2002) 'DuiRi guanxi xin siwei: ZhongRi minjian zhi you' (New thinking on relations with Japan), *Zhanlüe yu guanli*, 6, available HTTP: <www.gmdaily.com.cn/3_guancha/2002–12–30/021230–01.htm> (accessed 16 March 2003).

McCormack, G. (1998) 'The Japanese movement to "correct" history', *Bulletin of Concerned Asian Scholars*, 30 (2): 16–23.

Macdonald, S. and Fyfe, G. (eds) (1996) *Theorizing Museums: Representing Identity and Diversity in a Changing World*, Oxford: Blackwell.

McDougall, G. J. (1998) *Systematic Rape, Sexual Slavery and Slavery-Like Practices during Armed Conflict*, UN Commission on Human Rights (E/CN.4/Sub.2/1998/13).

Macintyre, D. (1996) 'Imperial Japan Inc. on trial', *Asiaweek*, 15 November.

Maga, T. (2001) *Judgment at Tokyo: The Japanese War Crimes Trials*, Lexington, KT: University Press of Kentucky.

Maier, C. S. (2003) 'Overcoming the past? Narrative and negotiation, remembering, and reparation: issues at the interface of history and the law', in J. Torpey (ed.) *Politics and the Past: On Repairing Historical Injustices.* Lanham, MD: Rowman & Littlefield.

Matsuo S. (1998) *Chūgokujin sensō higaisha to sengo hoshō* (Chinese war victims and post-war compensation), Tokyo: Iwanami (Iwanami Bukuretto 466).

Midford, P. (2000) 'Chinese perceptions of Japan as a military power: balance of power, balance of threat and the psychological dynamics of reputation', paper presented at Workshop on the Chinese-Japanese Relationship, Swedish Institute for International Affairs, Stockholm, August.

Miller, H. L. and Liu X. (2001) 'The foreign policy outlook of China's "third generation" elite', in D. M. Lampton, (ed.) *The Making of Chinese Foreign and Defence Policy in the Era of Reform, 1978–2000*, Stanford, CA: Stanford University Press.

Minear, R. H. (2001) *Victor's Justice: The Tokyo War Crimes Trial*, Ann Arbor, MI: Centre for Japanese Studies, The University of Michigan.

Ministry of Foreign Affairs of Japan (2002) *Diplomatic Bluebook, 2002*, available HTTP: <http://www.mofa.go.jp/policy/other/bluebook/2002/index.html> (accessed 1 August 2003).

—— (2003) 'Recent policy of the Government of Japan on the issue known as "wartime comfort women"', available HTTP: <http://www.mofa.go.jp/policy/women/fund/policy.html> (accessed 10 July 2003).

Mitter, R. (2000) 'Behind the scenes at the museum: nationalism, history and memory in the Beijing War of Resistance museum, 1987–1997', *China Quarterly*, 161: 279–93.

Moffett, S. (1996) 'Past perfect', *Far Eastern Economic Review*, 21 November: 26–8.

Morris-Suzuki, T. (2000) 'The view through the skylight: Nishio Kanji, textbook reform and the history of the world', *Japanese Studies*, 20 (2): 133–9.

Mukae R. (1996) 'Japan's Diet resolution on World War Two: keeping history at bay', *Asian Survey*, 36 (10): 1011–30.

Murayama A. (1993) 'Realities of war victims and Japan's measures for war responsibility', in Executive Committee, International Public Hearing Concerning the Post-war Compensation of Japan (ed.) *War Victimization and Japan: International Public Hearing Concerning the Post-war Compensation of Japan*, Tokyo: Tōhō Shuppan.

Nakajima M. (1986) 'Chūgoku ni jubaku sareta Nihon' (Japan spellbound by China) *Shokun*, March: 26–42.

Nakakita R. (2000) 'Heiwa hakubutsukan e no kōgeki o ikani hanekaesu ka' (How can the attack on peace museums be stopped?), *Sekai*, (5): 231–5.

Nakamura M. (1998) 'The history textbook controversy and nationalism', *Bulletin of Concerned Asian Scholars*, 30 (2): 24–9.

Nash, G. B., Crabtree, C. and Dunn, R. E. (1997) *History on Trial: Culture Wars and the Teaching of the Past*, New York: Vintage.

Nearey, J. P. (2001) 'Seeking reparations in the new millennium: will Japan compensate the "comfort women" of World War II?', *Temple International and Comparative Law Journal*, 15 (1): 121–46.

Negishi M. (1999) 'Education Ministry pushes pride in flag and national anthem in textbook screening', *Japan Times International*, 1–15 July: 5.

Neier, A. (1998) *War Crimes: Brutality, Genocide, Terror, and the Struggle for Justice.* New York: Random House.

Nelson, J. K. (2002) 'Tempest in a textbook: a report on the new middle-school history textbook in Japan', *Critical Asian Studies*, 34 (1): 129–48.

—— (2003) 'Social memory as ritual practice: commemorating the spirits of the military dead at Yasukuni Shinto Shrine', *The Journal of Asian Studies*, 62 (2): 443–67.

NHK (ed.) (1994) *Maboroshi no Gaimushō hōkokusho – chūgokujin kyōsei renkō no kiroku* (The Ministry of Foreign Affairs' mythical report – records of Chinese forced labourers), Tokyo: NHK.

Niimi T. (1998) 'Hanaoka jiken saiban ni tsuite' (On the Hanaoka incident court case), *Sensō sekinin kenkyū*, 20: 2–7.

Nishio K., Takahashi S., Fujioka N. *et al.* (1997) *Rekishi kyōkasho to no 15 nen sensō* (History textbooks and the 15-year war), Tokyo: PHP.

Nishio K. *et al.* (2001) *Atarashii rekishi kyōkasho* (New history textbook), Tokyo: Fusōsha.

Niven, B. (2002) *Facing the Nazi Past: United Germany and the Legacy of the Third Reich*, London and New York: Routledge.

Nomura T. (1997) 'Japan strafed by war victims', *Christian Science Monitor*, 25 August, available HTTP: <http://www.csmonitor.com/durable/1997/08/25/intl/intl.4.html> (accessed July 3 2002).

Nozaki Y. and Inokuchi H. (1998) 'Japanese education, nationalism, and Ienaga Saburō's court challenges', *Bulletin of Concerned Asian Scholars*, 30 (2): 37–46.

Nozoe K. (1995) *Liu Lianren: Ana no naka no sengo* (Liu Lianren: post-war days underground), Tokyo: San'ichi Shobo.

O'Brien, D. M. (1996) *To Dream of Dreams: Religious Freedom and Constitutional Politics in Postwar Japan*, Honolulu: University of Hawai'i Press.

Ogata S. (1988) *Normalization with China: A Comparative Study of U.S. and Japanese Processes*, Berkeley, CA: University of California, Institute of East Asian Studies.

Oguma E. (1998) '"Hidari" o kihi suru popyurizumu' (Populism which avoids 'the left'), *Sekai*, December (656): 94–105.

Okabe T. (2001) 'Historical remembering and forgetting in Sino-Japanese relations', *Memory and History in East and Southeast Asia*, 23 (3): 47–64.

Okuda Y. and Kawashima S. (eds) (2000) *Chūgoku sengo hoshō: rekishi, hō, saiban* (China's post-war compensation: history, law, and court cases), Tokyo: Akashi Shoten.

Orr, J. (2001) *The Victim as Hero: Ideologies of Peace and National Identity in Postwar Japan*, Richmond, Surrey: Curzon.

Osaki Y. (1998) 'China and Japan in the Asia Pacific: looking ahead', in Kokubun R. (ed.) *Challenges for China-Japan-US Cooperation*, Tokyo: Japan Centre for International Exchange.

Park, B. (2002) 'Comfort women during World War II: are US courts a final resort for justice?' *American University International Law Review*, 17 (2): 403–58.

Pempel, T. J. (ed.) (1977) *Policymaking in Contemporary Japan*, Ithaca, NY and London: Cornell University Press.

Piccigallo, P. R. (1979) *The Japanese on Trial: Allied War Crimes Operations in the East, 1945–1951*, Austin, TX: University of Texas Press.

Piper, N. (2001) 'War and memory: victim identity and the struggle for compensation in Japan', *War and Society*, 19 (1): 131–48.

Powell, J. W. (1981) 'Japan's biological weapons, 1930–1945: a hidden chapter in history', *Bulletin of the Atomic Scientists*, 37 (8): 44–53.

Preece, J. C. (2001) 'A funeral, three apologies and an imperial visit: the PoW issue in Anglo-Japanese relations, 1989–2001', unpublished MA dissertation, University of Leeds.

Price, J. (2001) 'A just peace? The 1951 San Francisco Peace Treaty in historical perspective', available HTTP: <http://www.gainfo.org/SFPT/aJustPeace.htm> (accessed 15 July 2003).

Przystup, J. (2001) 'Japan-China relations: spiraling downward', *Comparative Connections*, 3 (3), available on http://www.csis.org/pacfor/ccejournal.html .

—— (2002a) 'Japan-China relations: smoother sailing across occasional rough seas', *Comparative Connections*, 4 (1), available on http://www.csis.org/pacfor/ ccejournal.html.

—— (2003a) 'Japan-China relations: congratulations, concern, competition, and cooperation', *Comparative Connections*, 4 (4), available on http://www.csis.org/ pacfor/ccejournal.html.

—— (2003b) 'Japan-China relations: cross-currents', *Comparative Connections*, 5 (1), available on http://www.csis.org/pacfor/ccejournal.html.

—— (2003c) 'Japan-China relations: political breathrough and the SARS outbreak', *Comparative Connections*, 5 (2), available on http://www.csis.org/pacfor/ ccejournal.html.

Qi L. (2003) *Jingguo shenshe jiemi* (The Yasukuni Shrine exposed), Beijing: Shin shijie chubanshe.

Rekishi Kentō Iinkai (1995) *Daitōā sensō no sōkatsu* (Summary of the Greater East Asia War), Tokyo: Tendensha.

Rekishi kyōikusha kyōgikai (ed.) (1997) *Rekishi kyōiku gojū nen no ayumi to kadai* (50 years of history education: overview and issues), Tokyo: Miraisha.

Rigby, A. (2000) ' "Forgiving the Past": paths towards a culture of reconciliation', paper presented at IPRA, Tampere, available HTTP: <http://www.coventry-isl.org.uk/forgive/about/ipra2.doc > (accessed 18 March 2002).

—— (2001) *Justice and Reconciliation: After the Violence*, Boulder, CO: Lynne Rienner.

Rose, C. (1998) *Interpreting History in Sino-Japanese Relations*, London and New York: Routledge.

—— (2000) ' "Patriotism is not taboo": nationalism in China and Japan and implications for Sino-Japanese relations', *Japan Forum*, 12 (2): 169–81.

Rozman, G. (1999) 'China's quest for great power identity', *Orbis*, 43 (3): 383–402.

Ryū K. (Liu Jie) (1999) *Chūgokujin no rekishikan* (The Chinese view of history), Tokyo: Bungei Shunju.

Satō K. (2001) 'The Japan-China summit and joint declaration of 1998: a watershed for Japan-China relations in the 21st century?', *Brookings Institution Working Papers*, available HTTP: <http://www.ciaonet.org> (accessed 1 March 2002).

Senda, K. (1973) *Jūgun ianfu* (Military comfort women), Tokyo: Futabasha.

Sensō giseisha o kokoro ni kizamu Nankin shūkaihen (Nanjing Committee for Remembering War Victims) (ed.) (1995) *Chūgokujin kyōsei renkō* (Chinese forced labourers), Tokyo: Tōhō shuppan.

Shi J. (2000) *Yubiweilin: Zhongguo gaosu Riben* (Those neighbours: China warns Japan), Beijing: Kunlun.

Shimida M. and Tian J. (1997) *Sengo nitchū kankei gojūnen* (Fifty years of post-war Sino-Japanese relations), Tokyo: Tōhō shuppan.

Shimizu M. (1994) 'Sensō hoshō no kokusai hikō' (An international comparison of post-war compensation), *Sekai*, 591: 133–43.

Shōwa kōkō chiri rekishi kenkyūbu (ed.) (1998) *Kōkōsei ga mita saikinsen* (Chemical warfare: how high school students see it), Urawa, Saitama: Yunion Puresu.

Shūkan Kinyōbi (1994) 'Sengo hoshō wa owatte inai' (Post-war compensation is not settled), *Shūkan Kinyōbi*, 8 December: 14–39.

Shuppan Rōren (ed.) (1997) 'Chūgakkō rekishi kyōkasho ni ima nani ga okotteiru ka' (What's happening with middle-school history textbooks?), *Kyōkasho Repōto* (Textbook report 1997): 2–15.

—— (2002) '2002 nendo yō kyōkasho no saitaku kekka' (Results of textbook selection for use in 2002), *Kyōkasho Repōto* (Textbook report 2002): 64–8.

Smith, C. (1994) 'The textbook truth', *Far Eastern Economic Review*, 25 August: 26.

Sō S. (Song Zhiyong), (2000) 'Sengo Chūgoku ni okeru Nihonjin senpan saiban' (Japanese war crimes trials in post-war China), *Sensō sekinin kenkyū*, 30: 62–8.

Söderberg, M. (ed.) (2001) *Chinese-Japanese Relations in the Twenty-first Century*, London and New York: Routledge.

Soh C. S. (1996) 'The Korean "comfort women"', *Asian Survey*, 36 (12): 1227–40.

—— (2001) 'Japan's responsibility toward comfort women survivors', available HTTP: <http://www.icasinc.org/lectures/soh3.html> (accessed 6 July 2003).

Song Q., Zhang Z., Qiao B. *et al.* (1996) *Zhongguo keyi shuo bu* (A China that can say no), Beijing: Zhonghua gonshang lianhe chubanshe.

State Council of the People's Republic of China (1991) *Human Rights in China*, available HTTP: <http://english.peopledaily.com.cn/whitepaper/4.html> (accessed 13 August 2002).

Su S. (1992) 'Riben qinlüezhi qiangpo zhongguo funu zuo rijunweianfu shilu' (True records of Japanese invaders forcing Chinese women to become comfort women for the Japanese army), *KangRi zhanzheng yanjiu*, 4: 10–9.

Su, Z. (1999) *Weianfu yanjiu* (Studies on comfort women), Shanghai: Shanghai shudian.

—— (2000a) 'Ianfu no kinkyūchōsa' (Urgent survey of comfort women), *Sensō sekinin kenkyū*, 27: 19–23.

—— (2000b) *Rijun xingnüli: Zhongguo 'weianfu' zhenxiang* (Japan's military sex slaves: The truth about China's 'comfort women'), Beijing: Renmin chubanshe.

—— (2001a) *Riben lishi jiaokeshu fengbo de zhenxiang* (The truth about the Japanese history textbook crisis), Beijing: Renmin chubanshe.

—— (2001b) '2000 nian Dongjing nüxing guoji zhanfan fating jishi' (Notes on the 2000 Tokyo Women's International War Crimes Tribunal), *KangRi zhanzheng yanjiu*, 1: 224–33.

Su Z. and Chen L. (1998a) 'Present situation and perspectives of the researches [*sic*] of the comfort women issue in mainland China', available HTTP: <http://www.korea-np.co.jp/pk/074th_issue/98121607.htm> (accessed 3 August 2002).

—— (1998b) 'Qinhua rijun weianfu zhidu lüelun' (Overview of the comfort woman system during Japan's invasion of China), *Xinhua Wenzhai: Lishi*, November: 68–73.

Suzuki A. (1973) *Nankin daigyakusatsu no maboroshi* (The myth of the Nanjing massacre), Tokyo: Bungei Shunju.

Taigai kankei tasuku fōsu (2002) '21 seiki Nihon gaikō no kihon senryaku' (Basic

strategies for Japan's Foreign Policy), available HTTP: <http://www.kantei.go.jp/jp/kakugikettei/2002/1128tf.html#2–2> (accessed 1 August 2003).

Takahashi T. (2003) 'The Emperor Showa standing at ground zero: on the (re-) configuration of a national "memory" of the Japanese people', *Japan Forum*, 15 (1): 3–14.

Tamanoi M.A. (2000) 'War responsibility and Japanese civilian victims of biological warfare in China', *Bulletin of Concerned Asian Scholars*, 32 (3): 13–22.

Tanaka H. (1991) 'Nitchū baishō mondai to rekishi ninshiki' (The Sino-Japanese compensation problem and historical awareness), *Chūgoku kenkyū*, 21: 34–62.

—— (1992) 'Unfinished business: Japan and war compensation', *AMPO*, 23 (2): 18–20.

—— (1994a) 'Chūgoku: kokka baishō wa haishi shita ga, kongo wa minkan baishō ga kiiwādo' (China: state compensation was waived, but now the keyword is private compensation), *Shūkan kinyōbi tokushū*: 12 August 16–17.

—— (1994b) 'Nihon wa sensō sekinin ni dō taishitekita ka' (How has Japan dealt with its war responsibility?), *Sekai*, 591: 122–32.

—— (1994c) 'Nihon no sengo hoshō to rekishi ninshiki (Japan's post-war compensation and historical awareness)', in K. Awaya (ed.) *Sensō sekinin, sengo sekinin* (War responsibility, post-war responsibility), Tokyo: Asahi shinbunsha.

—— (1995) 'Koredewa, sengo gojūnen no kukiri wa tsukanai' (No end to the post-war period 50 years on), *Sekai*, 606: 168–75.

—— (1996) 'Why is Asia demanding postwar compensation now?' *Hitotsubashi Journal of Social Studies*, 28: 1–14.

—— (2002) 'Kōkai sareta "Shinkaku Nichigun dai nana san ichi butai iseki"' (The opening of the 'Ruins of the Japanese Invading Army's Unit 731'), *Chūgoku kenkyū geppō* 56 (4): 42- 48.

Tanaka H. and Matsuzawa T. (eds) (1995) *Chūgokujin kyōsei renkō shiryō: Gaimushō hōkokusho* (Materials concerning the forcible seizure of the Chinese: the Ministry of Foreign Affairs report), Tokyo: Gendai shokan.

Tanaka N. (2000) 'What is the Yasukuni problem?', available HTTP: <http://www.iwanami.co.jp/jpworld/text/yasukuni01.html> (accessed 23 July 2001).

—— (2002) *Yasukuni no sengoshi* (A post-war history of Yasukuni), Tokyo: Iwanami.

Tanaka Y. (2001) *Japan's Comfort Women*, London and New York: Routledge.

Task Force on Foreign Relations for the Prime Minister (2002) 'Basic strategies for Japan's foreign policy in the 21st century: new era, new vision, new diplomacy (executive summary)', available HTTP: <http://www.kantei.go.jp/foreign/policy/2002/1128tf_e.html> (accessed 1 August 2003).

Tavuchis, N. (1991) *Mea Culpa: A Sociology of Apology and Reconciliation*, Stanford, CA: Stanford University Press.

Tawara Y. (1998) 'Sengo hoshō mondai no genjō to kyōkasho (Textbooks and the current state of post-war compensation)', in Kyōkasho ni shinjitsu to jiyū o renrakukai (ed.) *Ima naze sensō sekinin o mondai ni suru no ka* (Why is war responsibility a problem now?), Tokyo: Kyoiku Shiryo Shuppankai.

—— (2000) 'Kenpō ihan, shinryaku sensō kōtei no "abunai kyōkasho" no jittai' (The truth about a 'dangerous textbook' that violates the Constitution and affirms the war of aggression), *Sensō sekinin kenkyū*, 30: 28–49.

—— (2001) *(Tettei Kensho) Abunai kyōkasho* (Dangerous textbooks – a thorough inspection), Tokyo: Gakushū no yūsha.

Tawara Y. and Ishiyama H. (1995) *Kyōkasho kentei to kyō no kyōkasho mondai no shoten* (Focus on textbook authorisation and today's textbook problem), Tokyo: Gakushū no yūsha.

Taylor, R. (2000) 'Sino-Japanese economic cooperation since 1978', in P. Drysdale, and D. Zhang (eds) *Japan and China: Rivalry or Cooperation in East Asia?*, Canberra: Asia Pacific Press.

Tian, H. (1997) *Zhanhou Zhong Ri guanxi wenxianji 1971–1995* (Collected documents on post-war Sino-Japanese relations 1971–1995), Beihing: Zhonggho shehui kexue chubanshe.

—— (2002) *Zhanhou ZhongRi guanxi shi 1945–1995* (A history of post-war Sino-Japanese relations 1945–1995), Beijing: Zhongguo shehui kexue chubanshe.

Torpey, J. (ed.) (2003) *Politics and the Past: On Repairing Historical Injustices*. Lanham, MD: Rowman & Littlefield.

Totman, C. (2000) *A History of Japan*, Oxford: Blackwell.

Totsuka, E. (1999) 'War crimes Japan ignores: the issue of "comfort women"', available HTTP: <http://www.jca.ax.apc.org/JWRC/center/english/Warcrime.htm> (accessed 5 March 2004).

Toyama K. (forthcoming) *War and Responsibility in Japan*, London and New York: Routledge.

Ts'ai H. Y. C. (2001) 'The war never ended: the war compensation movement in Taiwan', in D. P. Barrett and L. N. Shyu (eds) *China in the Anti-Japanese War, 1937–1945: Politics, Culture, and Society*, New York: Peter Lang.

Uchida M. (2001a) 'The Hanaoka incident: corporate compensation for forced labor', available HTTP: <http://www.iwanami.co.jp/jpworld/text/hanaoka01.html> (accessed 23 July 2001).

—— (2001b) '"Hanaoka jiken" wakai seiritsu no imi suru mono' (What the 'Hanaoka incident' settlement means), *Sekai*, 684: 30–3.

Unger, J. (ed.) (1993) *Using the Past to Serve the Present: Historiography and Politics in Contemporary China*, Armonk, NY: M. E. Sharpe.

—— (1996) *Chinese Nationalism*, London and New York: M.E. Sharpe.

Valencia, M. J. (2000) 'Domestic politics fuels Northeast Asian maritime disputes', Available HTTP: <http://EastWestCenter.org/stored/pdfs/api043.pdf> (accessed 10 October 2000).

Wada J. (2000) 'Applying track two to China-Japan-US relations', in R. Kokubun (ed.) *Challenges for China-Japan-US Cooperation*, Tokyo: Japan Centre for International Exchange.

Wakabayashi B. T. (2000) 'The Nanking 100-man killing contest debate: war guilt amid fabricated illusions, 1971–75', *Journal of Japanese Studies*, 26 (2): 307–40.

Wakamiya Y. (1995) *Sengo hōshū no Ajiakan* (The postwar conservative view of Asia), Tokyo: Asahi shinbun.

—— (1998) *The Post-war Conservative View of Asia: How the Political Right has Delayed Coming to Terms with its History of Aggression in Asia*, Tokyo: LTCB International Library Foundation.

Waldron, A. (1996) 'China's new remembering of World War II: the case of Zhang Zizhong', *Modern Asian Studies*, 30 (4): 945–78.

Walt, S. M. (1987) *The Origins of Alliances*, Ithaca, NY: Cornell University Press.

Wanandi, J. (2000) 'Regionalism in Asia Pacific', in JCIE (eds) *Community Building in Asia Pacific: Dialogue in Okinawa*, Tokyo: Japan Centre for International Exchange.

Wang X. (2001) 'Ping Riben dangdai lishi xiuzhengzhuyi' (On Japan's contemporary historical revisionism), *KangRi zhanzheng yanjiu*, 2: 160–83.

—— (2002) '"Huagang hejie" iwei zhe shenme' (What does the 'Hanaoka settlement' signify?), *Dongbei lunxianshi yanjiu*, 23 (2): 6–9.

White, G., Howell, J. and Shang, X. (eds) (1996) *In Search of Civil Society: Market Reform and Social Change in Contemporary China*, Oxford: Clarendon Press.

Whiting, A. S. (1989) *China Eyes Japan*, Berkeley, CA: University of California Press.

Williams, P. and Wallace, D. (1989) *Unit 731: Japan's Secret Bacteriological Warfare in World War II*, New York: Free Press.

Wilson, S. (2001) 'Rethinking the 1930s and the "15-Year War" in Japan', *Japanese Studies*, 21 (2): 155–64.

Winter, J. and Sivan, E. (eds) (1999) *War and Remembrance in the Twentieth Century*, Cambridge: Cambridge University Press.

Wu G. (2002) 'Guanyu "Huaguang hejie" de taolun' (On the debate about the 'Hanaoka settlement', *Dongbei lunxianshi yanjiu*, 23 (2): 1–2.

Wu G. and Zhu C. (2000) 'Ping dongjing difang fayuan guanyu qisanyao xijun duibu deng shouhaizhe suopeian de panjueshu' (A discussion of the Tokyo District Court's verdict in the Unit 731 compensation claims), *KangRi zhanzheng yanjiu*, 1: 155–73.

Wu X. (2000) 'The security dimensions of Sino-Japanese relations: warily watching one another', *Asian Survey*, 40 (2): 296–310.

Yahuda, M. (2001) 'The limits of economic interdependence: Sino-Japanese relations', available HTTP: <http://www.isanet.org/archive/yahuda.doc> (accessed 9 January 2002).

Yamagiwa A. (1991) 'Gendaishi ni okeru baishō mondai' (The reparations issue in contemporary history), *Chūgoku kenkyū*, 21: 12–33.

Yamamoto T. (ed.) (1999) *Deciding the Public Good: Governance and Civil Society in Japan*, Tokyo: Japan Centre for International Exchange.

Yamamoto M. (2000) *Nanking: Anatomy of an Atrocity*, Westport, CT: Praeger.

Yang D. (1999) 'Convergence or divergence? Recent historical writings on the Rape of Nanjing', *The American Historical Review*, 104 (3): 842–865.

—— (2002) 'Mirror for the future or the history card? Understanding the "history problem" in Japan-China relations', in M. Söderberg (ed.) *Chinese-Japanese Relations in the Twenty-first Century*, London and New York: Routledge.

Yee, H. and Storey, I. (eds) (2002) *The China Threat: Perceptions, Myths and Reality*, London and New York: RoutledgeCurzon.

Yin Y. (1996) *Chūnichi sensō baishō mondai* (The problem of Sino-Japanese war reparations), Tokyo: Ochanomizu Shobō.

Yokoyama H. (1994) *Nitchū no shōheki: sensō to yūkō no taishō* (The invisible wall between Japan and China: a legacy of the war), Tokyo: Simul Press.

Yoneyama, L. (1999) *Hiroshima Traces: Time, Space, and the Dialectics of Memory*, Berkeley, CA: University of California.

Yoshida Y. (1995) *Nihonjin no sensōkan* (Japanese views of the war), Tokyo: Iwanami Shoten.

Yoshimi Y. (2000) *Comfort Women: Sexual Slavery in the Japanese Military during World War II*, New York: Columbia University Press.

Zenkokukyō (731 butai shinsō chōsa zenkoku renraku kyōgikai) (ed.) (1997) *731 butai, iki doku gasu mondai* (Unit 731 and abandoned chemical weapons), Tokyo: 731 butai shinsō chōsa zenkoku renraku kyōgikai.

Zhang D. (2000) 'Managing bilateral economic differences', in P. Drysdale and D. Zhang (eds) *Japan and China: Rivalry or Cooperation in East Asia?*, Canberra: Asia Pacific Press.

Zhang J. (2002) 'Zuoyong juda renzhongdaoyuan: lengzhanhou ZhongRi minjian jiaolu de tezheng yu zuoyong' (Shouldering tremendous reponsibility: characteristics and functions of people exchange in post-Cold War Sino-Japanese relations), *Riben xuekan*, 4: 38–49.

Zhao L. (2000) 'Guanyu Jilin Dunhua Ri yidudan de liang ge xianchang' (Concerning the two sites in Dunhua, Jilin, where Japan abandoned chemical weapons), *KangRi zhanzheng yanjiu*, 1: 183–95.

Zhao Q. (1993) *Japanese Policymaking: The Politics behind Politics, Informal Mechanisms and the Making of China Policy*, Westport, CT: Praeger.

—— (2002) 'Sino-Japanese relations in the context of the Beijing-Tokyo-Washington strategic triangle', in M. Söderberg (ed.) *Chinese-Japanese Relations in the Twenty-first Century*, London and New York: Routledge..

Zhao S. (1997) 'Chinese intellectuals' quest for national greatness and nationalistic writing in the 1990s', *China Quarterly*, 152: 725–45.

Zhu J. (1992) 'Chūgoku wa naze baishō o hōki shita ka' (Why did China waive reparations?), *Gaikō Fōramu*, 92 (10): 27–40.

Zolberg, V. (1996) 'Museums as contested sites of remembrance: the Enola Gay affair'', in S. Macdonald (ed.) *Theorizing Museums: Representing Identity and Diversity in a Changing World*, Oxford: Blackwell.

Index

abandoned chemical weapons:
agreement to destroy 92; disposal of 2,
4, 5, 92; compensation cases 95–6
Abe Shinzō 114
Advisory Committee for Discussing
Social Studies Textbook Problems
(Shakai kyōkasho kondankai
sewaninkai) 61
'age of apology' 16, 19–20
All China Lawyers' Association 76, 90,
139n4
All-China Women's Federation 29, 90
Anami Koreshige 63, 115
anti-Japanism (in China) 52–3
Aoki Mikio 113
APEC 116
apologies (Japanese): to Asian countries
101; as issue in Sino-Japanese relations
2, 6, 9, 12, 13, 14, 16, 19–20, 27, 48–9,
100–3; by Koizumi Junichirō 101, 103,
108, 125; by Murayama Tomiichi 101;
by Obuchi Keizō 101, 103–7
apology, criteria of 100
Asahi shinbun 106
ASEAN + 3, 6, 7
Asian Network on History Education
(Rekishi kyōiku Ajia nettowāku) 62,
66
Asian Solidarity Conference on
Textbook Issues in Japan (Ajia rentai
kinkyū kaigi) 62, 66
Asian Women's Fund (AWF) 71, 85, 90,
147n39
Association for the Advancement of a
Liberalist View of History (Jiyūshugi
shikan kenkyūkai), *see* Jiyūshugi
shikan kenkyūkai
Association to Clarify Post-war
Responsibility of Japan (Nihon no
sengo sekinin o hakkiri saseru kai) 72

Atarashii rekishi kyōkasho (New History
Textbook) 60, 61, 65; adoption of
61; authorisation of 61, 62; criticism
of 61
Awaya Kentarō 9

Barkan, Elazar 16, 18, 22, 70, 99, 100
Barmé, Geremie 9, 40
Bazyler, Michael 81
B/C trials, *see* war crimes trials
'biased textbooks' campaign, *see*
textbook offensives
biological and chemical warfare
programme (Japan), *see* chemical and
biological warfare
Beal, Timothy 9
Bix, Herbert P. 9
Brooks, Roy 16, 19, 77, 85, 97
Bu Ping 9, 51, 65, 87, 95
Bungei Shunjū 59
Bush, George W. 91

Cairns, Alan 20
Cairo declaration 74
Canada Alpha 33
Centre for Research and Documentation
on Japan's War Responsibility (Nihon
sensō sekinin shiryō sentā) 62, 72
Chang, Iris 38
chemical and biological warfare (CBW),
Japan 5, 35, 91–2, *see also* Unit 731
chemical weapons, *see* abandoned
chemical weapons
Chemical Weapons Convention (1993)
12, 92, 147n.
Chen Jian 63
Chen Lifei 87, 89
Chen Lintao 88
Chen Yi 46
Chen Yufang 93

restitution 16, 18–19, 21
revisionism (Japan) 12, 14, 18, 53, 66,
  see also neo-nationalist groups,
  Tsukuru kai
Rigby, Andrew 16, 21, 22, 23, 24, 34, 40,
  47, 50
Roh Taewoo 58

Sakigake 102
San Francisco Peace Treaty (SFPT) 42,
  43, 45, 47, 80, 140n17
Sankei shinbun 58, 59
Satō Kazuo 104, 105
Seiron 58
Senda Kakō 39
settling the past 4, 13, 25, 48–9, 99, *see
  also* reconciliation
Shenyang consulate issue 1, 137n
Shenyang September 18th History
  Exhibition Hall 119
Shinshintō 59; Dietmembers' League for
  Teaching Correct History (Tadashii
  rekishi o tsutaeru kokkai giin renmei)
  59
Shokun 58
Shōwa Hall (Shōwa kan) 118, 119, 120
Sino-Japanese relations: economic
  relations 6–7; informal groups in
  31–3; normalisation of 5, 16; Taiwan
  and 7, 9; thirtieth anniversary of
  normalisation 1, 8, 116; Track
  Two diplomacy in 32, *see also*
  reconciliation
Sivan, Emmanuel 22, 125
Social Democratic Party (SDP) 97, 102;
  and Diet Resolution 103
Society to Honour the Glorious War
  Dead (Eirei ni kotaeru kai) 111
Society to Support the Demands of
  Chinese War Victims (Chūgokujin
  sensō higaisha yōkyū o sasaerukai),
  see Suopei
Soviet Union 36, 42, 43, 47, 139n6
Su Shi 87
Su Zhiliang 9, 51, 66, 68, 87, 88
Sumitomo Coal Mining 86
Sun Pinghua 32
Suopei 77, 85, 88, 95
Supreme Commander of the Allied
  Powers (SCAP) 38, 42, 111
Suzuki Zenkō 113

Tachiki Toyoji 85
Taiwan 26, 64, 104, 105, 106

Taiwan Comfort Women Legal Support
  Group (Taiwan no moto ianfu saiban
  o shi'en suru kai) 72
Takagi Ken'ichi
Takahashi Shirō 53, 141n1
Takeiri Yoshikatsu 46
Takeshita Noboru 27
Tanaka Hiroshi 9, 47, 96, 111
Tanaka Kakuei 46, 48–9, 64
Tanaka Makiko 64, 116
Tang Jiaxuan 27, 63, 64, 105, 114
Tavuchis, Nicolas 19, 23, 100
Tawara Yoshifumi 9, 47, 57, 58, 60, 61
textbook authorisation (Japan) 54, 55,
  141n4
Textbook Authorisation Research
  Council (TARC) 57
textbook issues 11; (1982) 50, 55, 56, 57,
  142n7; (1984) 142n7; (1986) 56–7
textbook offensives 55, 56, 128–9
textbook screening system, *see* textbook
  authorisation
textbook trials, *see* Ienaga Saburō
third textbook offensive 51, 57–61;
  Chinese and Korean response to 63–5;
  counter-offensive 61–3
Tian Huan 46
Tōjō Hideki 113
Tokyo trial 24, 35–6, 58, 64, 73
Tong Zeng 74–5, 145n7
Torpey, John 21, 23, 24, 34, 50
Totman, Conrad 110
Treaty of Peace and Friendship (1978) 24
Treaty of Peace between Japan and the
  Republic of China (1952) 42, 47;
  negotiations 43–45
Tsuchiya Kōken 93
Tsukuru kai 18, 53, 54, 59, 60, 61, 67, 68,
  129
Tsurumi Shunsuke 38

Uchida Masatoshi 83
UN Commission on Human Rights 33,
  63, 68, 72
UN Conference on Environment and
  Development (Rio de Janeiro) 29
Unit 731, 67, 91; and compensation case
  93–4; Crime Evidence Exhibition Hall
  118, 119; in history textbooks 58, 60;
  and war crimes trials 35–6
United Nations Security Council
  (UNSC) 63
United States: and alliance with Japan
  53, 60, 73; and compensation cases 69,